Praise for the first edition:

'In this book, Cetindamar, Phaal and Probert arrive at the ı
vative ideas about the way successful technology management is practised. They further offer
a set of key tools that will be helpful in the everyday managerial processes of technology and
innovation-driven companies. Their ideas have novel and significant implications for teaching
and management.

What the authors found was startlingly simple: the base of technology management is
a function of six processes and six tools. While there are numerous books on the topic of
innovation, this volume's real value is its exposition of the two sides of the same coin and the
illustration of these processes through exhaustive case studies.

This most stimulating book offers companies a convincing way to make technological
innovations more effective in boosting their competitiveness. It therefore must be read by
managers and students who plan a managerial career in the coming innovation age.' – **Hugo
P. Tschirky**, *Professor Emeritus Swiss Federal Institute of Technology (ETH), founding member of
the European Institute of Technology and Innovation Management (EITIM)*

'An excellent and well organized resource for people wanting to understand the complexities
of technology management. Because the book is structured around a framework and offers
a range of tools and techniques, it is also essential for those already working in technology
management who want to ensure they follow a structured approach to decision making. I
was impressed by the comprehensive coverage of key definitions and concepts, and the application of these concepts to case examples.' – **Jenny Darroch**, *author of* Marketing through
Turbulent Times *and Professor of Marketing at Drucker Graduate School of Management, USA*

'This volume delivers an excellent guide for managers and for final year undergraduate
and postgraduate students who want to hit the ground running in firms driven by technology innovation. It describes Technology Management as rooted in a particular set of
management competencies delivered through a related set of management tools and is
based on detailed extended case studies. The book fills a gap between general Operations
Management texts and more diffuse Innovation Management texts.' – **Chris Ivory**, *Degree
Programme Director, Masters in Innovation, Creativity and Entrepreneurship, Newcastle
University Business School, UK*

'A much needed update on the field of technology and innovation management, written by a
team of academics with a keen sense of industry needs. It provides an accessible and clear-cut
picture of state-of-the-art TM frameworks, and offers theoretically grounded yet hands-on
illustrations of how to apply the field's most central tools. This book will be of great value to
students of technology and innovation management, as well as its practitioners.' – **Tomas
Hellström**, *Professor at CIRCLE, Lund University, Sweden*

'Cetindamar, Phaal and Probert provide the reader with a clear and comprehensive guide to
the theory and practice of technology management. Not only is this book a useful collection
of the best approaches and analytical frameworks, but the structure adopted by the authors
connects a generic process model with valuable tools and techniques in an integrated
approach. We are taken through a series of six technology management activities in Part I,
followed by six tools for the manager in Part II, including patent analysis, the S-curve and the
stage-gate framework. Each of these is illustrated with related case studies, linking a specific
analytical approach to business strategies more generally. The chapter structure provides a
useful framework for linking past studies with key academic concepts and practice, whilst

the style and content are both hugely engaging. It is an excellent book in an important field for both aspiring and practising managers in technology management.' – **Simon Collinson**, *Professor of International Business and Innovation, Warwick Business School, UK*

'The reputation of this book's international author team promises academic depth and practitioner value. It does not disappoint on either count. Its technology management framework articulates six linked activities which are then mapped to practical technology management tools. This integrated approach provides both a solid basis on which readers may understand the technology management concept and guidance on how they may manage technology within their own environments. The book draws on a wealth of traditional and contemporary work from the field, and includes a comprehensive bibliography of technology management sources. It is a valuable mine of information for scholars, managers and technologists worldwide.' – **Margaret Taylor**, *Professor of Operations and Technology Management, Bradford University School of Management, UK*

'Grounded in dynamic capabilities theory, Dilek Cetindamar, Robert Phaal and David Probert focus on the often overlooked micro-level analysis of Technology Management. Their book explains how a carefully selected set of tools (patent analysis, portfolio management, roadmapping, S-curve, stage-gate and value analysis) can help technology managers successfully conduct the key technology processes (acquisition, exploitation, identification, protection and selection).

This book is an insightful resource for the technology management student and the professional. The student can benefit from the practical examples that bring the technology management tools and processes to life. The professional can benefit from the clearly written processes that explain the applicability of the presented tools. It makes frequent reference to relevant theoretical concepts and as a result it also serves as an excellent guide for the interested reader who wants to learn more about the discipline. Overall, this is an exciting book that provides a sophisticated, yet simple account of technology management.' – **Christos-Dimitris Tsinopoulos**, *Lecturer in Operations & Project Management, Durham Business School, Durham University, UK*

DILEK CETINDAMAR
ROB PHAAL
DAVID PROBERT

IN ASSOCIATION WITH EITIM

TECHNOLOGY MANAGEMENT

ACTIVITIES AND TOOLS

Second edition

© Dilek Cetindamar, Rob Phaal and David Probert 2016

All rights reserved. No reproduction, copy or transmission of this publication may be made without written permission.

No portion of this publication may be reproduced, copied or transmitted save with written permission or in accordance with the provisions of the Copyright, Designs and Patents Act 1988, or under the terms of any licence permitting limited copying issued by the Copyright Licensing Agency, Saffron House, 6–10 Kirby Street, London EC1N 8TS.

Any person who does any unauthorized act in relation to this publication may be liable to criminal prosecution and civil claims for damages.

The author(s) has/have asserted his/her/their right(s) to be identified as the author(s) of this work in accordance with the Copyright, Designs and Patents Act 1988.

First published 2016 by
PALGRAVE

Palgrave in the UK is an imprint of Macmillan Publishers Limited, registered in England, company number 785998, of 4 Crinan Street, London, N1 9XW.

Palgrave Macmillan in the US is a division of St Martin's Press LLC, 175 Fifth Avenue, New York, NY 10010.

Palgrave is a global imprint of the above companies and is represented throughout the world.

Palgrave® and Macmillan® are registered trademarks in the United States, the United Kingdom, Europe and other countries.

ISBN 978–1–137–43185–1 paperback

This book is printed on paper suitable for recycling and made from fully managed and sustained forest sources. Logging, pulping and manufacturing processes are expected to conform to the environmental regulations of the country of origin.

A catalogue record for this book is available from the British Library.

A catalog record for this book is available from the Library of Congress.

Printed in China

'To our children and students, who are our source of energy and stimulation'

TABLE OF CONTENTS

LIST OF FIGURES

LIST OF TABLES

NOTES ON THE AUTHORS

Dilek Cetindamar is Professor at the School of Management and the Academic Director of Entrepreneurship Committee, Sabanci University, Turkey. She conducts research in the area of entrepreneurship and technology management. She has been a visiting scholar in several US and European universities. She has published many books and journal articles and was the recipient of the Encouragement Award from the Turkish Academy of Sciences.

Robert Phaal is based at the Centre for Technology Management, part of the Engineering Department at the University of Cambridge, where he conducts research in the area of strategic technology and innovation management. He has industrial experience in technical consulting, contract research and software development, and has a PhD in computational mechanics.

David Probert is Reader in Technology Management and founder of the Centre for Technology Management at the University of Cambridge. He teaches on the Manufacturing Engineering Tripos, and his research interests are in technology and innovation management. His earlier industrial career was with Marks & Spencer and Philips Electronics.

PREFACE

The technology management (TM) discipline has a history of more than 50 years, becoming self-sustaining in the past 20 years with the emergence of specialized professional organizations and a rapid increase in the number of publications and degree programmes. TM is inherently interdisciplinary and multifunctional, but much of the existing literature looks at technological issues from either a restricted or a broad perspective. Some authors are concerned with the internal company management of research and development or technology strategy alone, while others concentrate on the broader topic of innovation and blur the boundaries between TM and other disciplines such as innovation management. In contrast, by trying to avoid both these traps, we aim to provide an integrative approach to the management of technology.

Although TM has become popular in the business community, an accessible handbook of practical frameworks and management tools is not available. Also, considering the rapidly evolving nature of the discipline, the majority of existing TM textbooks are outdated, mostly published before 2000. This book will focus on the micro-level analysis of TM as a dynamic capability. It attempts to link how firms carry out their TM activities with the major tools and techniques needed to succeed in conducting these activities. There is no single best way to manage technology in a company and there is no mechanistic route to success. There are, however, lessons that can be learned from other companies and theoretical frameworks to guide thinking and decision making, and tools and techniques to assist analysis.

The book is arranged in two integrated parts. Chapter 1 gives a full account of the authors' understanding of TM, outlined in a comprehensive process model that includes six specific TM activities – acquisition, exploitation, identification, learning, protection and selection. We argue that the process of TM is essentially generic, although organization and market-specific factors will constrain choices and actions. Part I (Chapters 2–7) covers all these TM activities/processes. Each chapter deals with a specific TM activity, comprising the definition of the activity, how to carry out the activity and a case study. In Part II, Chapters 8–13 provide a description of six major TM tools and techniques – patent analysis, portfolio management, roadmapping, S-curve, stage-gate and value analysis. These tools are useful to carry out the TM activities outlined in the first part. Chapter 14 introduces challenges to technology managers as a profession and offers suggestions how to deal with them. We hope that this integrated approach will help the reader to increase their understanding of the subject, breadth of potential analysis and scope for creativity in the application of these ideas.

Likely audience

This book will be useful to several types of reader:

- Students on management and engineering education programmes.
- Students on other courses that include business, organization or technology units.
- Former students who wish to keep a reference of the main concepts they have studied and also wish to keep up to date with current ideas in the field of TM.
- Practising managers who wish to apply a more rigorous approach in their work.
- Consultants concerned with TM.

Taken as a whole, this book is written with the needs of two main target audiences in mind: students in engineering and management programmes who plan to become managers of technology in the future and technologists and managers at all levels. Our analysis is based on the systematic analysis of the latest management research and our own research, consulting and teaching experience. The idea is to balance sound research and relevant theory with up-to-date practical applications and hands-on techniques. Managers, consultants and students looking for a broad yet integrated approach should find that this book provides a view of the subject that is both timely and of enduring value. We hope that the book will become a primary source of information within the TM community.

ACKNOWLEDGEMENTS

We are fortunate to have supportive colleagues who reviewed drafts and contributed many useful ideas. We are particularly grateful to Michael Gregory, Clive Kerr, Clare Farrukh and Letizia Mortara at the University of Cambridge. Students attending our courses, and participants from industry who joined our seminars, have all contributed to developing and shaping our knowledge of TM.

Valuable comments were also given by Jeff Butler, Michael Best and Mike Hobday.

Martin Drewe of Palgrave Macmillan read and commented on our work and provided helpful guidance on how to develop the style of this book. Jenny Hindley made our life easy in getting the second edition ready. Batuhan Gultakan and Turkan Yosun were the assistants for the figures and tables, while Aysegul Boz designed two figures showing the TM activities and tools.

The University of Cambridge provided us with a congenial atmosphere for research. Dilek Cetindamar would especially like to thank the director of the Centre for Technology Management and his colleagues and Geraldine Guceri for their hospitality and engagement with itinerant visitors. In addition, Dilek Cetindamar is grateful to three teachers from whom she has learned much: Hacer Ansal, Bo Carlsson and Dundar Kocaoglu. Particular thanks are due to TUBITAK for its financial support (2219 scholarship programme) for Dr Cetindamar's time in Cambridge.

PUBLISHER'S ACKNOWLEDGEMENTS

The authors and publishers are grateful to the following organizations for permission to reproduce copyright material, listed in alphabetical order of the organization.

Elsevier: Figure 9.2, Technology assessment for scenario A (season in the sun), Chen, T.-Y., Yu, O.-S., Hsu, G. J.-Y., Hsu, F.-M. and Sung, W.-N. (2009) 'Renewable Energy Technology Portfolio Planning with Scenario Analysis: A Case Study for Taiwan', *Energy Policy*, **37**(8), 2900–2906. Figure 7.4, Strategy-technology firm fit audit, Walsh, S. and Linton, J. (2011) 'The Strategy-Technology Firm Fit Audit: A guide to Opportunity Assessment and Selection', *Technological Forecasting and Social Change*, **78**(2), 199–216. Figure 2.4, Technical, environmental and economical performance evaluation, Pecas, P., Ribeiro, I., Folgado, R. and Henriques, E. (2009) 'A Life Cycle Engineering Model for Technology Selection', *Journal of Cleaner Production*, **17**(9), 846–856.

PD-Trak Solutions: Figure 9.1, Portfolio bubble chart showing risk–reward balance of the portfolio, PD-Trak Solutions (2006) *A Practical Approach to Portfolio Management*.

Wiley: Figure 11.2, Dynamic imitator-to-innovator S curve chasms, Ouyang, H. S. (2010) 'Imitator-to-Innovator S Curve and Chasms', *Thunderbird International Business Review*, **52**(1), 31–45.

All case studies in Chapters 1–13 are reprinted as a summary/excerpt (with small modifications) by permission of the Industrial Research Institute, which publishes the *Research-Technology Management* journal.

ABBREVIATIONS

CEO	Chief Executive Officer
CR&D	Corporate Research and Development
CTO	Chief Technology Officer
EC	European Commission
EITIM	European Institute for Technology and Innovation Management
EU	European Union
HR	Human Resources
HRM	Human Resource Management
IAMOT	International Association for Management of Technology
ICT	Information and Communication Technologies
IP	Intellectual Property
IPR	Intellectual Property Rights
IRI	Industrial Research Institute
IT	Information Technology
KM	Knowledge Management
LBD	Learning-By-Doing
M&A	Mergers and Acquisitions
NPV	Net Present Value
OEMs	Original Equipment Manufacturers
R&D	Research and Development
ROI	Return On Investment
SMEs	Small and Medium-sized Enterprises
TM	Technology Management
TQM	Total Quality Management

1

INTRODUCTION: A FRAMEWORK FOR UNDERSTANDING TM ACTIVITIES AND TOOLS

Technology can represent a major source of competitive advantage and growth for companies. However, effectively integrating technological considerations into business processes is a complex task, requiring consideration of multiple functions, including technical, marketing, finance and human resources. Technology, combined with highly motivated and properly trained people, enables a business to respond rapidly to changing customer demands and to access and develop new market opportunities.

The challenges associated with the management of technology are compounded by a number of factors, including the increasing cost, complexity and pace of technology advancement, the diversity of technology sources, the globalization of competition and alliances and the impact of information technology (IT). These challenges also represent a great opportunity for organizations that can fully harness their technological potential.

To compete successfully, companies must assess their **technology management** (TM) strategy and practice and address how they:

- Recognize technological opportunities and threats and convert them into sales and profit.
- Exploit existing technology by the effective translation of strategy into operational performance.
- Differentiate products using cost-effective technological product and process solutions.
- Identify and evaluate alternative and emerging technologies in the light of company policy and strategy and their impact on the business and society.
- Reduce the risks inherent in new or unfamiliar technologies.
- Harness technology that supports improvement in processes, information and other systems.
- Decrease the time to market of new products and services through effective identification and exploitation of technologies that provide competitive advantage.
- Protect and exploit **intellectual property** (IP).

Six key questions must be answered if the full potential of technology investment is to be realized:

1 How do we exploit our technology assets?
2 How do we identify technology that will have a future impact on our business?
3 How do we select technology for business benefit?
4 How should we acquire new technology?
5 How can we protect our technology assets?
6 How can we learn from our experience to improve our ability to develop and exploit the value of technology?

This chapter explores the theoretical perspectives that underpin the practice of TM, providing the pillars of a technology system upon which the structure of the book is based, with practical examples included to illustrate the application of these concepts. This book will focus on the micro-level analysis of TM in order to understand how firms carry out their TM activities and what tools and techniques are needed. Technological changes are continuously creating new challenges and opportunities for application to new product, service and process development. However, these opportunities need to be captured and turned into value through effective TM.

After the definitions of key concepts, the **TM framework** will be introduced. This framework will show the context within which TM activities take place. The description of each TM **activity** will then become a separate chapter in Part I. Following the TM activities, the chapter will discuss which TM tools and techniques are useful to carry out TM activities and introduce the rationale behind selecting key tools, which are given at length in Part II of the book. Two case studies at the end of this chapter illustrate the TM system.

1.1 Definition

The definition of TM includes planning, directing, control and coordination of the development and implementation of **technological capabilities** so that firms can shape and accomplish their strategic and operational objectives (NRC, 1987). This definition attempts to combine both 'hard' aspects of technology (science and engineering) and 'soft' dimensions such as the processes enabling its effective application (Phaal et al., 2004). However, it does not make an explicit distinction between the technical and managerial issues associated with TM, and is a rather static definition. Technological changes are continuously creating new challenges and opportunities for new product, service, process and organizational development and industrial diversification. In order to capture and convert these opportunities into value through effective and dynamic TM, a new definition is needed.

An appropriate paradigm or perspective on understanding TM could be the **dynamic-capabilities** theory. Capability implies an ability to do something and is constituted both by strategies and operational activities (Teece, 2014). In its most elaborate form, dynamic capabilities are the ability to reconfigure, redirect, transform and appropriately shape and integrate existing **core competencies** with external resources and strategic and **complementary assets** to meet the challenges of a time-pressured, rapidly changing world of competition and imitation (Teece et al., 2000; Teece, 2014). Three main reasons explain why the dynamic-capabilities theory could enhance the understanding of TM (Cetindamar et al., 2009):

1 It is not specific technological innovations but rather the capability to generate a stream of product, service and process changes that matter for long-term firm performance (Rush et al., 2007).
2 It is possible to observe the dynamics taking place in the organization of firms, since the unit of analysis is the capabilities (Best, 2001).
3 Dynamic-capabilities theory considers the market or the product as objects of strategic reconstruction and thus emphasizes the key role of strategic management in appropriately adapting, integrating and reconfiguring internal and external

organizational skills, resources and functional competencies towards a changing environment (Teece, 2014).

As firms develop and respond to productive opportunities, they alter and further differentiate and, in the process, recharacterize the market parameters, such as those related to technology, product, service or organization (Best, 2001; Teece, 2007). In this evolutionary perspective, the firm shapes the market as much as vice versa. So success is achieved by developing distinctive organizational, technological and production capabilities. These different sets of capabilities affect each other in an evolutionary manner, as described in different production systems developed in the USA (Best, 2001).

Capabilities might be dynamic or operational (Helfat and Peteraf, 2003). Dynamic capabilities build, integrate or reconfigure operational capabilities, which are defined as:

[A] high-level routine (or collection of routines) that, together with its implementing input flows, confers upon an organization's management a set of decision options for producing significant outputs of a particular type. (Winter, 2000: 983)

A **routine** describes a 'repetitive pattern of activity'. Similarly, competencies refer to activities to be performed by assembling firm-specific assets/resources. This is why dynamic capabilities are conceived as the routines/activities/competencies embedded in firms (Eisenhardt and Martin, 2000; Bergek et al., 2008). Defined as such, technological capabilities consist of dynamic and operational capabilities, which are a collection of routines/activities to execute and coordinate the variety of tasks required to manage technology. Thus, this book will analyse the core activities that firms perform in order to achieve effective TM.

Dynamic-capabilities theory is not interested in fixed assets per se; rather, it aims to explain the way in which a firm allocates resources for innovation over time, how it deploys its existing resources and where it obtains new resources (Teece et al., 1997). This is relevant for understanding TM, helping to explain how combinations of resources and processes can be developed, deployed and protected for each TM activity.

Although this book will focus mainly on TM activities, resources and skills will be discussed within a specific activity whenever relevant. Therefore, the main elements of a TM system in this book will be TM activities that help to build technological capabilities. In order for the performance of an activity to constitute a capability, the capability must have reached some threshold level of practised or routine activity. Each TM activity is related to a certain technological capability, comprising one or more processes/routines/competencies. **Process** can be described as an approach to achieving a managerial objective through the transformation of inputs into outputs. So, the term 'activity' is used interchangeably with 'process' or 'routine', and is associated with the concept of capability.

Every firm is a collection of activities to design, produce, deliver and support its products and services. Individual activities are a reflection of their history, strategy, resources, approach to implementing their strategy and the underlying economics of the activities themselves. Dynamic-capabilities theory does not imply that any particular dynamic capability is exactly alike across firms. While dynamic capabilities are certainly distinctive in their details, specific dynamic capabilities exhibit common features that are associated with effective processes across firms (Eisenhardt and Martin, 2000). Thus, each chapter in Part I will describe general processes/routines to illustrate the set of tasks needed to be carried out in order to achieve a particular technological capability.

1.2 Differences between TM and innovation management

In the past 20 years, innovation has become the leading topic in TM (Cetindamar et al., 2009). However, the dominance of one topic starts to misrepresent the TM field, resulting in confusion about the borders between innovation and TM. This confusion is further strengthened with a popular new business concept – open innovation systems (Chesbrough, 2003). The central idea behind open innovation is that in a world of widely distributed knowledge, companies cannot afford to rely entirely on their own research, but should instead buy or license processes or inventions from other companies. In addition, internal inventions not being used in a firm's business should be taken outside the company through mechanisms such as licensing and spin-offs. Described as such, the concepts of innovation and technology become confusing, necessitating clarification.

In simple terms, **innovation** is doing something new such as a product, process or service, including newness in the firm (Hobday, 2005). Although implicit in this definition, the critical issue is the fact that innovation is not limited to technology. Innovations might be organizational and come from many sources. For example, Amazon's offering of book delivery over the Internet was a service-related innovation. So innovation management is the successful implementation of novel ideas that form different innovation types within an organization.

The Oslo Manual (OECD, 1995) lists the four main innovation types as follows:

1 A product innovation is the introduction of a good or service that is new or significantly improved with respect to its characteristics or intended uses. This includes significant improvements in technical specifications, components and materials, incorporated software, user-friendliness or other functional characteristics. Product innovations can utilize new knowledge or technologies, or can be based on new uses or combinations of existing knowledge or technologies.

2 A process innovation is the implementation of a new or significantly improved production, service or delivery method. This includes significant changes in techniques, equipment and/or software. Process innovations can be intended to decrease unit costs of production or delivery, to increase quality or to produce or deliver new or significantly improved products.

3 A marketing innovation ranges from a new marketing method involving significant changes in product design or packaging, product placement, product promotion to pricing. Marketing innovations are aimed at better addressing customer needs, opening up new markets or newly positioning a firm's product on the market, with the objective of increasing the firm's sales.

4 An organizational innovation is the implementation of a new organizational method in the firm's business practices, workplace organization or external relations. Organizational innovations can be intended to increase a firm's performance by reducing administrative costs or transaction costs, improving workplace satisfaction (and thus labour productivity), gaining access to non-tradable assets (such as non-codified external knowledge) or reducing costs of supplies.

In recent years, new types of innovations have been introduced; we will mention three popular ones in this book that are relevant to technology managers: eco-innovation, reverse innovation and design-driven innovation. The first category of innovations is described by the Europe INNOVA panel (Schiederig et al., 2012) as the creation of novel and competitively priced goods, processes, systems, services and procedures that can satisfy human needs and bring quality of life to all people with minimal use of natural resources per unit output, and a minimal release of toxic substances. The second type, reverse innovation, refers to product and service innovations aimed at resource-constrained customers in emerging markets (see details in Chapters 3 and 14). The final category, design-driven innovation, is based on user experience and meaning for products and services. It offers surprise and pleasure at the look and feel of a product or a service (see more discussion in Chapters 13 and 14).

Given all these innovation types mentioned above, it is no surprise that innovation management literature becomes inclusive of many disciplines including TM. However, TM is not about **technological innovations** and their management alone; rather, it is a specific discipline related to all sorts of decision making needed to develop and/or use technologies within a firm or organization as explained in the next section.

This book proposes the following solution for the confusing borders between TM and innovation management: TM and innovation management overlap when there is a technology innovation, otherwise they have their own unique disciplinary body of knowledge. For example, the development of a new TV screen technology involves a technology-based product innovation, so there is an overlap. But the development of a new sales channel for a TV screen falls into marketing innovation, whereas the acquisition of a process technology to produce TV screens is related to TM. When it comes to services, the same rule applies. For example, walk-in clinics accept patients on a walk-in basis and with no appointment required. They are innovative health care providers around the world but their innovation is not based on a technology. But the example of Airbnb that offers sharing rooms is a technology-based innovation in the hospitality business. Even though it was established in 2008, Airbnb became one of the world's largest hotel chains by the summer of 2014, comparable to Hilton Worldwide, but it does not own a single hotel since it allows users to rent out their spare rooms or vacant homes to strangers over its Internet platform. Airbnb surpassed ten million stays on its platform in 2014 and doubled its listings to 550,000 (in 192 countries). The company successfully used technologies and designed a new business model where experience has meant everything for its users and transformed the idea of hotel accommodation.

1.3   The TM framework to set the context

The TM discipline has a history of over 50 years (Kocaoglu, 1994; Roberts, 2004; Larson, 2007). The discipline has evolved from a stable and predictable situation within an R&D department to a discontinuous and unpredictable situation taking place at the strategic level (Drejer, 1996). However,

> TM studies offer few universally accepted conceptual models or frameworks to understand and communicate structures and relationships within a TM system (Phaal et al., 2004). This book integrates the theory of dynamic capabilities into a TM framework developed by Phaal et al. (2004) and offers a comprehensive framework in understanding TM (Cetindamar et al., 2009).

TM activities are based on technological capabilities. Due to the complex nature of firms and industries, it is difficult to describe where exactly firms exercise these activities. In the

TM framework presented in Figure 1.1, the TM activities – acquisition, exploitation, identification, learning, protection and selection – are typically linked to or embedded within three core business processes: strategy, innovation and operations (Phaal et al., 2004). For example, technology selection decisions are made during business strategy and new product/service development.

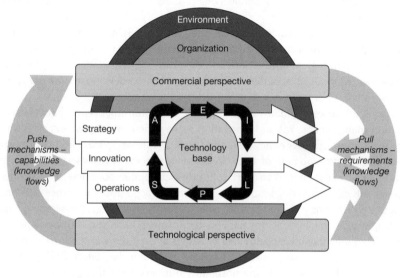

Figure 1.1   TM framework
Source: Based on Phaal et al. (2004).

Key aspects of the framework include:

- The linkage between technological and commercial perspectives in the firm.
- The knowledge flows (and other mechanisms) that support this linkage.
- The core business processes of strategy, innovation (including new product development) and operations.
- The TM processes: identification, selection, acquisition, exploitation, protection and learning.
- The organizational and environmental context in which the firm operates (the 'system'), which includes additional internal elements of the system, such as staff and other business processes and sub-systems, together with external elements such as customers, competitors, partners, government, etc.
- Time (change, trends, evolution and synchronization).

Time is implicitly included in the business and TM processes, together with the trends that are associated with the business environment.

At the heart of the framework are three core business processes – *strategy, innovation and operations*, operating at different business system 'levels' in the firm. The link to core business processes is important, as these are the focus of management and action in the business, and the means for ensuring sustainable productive output of the firm. One of the challenges of TM is that associated activities are distributed and embedded in these core business processes. The aim of effective TM is to ensure that technological issues are incorporated appropriately in these processes, to form a system that is coherent and integrated across and beyond specific business processes and activities.

The proposed TM framework offers many advantages. It allows us to conceive that TM activities might operate in any business process, department or business system level, for example project, corporate and strategic business units, in the firm. The framework does not differentiate with respect to the sector in which firms operate. It is valid for service firms as much as it is valid for firms in manufacturing sectors that are extensively discussed in Chapter 14.

The framework also indicates that the specific TM issues faced by firms depend on the context (internal and external), in terms of organizational structure, systems, infrastructure, culture and structure, and the particular business environment and challenges confronting the firm, which change over time. The time dimension concerns synchronizing technological developments and capabilities with business requirements, in the context of evolving markets, products and technology. Thus, the TM framework is in line with the dynamic-capabilities framework. While the former focuses on managing technological capabilities, the latter covers all capability types.

An advantage of the TM framework is its applicability to all firms regardless of their size, in contrast to the frameworks/models that implicitly assume firms with leadership status. Most are oriented towards large firms with R&D departments and elaborate organizational divisions of labour rather than small or medium-sized enterprises (SMEs) that might operate with more informal processes with perhaps no official R&D or engineering department. Many SMEs lack R&D departments and they are followers, but the TM framework can still apply in these firms.

Further, the framework considers technology as a resource. This is why the technology base of a company represents the technological knowledge that needs to be turned into products, processes and services through the technological capabilities developed by TM.

The framework emphasizes the dynamic nature of the knowledge flows that must occur between the commercial and technological functions in the firm, linking to the strategy, innovation and operational processes (Phaal et al., 2004). An appropriate balance must be struck between market 'pull' (requirements) and technology 'push' (capabilities). Regardless of the driver of technological change, managers need to link markets and technology through various mechanisms, including traditional communication channels, cross-functional teams or meetings, management tools, business processes, staff transfers and training.

Firms vary widely in size and scope, ranging from a one-person firm to a company with multi-department/multi-country operations. In each case, this basic TM framework can be applied, adapted appropriately for the particular organizational context. After identifying the business processes behind strategy, innovation and operations, managers could integrate TM processes into them. The next section focuses on the generic TM processes that can be observed within firms.

1.4 TM activities behind technological capabilities

Many TM handbooks consist of numerous managerial tasks that are very general and have no explicit link to specific TM concepts (Dorf, 1999). This results in no clear set of TM activities and confusion as to what technology managers need to do. This book considers the management of technology to be a professional task, and thus it focuses on a micro-level analysis of TM. This micro-focus makes it possible to understand how firms carry out their TM activities and what **tools** and techniques are needed to carry out these activities.

The initial step is to use the TM framework and dynamic-capabilities theory to find a set of core/generic technological capabilities. The firm's knowledge base includes its technological competencies as well as its knowledge of customer needs and supplier capabilities. These competencies reflect individual skills and experiences as well as distinctive ways of doing things inside firms. In other words, capabilities are gradually accumulated through various processes, procedures, routines and structures that are embedded in practice (Rush et al., 2007). Thus, the goal in this book is to identify the various common processes/routines forming the key technological capabilities that reflect what goes on within companies. An emphasis is given to processes since the dynamic-capabilities approach emphasizes the process rather than the asset per se.

Identifying a core set of TM activities naturally does not cover all possibilities. Managers can benefit from a general TM framework and its grouping of TM activities only when they consider their firms' own particular circumstances, resources and purposes. So the purpose here in offering a generic set of TM activities is to achieve four key learning objectives:

1 The core set of generic TM activities can be customized by any organization (manufacturing or services) and is applicable at any level, such as R&D unit or business unit, as well as at any size, either SMEs or large firms.
2 Knowing the main TM activities can reduce confusion between TM and other management activities such as innovation management.
3 Linear and limited perceptions on TM activities can be replaced with a dynamic view that emphasizes the links between activities.
4 Managers as well as engineers and management students who want to pursue careers in TM can conceive what skills and knowledge are necessary to manage technology.

Main TM activities

TM activities are abundant, but it is possible to identify a small set of processes/routines that address the fundamental and common tasks needed to manage technologies and build technological capabilities. Choosing the unit of analysis as technological capabilities, the activity name is the same as the specific technological capability it aims to develop. As shown in Figure 1.1, the general TM model is based on six generic TM activities (Gregory, 1995; Rush et al., 2007; Cetindamar et al., 2009):

1 **Acquisition**: Acquisition is how the company obtains the technologies valuable for its business. Acquisition is based on the buy–collaborate–make decision. In other words, technologies might be developed internally, by some form of collaboration, or acquired from external developers. The management of acquisition differs on the basis of the choice made.
2 **Exploitation**: Exploitation entails commercialization but first the expected benefits need to be realized through effective implementation, absorption and operation of the technology within the firm. Technologies are assimilated through technology transfer either from R&D to manufacturing or from external company/partner to internal manufacturing department. Exploitation processes include incremental developments, process improvements and marketing.

3 **Identification**: Identification is necessary for technologies at all stages of development and market life cycle. This process includes market changes as well as technological developments. Identification includes search, auditing, data collection and intelligence processes for technologies and markets.

4 **Learning**: Learning is a critical part of technological competency; it involves reflections on technology projects and processes carried out within or outside the firm. There is a strong link between this process and the broader field of knowledge management (KM).

5 **Protection**: Formal processes such as patenting and staff retention need to be in place in order to protect intellectual assets within a firm, including the knowledge and expertise embedded in products and manufacturing systems.

6 **Selection**: Selection takes account of company-level strategic issues, which requires a good grasp of strategic objectives and priorities developed at the business-strategy level. Then, the selection process aligns technology-related decisions with business strategy.

This list of TM capabilities does not include the innovation capability for two main reasons (Cetindamar et al., 2009). First, the innovation capability is the ability to mould and manage multiple capabilities (Wang and Ahmed, 2007). The set of TM capabilities is a subset of capabilities that are integrated within the innovation system. Depending on innovation type, the required technological knowledge set and the way they interact with each other will differ as well (Tödtling et al., 2008). Second, each of the TM capabilities involves an innovative element in itself. For example, the acquisition capability is to a large degree a major innovative activity, dealing with product, service, process and organizational innovations in a company.

As a final note, the level of TM activities will change over the life cycle of a firm for many reasons, such as product **diversification** or complexities in technologies. For example, Bell's (2003) study shows that organizations pass from the point of 'acquiring and assimilating imported technologies' to reach a stage where the organization is 'generating core advances at international frontiers'. Depending on the capability requirements, firms will naturally adapt their activities to meet the requirements. In addition, depending on where a firm operates (within an advanced or developing economy), the technological capabilities of firms and their degree of development will vary considerably, as shown by the mobile phone producers operating in China (Jin and Zedtwitz, 2008).

Nonlinearity of TM activities

In the TM activities model proposed here, TM activities corresponding to each technological capability are represented as individual processes like pieces of a jigsaw puzzle, as shown in Figure 1.2. The analogy of a jigsaw puzzle aims to avoid enforcing a hierarchy of processes. It also avoids a perception that 'one model fits all', as if all TM activities must exist in an organization. It is likely that some companies will focus on particular activities at any one time, and that the set might change over the course of time, depending on the needs and circumstances of the company. Another advantage of the jigsaw puzzle representation is its emphasis on showing TM as an art, where technology managers need to identify which processes are required and find ways of making them work properly together.

The links between TM activities might not necessarily follow a linear relationship. Naturally, there will be process flows among them but it is not possible to generalize the input–output relationships in a deterministic way. Any process might be the starting point that triggers a number of TM activities to take place. For example, in contrast to the traditional product development approach, where the starting point for concept creation is the improvement of functional benefits, it is possible to develop research, products and invention ideas from the patent strategy, regardless of whether or not there are functional benefits (Nissing, 2007).

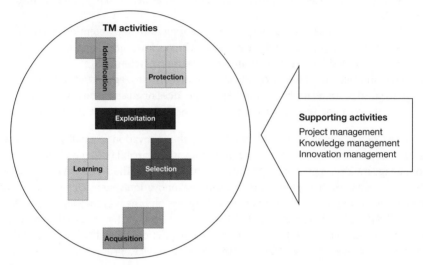

Figure 1.2   TM activities and supporting activities

The flexibility of the jigsaw puzzle concept indicates that each organization will have specific elements that show their own individual picture. If the organization is a large company with considerable R&D activity, the story/completed picture might include all elements in the TM activities model. However, if the organization has no R&D and the innovation is incremental, the corresponding activities will be different.

The recent criticisms of many innovation models focus on two critical concerns (Hobday, 2005): their static nature and their deterministic approach. The nonlinear feature of innovation activities has been highlighted. The TM activities model avoids these two criticisms at least for TM. In addition, the new model helps to draw the boundaries between different disciplines and TM activities by proposing two categories: primary/core and supporting activities, as shown in Figure 1.2.

Activities supporting TM

Drawing a basic framework for describing the core TM activities is useful for understanding the relationship between TM and other management activities, particularly project, knowledge and innovation management, as shown in Figure 1.2:

1 **Project management** refers to managerial activities associated with all types of projects such as product development. Each TM activity can be considered as a project, necessitating knowledge and skill to manage it.
2 **KM** is a widely used term for managing the knowledge accumulated in a company, including non-technology-based knowledge. Knowledge constitutes not only cognition or

recognition (know-what), but also the capacity to act (know-how) as well as understanding (know-why) that resides within the mind (Desouza, 2005). Therefore, all TM processes are involved with knowledge at some level and they necessitate adopting KM practices.

3 **Innovation management** is involved with various innovations being financial, organizational and technological, so it naturally shares common ground with TM but it is a broader management exercise, covering the management of all sorts of innovations.

Supporting activities will vary from case to case depending on the company size, objectives and technology characteristics. For example, an SME with a few small product development projects will have different project management needs from a multinational company with multiple projects. The latter will have more structured and formal project management exercises embedded in its processes used to manage technology.

1.5   TM tools

Once the general outlook of the TM field is sketched by presenting a generic set of TM activities, the next task is to identify the generic tools used in carrying out these activities. This will not only improve the understanding of TM in academic terms but also as a profession. TM needs to offer some practical guidelines to apply and reinforce TM concepts within the business so that managers can incorporate TM into their daily routines.

Brady et al.'s study (1997) clearly highlights the difficulty of precisely defining what a tool is, considering a variety of terms used interchangeably, such as 'tools', 'techniques', 'procedures', 'processes', 'models', 'maps' and 'frameworks'. This book adopts the definition used in Phaal et al.'s study (2006):

> [In] the broadest sense, tools include devices for supporting both action/practical application and frameworks for conceptual understanding.

The confusion is not only in definition but also in deciding on the list of TM tools. Most studies end up with such broad categories of tools that it is hard to consider the actual applications. The TM handbooks (Gaynor, 1996; Dorf, 1999) do not make life easier either. There is no clear description and discussion on the methodologies, tools and techniques published in these handbooks and no effort is made to link TM activities to the tools to be used to carry out these activities.

The only comprehensive coverage of TM tools was carried out by a European Commission (EC) project published in 1998. As the outcome of this project, *Temaguide* (Cotec, 1998) had the explicit goal of explaining different TM tools, and grouped them under six headings on the basis of their functions in a company:

1 Tools for external information analysis, such as technology forecast and benchmarking.
2 Tools for internal information analysis, such as skills and innovation audit.
3 Tools to calculate workload and resources needed in projects, such as project management and portfolio management.
4 Tools to manage working together, such as interface management and networking.
5 Idea creation and problem-solving techniques, such as creativity and value analysis.
6 Tools related to improving efficiency and flexibility, such as lean thinking and continuous improvement.

Even though the *Temaguide* list might seem coherent, it also poses problems in understanding TM for two reasons. First, the level of tools applicable to TM activities makes it difficult to grasp. For example, project management is a large discipline but is just one of the tools mentioned in *Temaguide*. Second, the wide spectrum of tools, from conjoint analysis used in market analysis to Delphi analysis for technology forecasting, raises the question of their relevance to TM. Some of these techniques, such as Delphi analysis, can be applied in any forecasting activity for any managerial problem. So these lists do not necessarily clarify which tools constitute the body of TM as a distinct discipline and which are not developed particularly for TM but are widely used in carrying out TM activities.

The lack of systematic gathering of tool lists makes it difficult to operationalize them. For example, Dorf's list (1999) in the tools section includes financial tools such as cash flow, legal issues (with no tool reference), information systems such as database and decision support systems and finally decision and simulation methods such as value-focused thinking and uncertainty.

The major confusion might be due to the multidisciplinary nature of TM. According to the International Association for Management of Technology (IAMOT), one of the most influential associations in the field of TM, four major disciplines are considered to constitute the basis for a master of science programme in a management of technology curriculum. These four disciplines show the wide spectrum of TM:

1 Management of technology-centred knowledge: management procedures associated with the exploitation of technological resources. Examples are technology acquisition, exploitation and transfer, new product development, project management, entrepreneurship, technology forecasting and planning, innovation and R&D management, KM, IP management and strategic management of technology.
2 Knowledge of corporate functions: classic business functions such as marketing, finance, accounting, operations, management information systems, human resource management and business strategy.
3 Technology-centred knowledge: topics that relate to specific technology fields or critical technology areas. Examples are information and computer technologies, pivotal and emerging technologies, manufacturing technology, petroleum and mining technology and production technologies.
4 Knowledge of supporting disciplines: important supporting topics such as national policy frameworks, economics, general systems theory, risk analysis, environmental management, ethics, human behaviour, quantitative methods, legal issues, research methods and statistics.

This book presents a small number of tools applicable specifically for managing technology, the first knowledge set mentioned above, namely management of technology-centred knowledge. Limiting the list of tools is a daunting task but it is necessary to reduce the confusion about what TM tools are.

What should be the criteria to decide on the tools that go into the TM toolkit? Obviously, the most critical tool is not the same as the most useful or the most important, neither is it the same as the most used or most popular. The toolkit will not make any reference to the quality of tools, since there are almost no studies measuring the performance of tools as such and it is outside the scope of this study. Even though a particular tool will be listed in a final tool set, there will be many others serving a similar purpose, for example capture of technology information, competitive analysis, creativity development and external R&D cooperation.

The goal of this study is to write a practical book that recommends certain tools and techniques with clear and rich content without confusing the concept of a tool. This is why it is good to borrow the carpenter analogy used by Straker (1997) in his book *Toolbook for Quality Improvement and Problem Solving*. Straker points out that there are a large number of possible tools that a carpenter could have in their toolbox, but the carpenter typically carries around only a small set of the most commonly used tools, keeping a larger set of more specialized tools at their workbench. Even then, the carpenter pays an occasional trip to the hardware store for special jobs. In the case of quality improvement and problem solving, Straker argues that the toolkit consists of seven tools and, interestingly, together they can solve 90% of all problems. So this book would like to suggest a toolkit for TM: a number of tools that will be handy when managers face decisions regarding TM.

Deciding which tools should be in the TM toolkit is a difficult task. A recent EC study published in the journal *R&D Management* (Hidalgo and Albors, 2008) uses three criteria as the basis for selecting the tools suggested:

1 The level of standardization of a tool.
2 The level of knowledge involved in the process.
3 The free accessibility of a tool, for example not subject to any copyright or licence restrictions.

In this book, we consider three criteria as the basis for delineating the six core tools of TM:

- Simplicity and flexibility of use.
- Degree of availability.
- Standardization level.

In addition, as this book is based on dynamic capabilities, key tools should be dynamic in nature and applicable in all TM activities. So key tools will also be:

- The prevailing ones across TM processes, which capture internal and external dynamics.

Accordingly, the final list consists of six tools listed in Table 1.1: **patent analysis, portfolio management, roadmapping, S-curve, stage-gate** and **value analysis**. The initial list was formed at a workshop organized at the Centre for Technology Management, University of Cambridge, and then it was circulated among prominent TM scholars who are members of the IAMOT and the European Institute for Technology and Innovation Management (EITIM) executive committees. The authors integrated the responses into the initial list and finalized it (for details see Appendix). Although the selected tools are applicable in all activities, it is possible to associate each tool with two major activities to which it is widely applied, as shown in Table 1.1. However, TM tools will include tools that are used in TM activities but not all of them are uniquely developed for TM. For example, stage-gate is a project management tool that is used extensively in the analysis of new product development.

Even though the book will cover these six TM tools in depth in Part II, some other tools to be used in TM activities are mentioned on the book's companion website (www.palgrave.com/companion/cetindamar2) with detailed reference lists. Some tools are available publicly in rich formats such as the T-catalogue, developed by the Centre for TM at the University of Cambridge. This catalogue and other public sources allow the reader to obtain more detailed information on topics of interest. It is possible to have a long list

Table 1.1   TM tools and their applications

Tools/activities	Patent analysis	Portfolio management	Roadmapping	S-curve	Stage-gate	Value analysis
Acquisition	★					★
Exploitation			★	★		
Identification				★	★	
Learning		★	★			
Protection	★				★	
Selection		★				★

of tools that might be used in individual TM activities such as decision-making tools or leadership tools. However, they are broad tools that any manager needs to know, so the list will be limited.

As a final remark, the tools are not off-the-shelf medicine, since TM problems are complex. So it cannot be claimed that each TM tool mentioned in this book would solve all the problems and challenges faced by business as a whole. TM tools act in combination with others, adapted and personalized to varying degrees for each specific case due to the diversity of firms and business circumstances. The benefit gained by the company depends on a combination of TM tools and the firm itself, and the mix of these two elements is what determines an effective outcome.

 Cases illustrating different TM system configurations

The characteristics of a TM system based on TM activities and tools can be observed in real-life cases. Two case studies are presented here: Glaxo Wellcome, whose TM system is closer to the idea of open innovation; Rolls-Royce, that is similar to this book's key activities, but learning activity is blended with other activities.

Glaxo Wellcome

In early 2000, Glaxo Wellcome (GW), a multinational pharmaceutical company, decided to implement a TM strategy across the development and manufacturing interface prior to its merger with SmithKline Beecham to form GlaxoSmithKline. This was to augment the new product delivery process that was being introduced.

TM activities

The resulting TM process is presented in Figure 1.3. When this process is compared with the six TM activities, it is observed that neither the acquisition nor the protection process is explicit in GW's TM processes. Although the names are different:

- The 'innovate, search and survey' step is similar to the identification activity.
- The 'evaluate and select' step is like the selection activity.

- The 'develop and execute' step corresponds to the acquisition and exploitation activities.
- The 'demonstrate benefits' step resembles the exploitation activity.

The process model is depicted in a linear format, without showing any feedback/learning loops – in this regard Figure 1.3 is a simplification of the real situation, aiming to provide an easy-to-understand framework for organizing the complex set of TM activities and interactions in the organization.

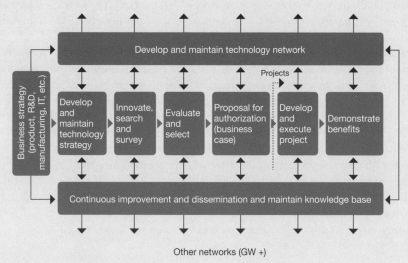

Figure 1.3   The TM system at GW

Resources

Technology domains, centred on strategic functions or processes in new product development, have overall accountability for the technology strategy for that part of the business. The technology domains operate through a number of technology networks whose members are experts drawn from global development and manufacturing. Each technology network implements the generic TM process. Interestingly, GW had linkages with extended teams in expert networks, or communities of practice, located not only within GW but also across the globe. This opens up possibilities for acquisitions and enriches the content of each TM process carried out in the company.

There are one or more domain leaders with budget responsibilities, who are full-time or part-time members of staff, depending on the size and scope of the domain. A new product development technology steering team was set up, consisting of the technology committee and the leaders of the technology domains. This team reviews and prioritizes the overall portfolio of technology projects.

Shared databases and IT infrastructures were used to support the networks and the TM system.

(Continued)

Tools

For each TM activity, inputs and outputs (such as information and resources), individual tasks and a list of information sources and available tools were developed. In particular, an appropriate methodology was selected for valuing potential initiatives and conducting the portfolio analysis and prioritization.

Farrukh et al. (2004) describe in detail how a TM system was developed within GW in a series of cross-functional workshops. This adopts a process-based framework, incorporating aspects of the five-process TM model (Gregory, 1995). The GW TM system builds on active technology networks within the company, with some parallels to open innovation, providing a rich case to illustrate the use of the TM framework presented in this book.

The GW case is an excellent example for highlighting the differences of core versus supporting TM activities as well as the relevance of the TM framework. The technology process in GW is embedded in one important business process: new product development process. This process is further integrated with strategy, project management, KM and networks. The importance of **open innovation systems** for GW can be seen in its structure – to develop and maintain the technology network in parallel with its internal TM activities, so that GW can tap into not only company resources but also the available knowledge base in the external environment. As a tool set, there is not much information on specific tools selected for each TM activity; however, it seems that portfolio management has particular importance at GW due to the use of process for new product development.

Source: Farrukh et al. (2004) 'Developing an Integrated Technology Management Process', *Research-Technology Management*, **47**(4), 39–46.

Rolls-Royce TM activities

Rolls-Royce is a leading provider of power systems and services for use on land, at sea and in the air. Its products serve civil aerospace, defence aerospace, marine industries and energy. Foden and Berends (2010) propose a TM framework driven from their exploratory interviews with the company's central technology managers as well as the survey of R&D engineers. As shown in Figure 1.4, there are six sub-processes that are aligned to the technology life cycle: (1) identification and monitoring; (2) selection and approval; (3) development research; (4) acquisition and adaptation; (5) exploitation and review; and (6) protection. The first five of these processes represent sequential stages, although several feedback loops exist, the most important being between the first and last stages. These represent the replacement of aging technologies by newer radical solutions.

The model does not directly cover learning but learning features exist in other activities, particularly in exploitation and acquisition. In exploitation and review process, the firm conducts continuous review of the ability of exploited technologies in order to continue to meet customer requirements and forward planning of more innovative replacement technologies. But more importantly, in acquisition activity, the goal is clearly set to develop capabilities of the firm that is not possible to do without learning embedded into the activity.

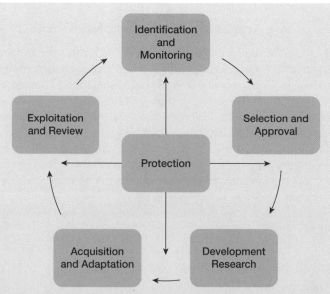

Figure 1.4 The integrated technology management framework developed for Rolls-Royce
Source: Adapted from Foden and Berends (2010), with permission.

Resources

TM is based on three groups. 'Strategic technical areas' are critical technology groups and combinations of technical skills for a particular application. They possess in-depth technical knowledge of a technology area and frequently engage with other experts (such as partners, suppliers and research centres) to explore internal and external environments. 'Product introduction engineers' lead the selection of technological solutions to satisfy new products. The final group is 'capability acquisition engineers' who own the existing technologies under study. They are responsible for technology capability acquisition by assessing the position of a technology's maturity along its S-curve/life cycle.

Tools

Effective TM requires the integration of multiple activities and tools. Examples of TM tools addressing each of the TM processes consist of the following:

Identification and monitoring: technology networking, technology watch, make-the-future (inward-facing technology opportunity identification aligned with product development programmes), technology maturity assessment (S-curve analysis), technology benchmarking.

Selection and approval: technology roadmapping

Acquisition and Exploitation: technology make-buy, capability acquisition, technology readiness scale (stage-gate).

(Continued)

Protection: technology risk management, knowledge base protection, IP protection.

Interestingly, these TM tools are associated not only with the activities they are used for but also with different engineering groups in the organization. Even though all tools are used with all levels of engineers and managers, some tools are used more than others by specific groups. For example, strategic technology area group is expected to use technology networking, technology watch, technology roadmapping and technology make-buy. Production introduction engineers are thought to use more of make-the-future and make-the-future selection. Capability acquisition engineers use technology benchmarking and technology maturity assessment. The tools such as risk management and IP protection are considered to be run by specialized teams central to the organization.

Source: Foden, J. and Berends, H. (2010) 'Technology Management at Rolls-Royce', *Research-Technology Management*, **53**(2), 33–42.

Summary

TM studies face three main problems:
1 A lack of distinction between concepts and practice in innovation, knowledge and TM.
2 A lack of universally accepted conceptual models or frameworks to understand the practical application of TM.
3 A lack of integration of key tools into the analysis of TM.

In order to tackle the first two problems, this study integrates the theory of dynamic capabilities into a TM framework and offers a model for explaining the core TM activities on the basis of technological capabilities. In this framework, TM is conceived as the development and exploitation of technological capabilities on a constant basis. Technological capabilities, being a subset of dynamic capabilities, require a capacity/ability to integrate, build and reconfigure internal and external competencies to address rapidly changing environments. Furthermore, competencies or routines refer to activities to be performed by assembling firm-specific assets/resources. Thus, the analysis of TM becomes the analysis of six generic TM activities: acquisition, exploitation, identification, learning, protection and selection. All these activities will help to build the technological capabilities associated with them.

The proposed TM framework offers several benefits in understanding TM:

1 It establishes boundaries and relationships between TM and other management principles, particularly with innovation. This is achieved by classifying TM activities into two categories: primary/core and supporting activities that come from other disciplines such as KM.
2 It helps to avoid two critical concerns: the static nature of innovation models and their deterministic approach, thanks to the explicit indication of the nonlinear feature of TM activities in the framework.
3 The framework is based on the management of technological capabilities, enabling the link between TM activities and technological capabilities to be established.

4   The use of the TM framework helps to develop a core set of generic TM activities that can be customized by any organization (manufacturing or services) and applicable at any level, such as R&D or business unit, and at any size.

The TM activities model is highly flexible, and offers a good starting point for managers as well as engineers and management students who want to pursue careers in TM. It shows what skills and knowledge are necessary to manage technology in order to develop and exploit particular technological capabilities within firms.

Regarding the problem of the integration of key tools that facilitate TM activities into the analysis of TM, the book offers six tools to be included in a toolkit for technology managers: patent analysis, portfolio management, road-mapping, S-curve, stage-gate and value analysis. These tools are the prevailing ones across TM processes and capture internal and external dynamics.

While Part I will present each TM activity, Part II is about the TM tools. Activities and tools are presented in alphabetical order. The links between activities and tools are highlighted whenever relevant (for details see Appendix). Understanding the generic TM activities and the tools used in carrying out these activities will not only improve the understanding of TM in academic terms but also as a profession. TM should offer some practical guidelines to apply and reinforce TM concepts within the business so that managers can incorporate TM into their daily routines.

Key Questions

Why does dynamic-capabilities theory improve the understanding of TM?
1   How has the TM discipline changed over the past 50 years?
2   What is the TM framework?
3   What are the main generic TM activities?
4   What are the main generic TM tools and what criteria are used to select them?

Further reading

Allen, J. T. and Varghese, G. (1989) 'Changes in the Field of R&D Management Over the Past 20 Years', *R&D Management*, **19**(2), 103–113.

Badawy, A. F. (2009) 'Technology Management Simply Defined: A Tweet Plus Two Characters', *Journal of Engineering and Technology Management*, **26**(4), 219–224.

Barney, J. B. and Clark, D. N. (2007) *Resource-Based Theory: Creating and Sustaining Competitive Advantage* (Oxford: Oxford University Press).

Christensen, J. F., Olesen, M. H. and Kjær, J. S. (2005) 'The Industrial Dynamics of Open Innovation: Evidence from the Transformation of Consumer Electronics', *Research Policy*, **34**(10), 1533–1549.

Dodgson, M. (2000) *The Management of Technological Innovation* (Oxford: Oxford University Press).

Euchner, J. (2014) 'Services-Led Business Models for Manufacturers', *Research-Technology Management*, **57**(2), 11–14.

(Continued)

Foden, J. and Berends, H. (2010) 'Technology Management at Rolls-Royce', *Research-Technology Management*, **53**(2), 33–42.

ICS UNIDO (2008) *Forum for Technology Transfer, Training Course on Technology Management*, www.ics.trieste.it/TP_TechnologyManagement/

Levin, D. Z. and Barnard, H. (2008) 'Technology Management Routines that Matter to Technology Managers', *International Journal of Technology Management*, **41**(1/2), 22–37.

OECD (2005) *Oslo Manual: Guidelines for Collecting and Interpreting Innovation Data*, 3rd edn (Paris: OECD).

Phaal, R., Farrukh, C. J. and Probert, D. R. (2004) 'A Framework for Supporting the Management of Technological Knowledge', *International Journal of Technology Management*, **27**(1), 1–15.

Rothwell, R. (1994) 'Towards the Fifth-Generation Innovation Process', *International Marketing Review*, **11**(1), 7–31.

Schiederig, T., Tietze, F. and Herstatt, C. (2012) 'Green Innovation in Technology and Innovation Management – An Exploratory Literature Review', *R&D Management*, **42**(2), 180–192.

Teece, D. J. (2007) 'Explicating Dynamic Capabilities: The Nature and Microfoundations of (Sustainable) Enterprise Performance', *Strategic Management Journal*, **28**(13), 1319–1350.

Teece, D. J. (2014) 'The Foundations of Enterprise Performance: Dynamic and Ordinary Capabilities in an (Economic) Theory of Firms', *Academy of Management Perspectives*, **28**(4), 328–352.

Thongpapanl, N. (2012) 'The Changing Landscape of Technology and Innovation Management: An Updated Ranking of Journals in the Field', *Technovation*, **32**(5), 257–271.

Tidd, J. and Bessant, J. (2013) *Managing Innovation: Integrating Technological, Market and Organizational Change*, 5th edn (Chichester: John Wiley).

Verganti, R. (2009) *Design Driven Innovation* (Cambridge, MA: Harvard Business School Press).

Part I

TECHNOLOGY MANAGEMENT ACTIVITIES

Part 1

1. TECHNOLOGY MANAGEMENT ACTIVITIES

Technology management (TM) is the management of technological capabilities to shape and accomplish the strategic and operational objectives of an organization. Knowing that technological capabilities comprise a collection of activities to explore and exploit technologies, TM can be conceived as a set of activities. In order for the performance of an activity to constitute a capability, the capability must have reached some threshold level of practised or routine activity. Each TM activity is related to a certain technological capability and thus it comprises a set of routines. Routines, repetitive pattern of activities, are similar to processes that achieve a managerial objective through the transformation of inputs into outputs. The term 'activity' is used interchangeably with process or routine throughout the text.

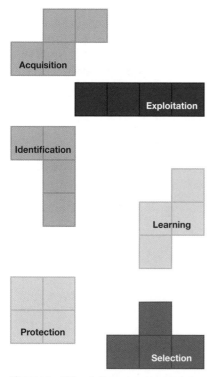

Figure I.1   TM activities

Part I consists of six chapters; each chapter is dedicated to a specific TM activity shown in Figure I.1 above, where the activity name is the same as the specific technological capability it aims to develop and exploit. The chapters are in alphabetical order to avoid any linear thinking about the sequence and hierarchy of each TM activity.

In this book, TM activities refer to the kinds of operations firms perform in their day-to-day routines. There might be multiple paths to the same dynamic capabilities and this is also true with technological capabilities. For example, the identification capability might be achieved with the formal establishment of an intelligence unit or just assigning one person. However, capabilities are similar in terms of key attributes, so each chapter is intended to exhibit common features associated with effective processes/routines across firms. These processes are drawn from the literature based on best practice. In other words, for simplicity, each chapter will describe generic processes/routines to illustrate the set of tasks needed to be carried out in order to achieve a particular technological capability.

It is important to remember, however, that these general processes aiming to achieve a goal might be carried out in many forms in real life. Managers need to realize that there is a degree of customization before any process is put into place in its context.

Chapters 2–7 have a similar format:

- Learning objectives.
- Introduction.
- Definition.
- Processes.
- Case study.
- Summary.

Case studies present real-life examples showing the different facets of each TM activity in varying detail. Almost all cases come from *Research-Technology Management*, a highly respected practice journal in the field of TM.

2

ACQUISITION

Learning objectives

After studying this chapter, you should be able to:

1 Differentiate between the two types of technology sourcing approaches: internal and external acquisition.
2 Identify advantages and disadvantages of acquisition types.
3 Understand the R&D capabilities and processes involved in producing new products, services and technologies.
4 Understand the relevance of open innovation in sourcing technology.
5 Learn about the variety of collaboration/alliance/network types and the process of external acquisition.
6 Observe the links between internal and external acquisitions.

2.1   Introduction

Acquisition relates to how the company will obtain the technologies needed for its business. Acquisition might be through internal technology development, collaborative development or purchasing from external developers. Depending on the type of acquisition, exemplar processes might be a simple purchasing act, internal R&D or complicated forms of collaborations that might range from a corporate merger to a research consortium. The concept of 'open innovation' also has implications for the acquisition and exploitation of technology, as organizations explore new ways to exchange ideas with a variety of new partners.

This chapter focuses on the internal development of technologies (internal R&D capability) as well as the co-development of technologies with outside partners/ collaborators (external acquisition capability). While the former is an in-house series of activities, the latter is based on activities involving inter-organizational relationships, popularly known as 'open innovation'. The chapter prefers to distinguish internal and external activities to understand distinct processes that are nested in real life. However acquisition takes place, the acquisition capability is the major base for building innovation capacity in an organization, but naturally innovation is generated across the borders of the R&D departments and can take place at any unit, department or staff level. Once the technology is acquired either internally or externally, it needs to be protected, as discussed in Chapter 6.

2.2 Internal acquisition: R&D

Definition

R&D encompasses a set of processes for creating a firm's technologies in-house. As its name shows, there are two main goals of R&D:

1 Doing research to generate new knowledge and technical ideas aimed at new and enhanced products, manufacturing processes and services.
2 Development activities where ideas are transformed into working prototypes and embodied in new products and services, including manufacturing, distribution and use.

In open innovation systems, the technology creation function has evolved into a broader context where both in-house and collaborative technology creation activities fall into the realm of R&D management, but as the case of Procter & Gamble (P&G) given at the end of the chapter indicates, firms organize their R&D along the lines of internal and external activities. Thus, external acquisition is discussed in the next section to accommodate all forms of collaborative means of inter-firm/inter-organizational R&D activities.

Radical technological changes and open innovation systems do not reduce the role of R&D departments of firms, rather they change and strengthen it. While open innovation systems do not focus exclusively on technology as the source of innovation, the implementation of such an approach may well have implications for internal resources and routines, leading to a higher return on R&D investments (Drake et al., 2006). This is clearly indicated in discussions about **absorptive capacity** (Cohen and Levinthal, 1990). There may be many external technological opportunities available for exploitation by firms, but this happens only if companies have strong knowledge capabilities/competencies that can recognize opportunities and transfer them into their context-specific/system knowledge (Larson, 2007). This kind of absorptive capacity requires an R&D department and related capabilities.

2.3 R&D processes

When technology strategy is developed, the broad goals for technologies are decided at the corporate level. These goals are transferred to the R&D department, starting a chain effect of generation and selection of projects on the basis of the general goals. The ultimate aim is to identify and deliver a portfolio of R&D projects that will satisfy the strategic needs. Once projects are identified and agreed upon, the R&D department implements them, managing the selected projects. Some of these projects might be chosen strategically to be carried out in collaboration with external partners.

R&D managers need to develop projects and manage them properly following project management guidelines. Projects might be different depending on the goal. The degree of process innovations combined with the level of product changes can help to describe the R&D management projects (Wheelwright and Clark, 1992). Accordingly, there are three main research project types: incremental, platform and radical. Besides this categorization, another set of projects might be basic research projects that are not necessarily product and process oriented. This type of blue-sky scientific project can result in new breakthroughs applicable to company-specific knowledge.

In addition to research projects, companies may have R&D projects devoted to ensuring that production and other operational systems continue to function and improve. These 'sustaining' or 'technical service' projects are required to solve unexpected problems or enable equipment maintenance (Burgelman et al., 2004). This group of projects relate to continuous improvement – as part of the 'D' in R&D. The details of these types of project are discussed in Chapter 3.

Once R&D projects are identified and feasible projects selected, their management is similar to other project management activities (Scott, 2000). However, the generation of R&D projects has characteristics different from other types of project, namely marketing projects. Because of the distinct features of R&D, this section focuses on three main processes within the R&D context:

1 R&D portfolio management.
2 New product/service development.
3 New process development.

R&D portfolio management

The expectation from an R&D manager is to develop a set of R&D projects that will form a **portfolio**. In the finance domain, the goal of portfolio management is to decide what assets to include in the portfolio, given the goals of the portfolio owner and changing economic conditions. Selection involves deciding which assets to purchase, how many to purchase, when to purchase them and which assets to divest. In addition, decisions about portfolio projects always involve some sort of performance measurement, most typically expected return on the portfolio and the risk associated with this return. Similar thinking applies to R&D portfolios, although the type of assets, risks and returns are different.

Portfolio management will be discussed as an approach that helps R&D processes in **Chapter 9**. In general, the challenge of R&D portfolio management is one of constrained optimization under conditions of uncertainty: a multi-project and multi-stage decision model. R&D needs to be carried out under a complex set of conditions (Cooper and Edgett, 1997; Kim and Wilemon, 2002):

- Uncertain and changing information about technologies.
- The existence of dynamic opportunities, multiple goals and the strategic considerations of firms' managers.
- High interdependence among projects.
- Multiple decision makers from different management units.

This picture becomes even more complicated when R&D projects are carried out in collaboration with external partners, ranging from customers to universities. Further, strategic decisions about R&D projects are tied in with the management of **intellectual property rights** (IPR). Without a proper protection strategy, as discussed in Chapter 6, the formation of a project portfolio is difficult.

New product/service development

'New product development' is the term used to describe the complete process of bringing a new product or service to market. There are several ways of classifying the type of new product or service. A classical approach shows the types on the basis of a product's newness to the market and company (Burgelman et al., 2004). Accordingly, some products are completely new products, since they are new not only to the company but also to the market. Some products may be new to the particular market but not to the company; these might be referred to as 'repositioned' products. In some cases, products may be neither new to the market nor the company, where product changes are incremental. New product development activities form part of the broader process of innovation management (Lehmann and Winer, 2004).

In general, the new product development process aims to capture the exploitable knowledge that is generated by R&D activities and can be divided into six phases/stages (Kahn, 2004). These basic stages start with ideation and move into preliminary and detailed investigation stages that build the basis for the feasibility reports. Development then takes place and the results are tested through a pilot run. Depending on the results, the final stage, full production, takes place or some further refinement/development studies are carried out. In this book, any activity carried out after development, such as commercialization, is considered under the topic of exploitation.

Formal product/service and process development systems have been widely adopted by industry, often based on the Stage-Gate system® (Cooper and Kleinschmidt, 1994; Cooper, 2008). There are many versions and adaptations of this process, based on the common principle of separating the various stages by gates where product development activities are evaluated according to the performance achieved, leading to a decision as to whether and how to continue or to stop. The details of the Stage-Gate process are given in **Chapter 12**. As a product moves from idea to commercialization, the Stage-Gate model achieves two primary functions: it provides parallel processing of all the elements impacting on the development of the product, such as technology and market, while ensuring a gradual increase in the project's probability of success as one moves to later stages and larger amounts of capital are committed.

The phases of new product development are often depicted as a **development funnel** that consists of research, development and commercialization. It is also known as the 'idea/project funnel'. Broadly speaking, there are two parallel paths involved in the new product development process: one involves idea generation, product design and detailed engineering; while the other involves **market research** and marketing analysis. This simplification shows that R&D activities are very much integrated with creativity and commercialization. Creativity is particularly important for generating ideas at the early stage. This is mainly tackled in Chapter 5, while commercialization is discussed in Chapter 3. More recently, the development funnel has been adapted (Figure 2.1) to accommodate the implications of open innovation and show the exchange of ideas, technology and other IP with external organizations. This transition from a closed to an open system, based on permeable company boundaries, has procedural and cultural consequences for the individuals involved. Previous training to be secretive about confidential information will need to be modified to encourage a (safe) exchange with the outside world.

Even though the idea/project funnel seems to be a simple process, the new product development process can be divided into highly detailed sub-processes, as described in **Chapter 12**. But it is important to remember that these sub-processes are not always followed in a linear sequence as implied by the funnel model. In fact, many companies engage in several new product development stages at the same time, referred to as **concurrent engineering** (Cooper, 2008).

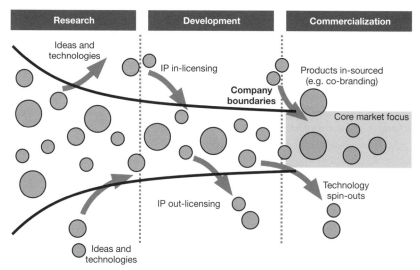

Figure 2.1 The model of open innovation
Source: Based on Hayes et al. (1988); Chesbrough (2003); Docherty (2006).

Even though the new product development phases are, in general, described just for one product or a service, it is important to consider the whole product life cycle (Burgelman et al., 2004). In particular, new product development analysis should incorporate product-family/platforms thinking. A **product family** consists of products that have similar features, typically with a shared technology basis. It provides an architecture based on commonality and similarity. The various product variants can be derived from the basic product family, which creates the opportunity to reuse and differentiate products in the family (Meyer et al., 2005). The approach focuses on the process of engineering new products in such a way that enables the reuse of product components, with the benefits of increased variability and decreased costs and time.

A company can develop its product-family structure by mapping existing products and comparing the assumptions underlying current product lines. By observing the evolution of a company's product lines, it is possible to expose products to different markets and understand the technologies that have been driving the evolution of the products.

New process development

In general, certain product strategies may necessitate a corresponding process technology. However, as the level of technological sophistication increases, these relationships are altered (Hayes et al., 1984, 1988). For example, historically, project-type product and job-shop processes corresponded to craft production, whereas assembly line and continuous processes have been associated with mass production technology. Mass customization has challenged these linkages. Mass customization makes it economically possible to consider the commercialization of less standardized products in a quasi-continuous process.

Besides searching for a fit between product and process, process innovations are an important element of any product innovation. Over time the dynamics of innovation shift from product innovation to process innovation (Utterback, 1994). In other words, innovations start with a new product idea but when production starts, actual problems on the shop floor trigger the need for adjustments, as well as feedback from customers/markets that call for process improvements such as quality. All these various reasons result in an intensified need for process innovations.

New process development can be characterized in terms of the degree of innovation in the process, ranging from incremental to radical process change. Similar to product families, processes can form platforms as well. Stretching the idea of individual processes into a set of related processes increases the **utilization** of common technologies across these processes by creating synergies and optimization. This is why any project involving process development should take into consideration the concept of process families, such as process architectures.

The key tasks in designing a new process are as follows (Tushman and Andersen, 2004):

- Identifying processes for innovation.
- Identifying change elements.
- Developing process visions.
- Defining business strategy and process vision.
- Understanding existing processes.
- Understanding the structure and flow of the current process.
- Measuring the performance of the current process.
- Designing and prototyping the new process.
- Implementing and operationalizing the process and associated systems.
- Communicating results and building commitment.

The tools applicable for new process and product development range from activity-based costing to **business process re-engineering**. The majority of the available tools have emerged from the total quality management field. Some of the most popular and powerful methods are (Melnyk and Denzler, 1996; Burgelman et al., 2004):

- Taguchi's methods of parameter design (for the product and process domains) and tolerance design (for the product domain).
- Design for assembly.
- Design for manufacturing.
- Design for serviceability.
- Design for testability.
- Design for environment.
- System engineering.
- Value analysis and value engineering.

2.4 External technology acquisition

Definition

An enterprise can either develop its technological products, processes or services internally or acquire them externally. Technology acquisition might range from buying skills and know-how to embedded technologies in components and products. It includes the use of external sources not only for well-defined technology needs but also emerging technology development. In recent years, there has been a dramatic increase in sourcing innovation externally, referred to as 'open innovation', where firms collaborate with external organizations ranging from universities to research companies across the globe (Chesbrough, 2003). This is why external technology acquisition consists of 'buy' and 'collaborate' options.

Even though the set of technologies to be sourced externally might be decided at the strategy level, there is a need for an integrated plan of acquisition which optimizes the benefits of buying in. When there are a number of technologies to be outsourced, there is a need to manage the portfolio and review it on a regular basis in the light of new information on markets, competitors and technologies, as the relative strategic importance of technologies will change over time. But more importantly, the external innovation activities need to be integrated into processes such as the firm's budget processes and R&D systems.

In general, companies might prefer to acquire technologies because of limited internal resources, time pressure, lack of complementary assets, diversification, influence over standards or to protect internal technologies and avoid development risks (Johnes et al., 2001). But the acquisition decision cannot be done alone. As discussed in **Chapter 7**, the make-buy-collaborate decision is a difficult one and managers might follow different criteria to find an optimum solution of these integrated decisions.

Sourcing technology externally demands relationships with other organizations and managers need to choose among different forms of inter-firm collaborations/**alliances**, known as 'acquisition channels' (Slowinski et al., 2009). The forms of alliances may vary according to how they are defined. One classification is based on the two key dimensions (Spekman and Isabella, 2000): the degree of control (from arm's length to full mergers and acquisitions – **M&A**) and the duration of the commitment (either short or long). Control refers to the legal ownership; for example an arm's-length relationship indicates no ownership relationship between parties involved in the alliance, while M&A result in one legal entity being formed through complete equity ownership of the parties taking part in the alliance.

All forms of inter-firm collaborations have certain advantages and disadvantages to firms. A basic categorization of alliance options includes (Chiesa and Manzini, 1998; Spekman and Isabella, 2000):

- Purchasing.
- Subcontracting/outsourcing/contracted-out R&D.
- **Licensing.**
- Alliances.
- M&A.

Purchasing/arm's-length transactions

Purchasing has clear-cut processes and the degree of collaboration is the least among the five collaboration options. After the company searches for what is available in the market, it decides whether or not to buy a technology and then negotiates on price with the supplier/vendor. In broad terms, what you see should be what you get. A purchasing act is, by and large, a one-time event and does not require a close relationship. However, continuous purchasing from one technology supplier might result in a relationship developing over time.

In a purchase, a company buys a product or service that embodies technologies. In some cases, vendors/suppliers may initiate the transaction. Large suppliers, in particular, who are leaders in their sector, may have innovations that are appropriate for the company, which they will proactively market and sell.

Contracted-out R&D

Contracting R&D is where a company uses the services of a contract research organization or some other party to develop a new process or product. In some cases, companies contract out R&D to individual consultants/experts/researchers in order to tap into distinct competencies that the company lacks. Contracting is suitable for those situations where the company has a low standing in the technological area. As it is contracted out, the company has little managerial input in the process. The third party might be a commercial company, a commercial R&D laboratory, a university or even a competitor. The goal of the contract might be to gain an experiment result, a proof-of-principle demonstrator, a prototype, a solution to a problem or machinery.

In rare cases, companies may choose to sponsor blue-sky projects in universities so that the results might be useful in the long term for their internal R&D.

Licensing

Licensing refers to the conventional situation where a company holds a licence for the use of a product design, a process or a marketing package or some combination of all three, on a franchise basis. The licensee company looks at what is available, deciding whether or not to buy and then negotiates on price. In broad terms, what you see should be what you get, but in practice technology can rarely be readily packaged, requiring a combination of drawings, documents, experience and know-how to be transferred to the purchasing company context.

Licensing initiates a long-term relationship between licensor and licensee companies equivalent to the licence duration. By licensing, a company confirms that it has no objective of being a leader in the licensed technology, at least in the short term. The major advantages are to speed the technology adoption and reduce the risk and cost of developing the technology.

Alliances

Several types of alliance are possible, ranging from ad-hoc partnerships formed to solve specific problems, through to complex alliances and joint ventures, to complete acquisitions. Ad-hoc alliances are flexible and are normally used to develop a technology that is critical to two or more businesses. Forming a consortium is another flexible alliance form, where many partners come together for pre-competitive R&D with no equity relationship involved. More complex alliance forms may be used to help two or more businesses operating in different sectors to pool their resources and generate synergy so that the companies can gain access to a critical technology in which they are weak. The joint venture is a type of complex alliance in which the area of cooperation is well defined and sufficiently long term to merit the creation of a separate legal entity. A joint venture shares the risks and costs of acquisition between two or more partners and is valuable when these are high.

For example, while developing the iPod music player, Apple did not develop the player in-house but created an alliance. It used a Toshiba disk drive, based the iPod software on a platform developed by Portal-Player and the music management software was developed by Pixo (Terwiesch and Ulrich, 2008).

M&A

Acquisition of a company is the most certain way of securing a technology and preventing others from acquiring it, although if the two companies are of roughly equivalent size, a merger may be appropriate. The goal in all M&A activity is to acquire and integrate an external entity into the existing company.

Acquisition is the fastest way of transferring required external critical capabilities and resources into the firm to support and help internal core competencies. However, the post-acquisition/merger of two companies can be slow and difficult. Particular challenges include potential organizational culture clashes and managerial problems that might result in a failure of the merger.

2.5   External acquisition processes

Managing technology acquisition is a multifaceted process. For example, Daim and Kocao-glu (2008) offer the following steps to be taken in technology acquisition:

- Technology gap analysis/problem identification.
- Identification of the technology alternatives.
- Evaluation of the technology alternatives.
- Acquisition of the technologies.
- Impacts through the acquisition of technologies.

However, this process flow applies to purchasing/arm's-length relationships rather than other forms of external acquisition processes, including collaborations. Therefore, for each technology and situation, there is a need to choose which acquisition approach to follow. The following six phases provide a useful framework for structuring acquisition processes (Chiesa and Manzini, 1998; Slowinski and Zerby, 2008; Slowinski et al., 2009):

1 Goal setting.
2 Finding technology suppliers.
3 Choosing acquisition method.
4 Contract preparation and negotiation.
5 Technology transfer.
6 Managing long-term collaboration.

Goal setting

Companies cannot afford to develop all technologies in-house but equally companies should not outsource everything. That is why technology forecasting and technology strategy activities supply important inputs when goals are set for technology acquisition. As discussed in Chapter 4, Clorox and Baxter Healthcare make explicit searches for opportunities outside the firm, regardless of who owns them.

Managers need to be aware of their current and future required technology portfolios and what they need to do to advance the competitive position of their companies. An important goal that is set during strategy development is to decide on what the core competencies of the company need to be. Having a core competence list helps managers to make technology acquisition decisions that are based on the degree to which the competencies support both current and future business activities and needs. So protecting core competencies is a critical goal in deciding which technologies to buy in.

Cost-benefit analysis is a useful decision tool when buying a technology. For example, buying in technology can be beneficial for base technologies, providing flexibility and saving time and money and can be beneficial for key and pacing technologies, facilitating cost sharing and increasing flexibility.

The goals for technology acquisition need to be coordinated with R&D management and decisions, considered in more detail in Chapter 7. The strategic goals will determine how the next processes in technology acquisition will be carried out.

Finding technology suppliers

Companies may utilize many different approaches to identify external technology. As discussed in Chapter 4, a formal intelligence unit might be established to keep an eye on the external environment, with the task of supplying information relating to potential technology suppliers and available technologies. If there is no formal forecasting/intelligence unit within an organization, then patent and literature searches, university and federal laboratory contacts as well as technology brokers and entrepreneurs all provide access to external technology. Some companies have dedicated individuals or teams who identify targeted technologies and acquire them with the involvement of the appropriate business units.

If there are a number of technology suppliers with different technology capabilities, as in any purchasing activity, an assessment will be needed for the technologies and the suppliers. For TM, any of the technology assessment techniques might be used. In the case of assessing suppliers, the situation can be complicated as suppliers might be customers, vendors, technology firms, universities and even competitors. Supplier assessment may depend on the potential supplier's experience, track record in technology, cultural fit with the company, geographical distance and its reputation. Success will be more likely for compatible partners that share similar aspirations, culture and strategic objectives. Mechanisms developed in advanced countries, such as innovation relay centres established by the European Union (EU), provide support for organizations seeking technology suppliers and customers.

Choosing acquisition method

Since technology acquisition options range from arm's-length transactions to M&A, the choice of acquisition method is a critical task. Among all potential forms of organizational collaborations, firms decide which form of collaboration is preferable on the basis of three main criteria:

1 The objectives of the collaboration.
2 The content of the collaboration.
3 The typology of partners involved in the process (Chiesa and Manzini, 1998).

An appropriate organizational form that matches all these criteria should be selected.

The objective of collaboration may be broad, limited or learning oriented. The content of the collaboration will depend on various aspects relating to the technology, such as the firm's familiarity with the technology, relevance to the firm's competitive position, technology life cycle, level of risk, appropriability/ownership of the innovation, phase of the innovation process, level of asset specialization and divisibility of assets (Teece, 1986). The typology of partners might be decided on the basis of the firm's characteristics, country location of the partner, sector of activity and contractual power.

The assessment and approach depend on a company's priorities. If a company wants to acquire technological competence by learning from a partner, it might choose to do an in-depth exchange through collaborative R&D, leading to a close form of alliance. Thus, a firm's technology strategy and the particular goals of the technology acquisition will influence the selection of the suitable collaboration form.

Contract preparation and negotiation

The purchasing option is relatively simple to manage, after identifying the potential sellers and agreeing on the conditions of purchase. However, acquisitions that require more complex organizational collaborations will typically involve more complicated arrangements, with a need to integrate a contract preparation process into the technology acquisition activity.

The formality of a contract will vary with the number of partners and the contents of the deal. Contracts are helpful in setting the boundaries of alliances in terms of:

- Scope and time.
- Describing the content of the collaboration.
- Defining IP.
- Indicating the division of labour among partners.
- The rules of funding/investment.
- Clarifying exit options and fall-back positions.
- The duties and responsibilities of partners including their investments.
- Penalties for not delivering on promises.

Contracts help to define and articulate the conditions of the interaction, but ultimately the key issue is one of trust and ethics.

The preparation of the contract is a negotiation process between partners. The degree to which they can influence the terms and conditions will depend on their relative power.

Technology transfer

After a technology is developed collaboratively or by the supplier, it is delivered to the buyer for use. However, technologies are not stand-alone hardware; on the contrary, they demand know-how and skills to apply them, as shown in Chapter 3 in the case of BICC in establishing its new cable plant. Moreover, emerging technologies have no clear product application, their application potential is ill-defined and they are not guaranteed to succeed. For knowledge created in a collaboration to become either a success or a failure is partly the responsibility of the technology manager. This is why its transfer into the buyer's own facilities needs to be managed as a distinct process, which is covered in more detail in Chapter 3.

Managing long-term collaboration

There are many critical managerial concerns in technology collaborations involving many partners. Depending on the size of the companies, there might be a need to have a lead company to balance the power and expectations among partners. Even though there might be symmetry with respect to the size of companies, there still might be a need to have a leader to represent the collaboration and to coordinate the interactions between the partners and maintain the balance (Spivey et al., 2009).

Activities within the collaborating network need to be managed, controlled and coordinated. Control implies measurement and evaluation, but for this type of technology collaboration, it may be challenging to define and agree on appropriate performance measures and evaluation mechanisms (Cetindamar and Ulusoy, 2008). Trust is another soft factor in running collaborations successfully and it is not developed overnight. Partners need to work on building trust explicitly and invest in building a common culture that promotes trust and common thinking. Learning is typically an issue for each partner, to varying degrees. They all have different sets of competencies and they exchange them throughout the relationship, but if learning is not set as a goal, many partners might fail to do it. Another problem with learning might be the different levels of knowledge in companies that limits their absorptive capacity.

In some cases, collaboration is done with competitors. In these cases, it is important to remember that collaboration is competition in a different form. Companies must defend themselves against competitive compromise and develop safeguards to protect core competencies. In addition, knowledge acquired from a competitor-partner needs to be diffused through the organization in order to utilize it in an optimum way.

Another dimension in collaborations is to consider the changes in managerial needs during the evolution of collaborations. Companies need to have cooperative relationships with some stakeholders and at the same time take precautions against competitors (Prahalad and Hamel, 1990; Chiesa and Manzini, 1998). These contradictions might also change over the life cycle of technology to protect core competencies. This is why management needs to take strategic actions to manage competition and cooperation over the life of the collaboration.

Even if all the processes of technology sourcing are well managed and effective, companies may suffer from the 'not-invented-here' syndrome, where employees reject the adoption and implementation of the purchased technology since it is not internally produced. Thus, change management is an important consideration in any technology acquisition activity.

2.6   The environment assessment in acquisition decisions

Managers increasingly face environmental problems as discussed in Chapter 14. That is why decisions regarding technology acquisition take into account environment as a new dimension while assessing the benefits of technologies before investing in them. In parallel to this, there are new tools that help managers to become sustainable. For example, environmentally conscious design (eco-design) or Design for Environment is becoming an increasingly important tool (Bevilacqua et al., 2007). The introduction of eco-design methodologies in manufacturing firms emphasized to environmental aspects right from the start of the design stage leading to a reduction in the materials used and the waste products, avoiding any future weaknesses and inefficiencies. Eco-design considers the potential environmental impact throughout the life cycle of the product: emission of harmful substances, excessive use of energy or nonrenewable energy sources. It also considers the life cycle of the materials from extraction to disposal. In this way the designers do not create just a product but a whole life cycle.

The life cycle engineering approach aims to integrate the technical, economical and environmental distinctive evaluations. There might be different ways of applying this approach. One such model will be summarized and its application will be shown. The exemplar approach is composed of three elements: a life cycle cost model, a life cycle assessment model and multiple attributes decision-making method (Pecas et al., 2009). The former includes and correlates the cost factors, allowing the economic performance assessment, while the latter allows the environmental performance evaluation. The final element, multiple attributes decision-making method, helps to assess the contribution of technical performance over the life cycle.

An example helps to illustrate how the life cycle engineering approach evaluates two candidate technologies to be used in the production of very small volumes of polymeric parts (Pecas et al., 2009). Accordingly, two rival moulds inject the same plastic part, but they differ essentially in the cavity and core materials as well as the technologies used to produce them. One is a mould made of a spray metal shell backfilled with resin and aluminium powder (STM mould) and the other is based on machined aluminium (CM mould).

The cost incurred during the overall life cycle is determined by the sum of the several cost items inherent to successive life cycle phases. The total cost in the mould example consists of three categories: the process costs, including machine and labour costs; the material costs, associated with the consumption of materials (raw materials and standard components); and the energy costs, related to the amount of energy consumed by the equipments. The costs are assumed for a production volume of 200 units.

The life cycle assessment uses internationally available standards (called ISO 14040-3 and Eco-Indicator 99) that consider several environmental impact categories, aggregating all the emissions and resources consumption into three areas: human health, ecosystem quality and resources.

The evaluation of the technical performance of a product, a tool or other equipment relies on the know-how of professionals (and users) to choose the relevant technical attributes for the application. Some of the selected attributes are technology availability, time-to-plastic part production, mould capability, mould robustness, mould durability, reusability and so on.

The assessment of the results achieved help to evaluate the alternatives. The outcomes of each individual dimension of analysis (technical, economical and environmental performance) are adimensionalized to allow the attribution of importance weights. The sum of the three dimensions' weights must be 100% and different combinations of weights might result in a different 'best mould'. The decision on weights to the dimensions of analysis reflects a corporation strategy. The possible 'best moulds' correlated to its domain of weights are shown in Figure 2.2 where each axis represents one dimension of analysis. The diagram illustrates the 'best mould' for a particular set of importance weights and the domain of weights for each 'best mould'.

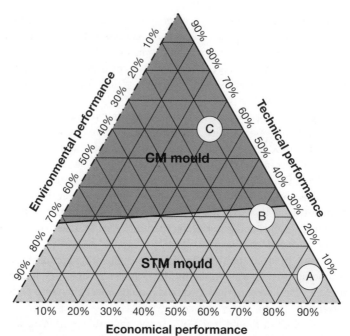

Figure 2.2 Technical, environmental and economical performance evaluation
Source: Pecas et al., 2009.

In general, Figure 2.2 shows that STM mould performs better both in economical and environmental terms, while CM mould performs better regarding technological issues. But the final selection of the best mould depends on the company strategy. For example, if a company gives high importance to cost and low importance to both environmental impact and technical performance, modelled with importance weights of 85%, 5% and 10% respectively, the STM mould would be the selected first (point A of Figure 2.2). Another scenario is illustrated in point C of Figure 2.2, where high importance is given to the mould technical performance (60%) and a lower importance is given to economic and environmental performance, 30% and 10% respectively. In this scenario it is clear that the best option is the CM mould.

As this case illustrates, there are many ways of incorporating environment dimension into the decision making of technology acquisitions. Depending on company strategy, the method to be deployed and the relative importance of environment dimension might show variance. In short, managers are equipped with many tools that could help them assess the impact of technology on environment before they invest in technologies.

 Case study

Technology acquisition consists of internal and external acquisition capabilities, as clearly shown in the case of P&G. In general, firms find different mechanisms to organize their R&D along the lines of internal and external activities ranging from centralized R&D departments to joint developments. By expanding their acquisition capabilities, firms manage to tap into a wide variety of opportunities.

P&G

P&G has 8,000 researchers, 40% of whom work outside North America. Consequently, P&G pursues a 'Connect + Develop' strategy that involves the use of corporate intranet and 'smart' reporting systems for knowledge sharing, communities of practice, technology entrepreneurs, joint technology development, liberal licensing of IP, government and university capabilities and a connection-making exposition, as shown in Figure 2.3.

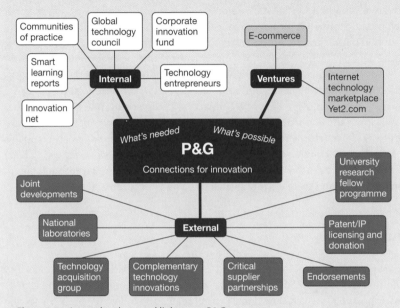

Figure 2.3 Internal and external linkages at P&G

Linking technologies in unexpected ways lies at the heart of breakthrough innovation in P&G products, packages and processes and it significantly reduces product costs, improves quality and speeds product delivery.

Examples of internal resources

P&G's Global Technology Council is made up of business unit technology directors, corporate R&D heads and key geographical R&D leaders to represent all the company competencies. This working forum explores how to leverage P&G technologies and serves as an 'incubator' for exploratory research and early-stage product development. There are 20 chartered communities of practice, sponsored by an R&D vice president appointed by the chief technology officer. Each represents a shared interest across P&G and has the budget and effective leadership to promote cross-fertilization and diffusion of expertise. Some of the larger communities of practice have full-time staff leading them. Their activities include active problem solving via email conferences, knowledge sharing via live seminars and websites, recognition for expert practitioners

(Continued)

and active seeking of internal and external expertise and tools for diffusion throughout the organization.

Examples of external resources

P&G employs a broad range of joint technology developments. Critical supplier partnerships are established so that staff are on site at supplier facilities, working together to develop and commercialize new chemicals, materials and mechanical processes. In effect, suppliers' R&D labs are now an extension of the company's innovating capability.

Complementary technology innovations involve joint developments with companies whose expertise is in strikingly different technical areas. The technology acquisition group actively seeks out new technologies and products. Stepping up the licensing of technologies allows P&G to access complementary technologies that would fill gaps in the IP portfolio. P&G is also actively licensing or donating P&G technologies to increase returns for the IP portfolios. P&G is a technology-rich company: 27,000 patents, 4,000 unique titles and 3,000 new patents each year. Even with a large $1.8bn annual investment in R&D, P&G uses less than 10% of its own technologies in company products and there is a lot of value to be had in the remaining 90%.

Resources/tools

P&G has a powerful internal website called 'InnovationNet', with a target audience of 18,000 innovators across R&D, engineering, market research, purchasing and patent divisions. It hosts 600 websites for global project teams and individual problem-solving and connection-making websites for 20 communities of practice. This adds up to nearly nine million documents online and growing daily. InnovationNet has automation and artificial intelligence that tracks users' interests, suggests reading material and identifies other users with similar interests.

As a means for stimulating technology awareness and innovation, P&G organized a deal-making/technology trading expo in 2000. This three-day event showcased over 100 of P&G's most promising, cutting-edge technologies with a global audience consisting of R&D, engineering, marketing and general management. Over 5,000 P&G researchers attended the expo. P&G used the latest in webcasting and satellite technology to create an internal innovation news network, complete with news anchors, reporters and even commercials. P&G invited external suppliers to showcase their technologies at the trading expo as well, with more than 600 representatives from 50 exhibitors of non-P&G technologies. Participants included developmental suppliers, university collaborators, federal laboratories and research institutes from around the world. As a result of the expo, over 2,200 ideas for new products and important new uses of P&G and external technologies were generated and entered into the Innovation 2000 database.

Source: Sakkab, N. Y. (2002) 'Connect & Develop Complements Research & Develop at P&G', *Research-Technology Management*, **45**(2), 38–45.

Summary

Acquisition is concerned with developing technologies internally or in some form of collaboration or buying from external developers. Examination of industrial R&D activity over the past 50 years highlights two pillars of acquisition. As observed in the 1970s, connecting R&D closely with manufacturing and marketing is the first important pillar of acquisition. Trying to make R&D work with other departments has led to a more team-based innovation process and this effort linked R&D to corporate business strategy. The other key pillar of acquisition is accessing external technology, which has become popular as open innovation in the 2000s. Open innovation, as described in the case of P&G through its Connect + Develop strategy, aims to stimulate radical innovation through different management techniques and organizational patterns where external players become important. This new approach is called 'fourth-generation innovation management', emphasizing dominant design, different management practices and strong chief executive officer (CEO) leadership.

Whatever developments take place in the future, it is clear that internal and external acquisition capabilities are crucial for long-term competitive advantage. If acquisition is done through collaboration, as in virtual organizations, coordination and integration become crucial as a managerial process, since the interests of all parties involved should be aligned. On the other hand, if the technology is bought, the integration of technology becomes harder since the tacit know-how is not found in the organization. Therefore, the integration and reconfiguration of existing organizational skills are vital and they are sustained by the dynamic capabilities of the organization. In other words, with static competencies, it is hard to achieve the integration of a technology bought from a third party with the existing internal technologies. If technology is developed in-house, the requirements differ from the other two options, since know-how is developed by the company itself, which results in a shorter period of integration of the new technology. On the other hand, internal acquisition usually requires installed R&D facilities, efficient methodologies and tacit knowledge obtained through a process of learning through experience.

? Key Questions

1 What differentiates the two types of technology sourcing approaches: internal and external acquisition?
2 What are the advantages and disadvantages of these two acquisition approaches?
3 What are the R&D capabilities and processes involved in producing new products, services and technologies?
4 What are the major types of collaboration/alliance/network used for external technology acquisition?
5 What is the process of external acquisition?

📖 Further reading

Badawy, M. K. (1995) *Developing Managerial Skills in Engineers and Scientists: Succeeding as a Technical Manager*, 2nd edn (Van Nostrand Reinhold Series in: Managerial Skill Development in Engineering and Science, New York: Van Nostrand Reinhold).

Bevilacqua, M., Ciarapica, F. E. and Giacchetta, G. (2007) 'Development of a Sustainable Product Lifecycle in Manufacturing Firms: A Case Study', *International Journal of Production Research*, **45**(18/19), 4073–4098.

Chesbrough, H. and Brunswicker, S. (2014) 'A Fad or a Phenomenon?', *Research-Technology Management*, **57**(2), 16–25.

Cooper, R. G. (2001) *Winning at New Products: Accelerating the Process from Idea to Launch*, 3rd edn (Cambridge, MA: Perseus Books).

Ford, S. J., Mortara, L. and Probert, D. R. (2012) 'Disentangling the Complexity of Early-Stage Technology Acquisitions', *Research-Technology Management*, **55**(3), 40–48.

Mortara, L. and Ford, S. (2012) *Technology Acquisitions: A Guided Approach to Technology Acquisition and Protection Decisions* (Cambridge: University of Cambridge).

Pecas, P., Ribeiro, I., Folgado, R. and Henriques, E. (2009) 'A Life Cycle Engineering Model for Technology Selection,' *Journal of Cleaner Production*, **17**(9), 846–856.

Roussel, P. A., Saad, K. N. and Erickson, T. J. (1991) *Third Generation R&D: Managing the Link to Corporate Strategy* (Boston, MA: Harvard Business School Press).

Spekman, R. E. and Isabella, L. A. (2000) *Alliance Competence: Maximising the Value of your Partnership* (New York: John Wiley & Sons).

3

EXPLOITATION

Learning objectives

After studying this chapter, you should be able to:

1 Understand the complexity of exploitation.
2 Identify the key features of exploitation.
3 Understand the three major sub-processes of an exploitation activity: commercialization/marketing, technology transfer and utilization.
4 Appreciate the role of commercialization/marketing.
5 Understand the role of technology transfer.
6 Understand the role of technology utilization.

3.1   Introduction

The process of exploitation is concerned with generating profit or achieving other benefits from technology. Exploitation can be defined as the utilization of new technology or scientific developments to improve the performance of products, services or manufacturing processes.

Exploitation of technological capability is more than just commercialization, since the expected benefits might be accrued through effective and efficient implementation, absorption and operation of the technology. If there is not a fully working product/process/service at hand, there will be no commercialization activity. So the exploitation activity includes three sets of sub-processes: commercialization/marketing, technology transfer and utilization.

The commercialization process is the launch of a product/service into the market based on a selected **business model**. Technology transfer consists of processes related to transferring technologies internally from an R&D unit to a manufacturing department, from an external company/partner to the internal manufacturing department or from an internal R&D unit to a partner company's manufacturing department. Utilization aims to put new technologies into use in such a way that they will be fully utilized. Utilization refers not only to adjusting/customizing/improving but also to maintaining and integrating technologies for synergy. The utilization process is intertwined with technology transfer activities, because each implementation or launch involves reconfigurations that will demand alignments between technology and its actual application.

In Chapter 2, the consequences of open innovation for technology acquisition were discussed and similar considerations also apply to technology exploitation. New routes to transfer technology may arise out of more open collaboration with a wider variety of partner organizations.

3.2   Commercialization/marketing

Definition

Commercialization is the process of introducing a new product or service into the market. The definition of innovation clearly indicates that the commercialization process turns an invention into an innovation, a sellable product or service in the marketplace. Many companies are good at producing inventions but not all their inventions are put into use. For example, the case of P&G discussed in Chapter 2 shows that the company uses less than 10% of its own technologies in company products (Sakkab, 2002). So the technology acquisition capability is a good start but not enough to turn inventions into profits.

The first task is to decide on the commercialization method; to a large degree, this is made at the strategy level, as described in Chapter 7.

Technology exploitation can take one of three possible routes:

1 *In-house development*: the production and distribution of technology are carried out within the company.
2 *Joint commercialization*: production and distribution are carried out in collaboration with other organizations through joint ventures or other forms of alliance.
3 *Selling technology*: can take place at any stage of technology development, including idea, prototype, patent and licence sales.

Making an analogy to the make-buy-collaborate decision, the exploitation activity is involved with a make-sell-collaborate decision. Exploitation options refer to selecting a different business model for the commercialization of technologies. In other words, exploitation requires strategic thinking. The sell option is discussed in Chapter 6, while in-house development and joint commercialization processes are discussed in Chapter 2.

A company chooses its exploitation method/business model on the basis of its strategy and core competencies. Accordingly, its core technologies must be produced in-house but technologies that do not fit into the company's overall strategy might be sold or collaboratively commercialized with partners. The collaborative alternatives such as mergers and consortia are covered in Chapter 2. Besides strategy, the level of exploitation will clearly depend on the geographical distribution of a company – being a multi-plant or international company will make a difference. The company might utilize local pockets of innovation around the country or nurture new technologies and cross-fertilize them for commercialization and global distribution.

Ford and Saren (1996) provide a framework for choosing an exploitation method based on seven criteria:

- Company's relative standing.
- Categories of technology.
- Urgency of exploitation.
- Need for support technologies.
- Commitment/investment.
- Technology life cycle position.
- Potential application.

Based on these criteria, a company might choose its exploitation method among the following available options: (1) internal employment in own products/processes/marketing,

(2) external contract out manufacture or marketing to others, (3) contract in manufacture, marketing or product design for others, (4) joint venture and (5) licensing out.

For example, the internal commercialization or make decision takes place when a company's relative standing is at all levels – technology is basic, urgency is the lowest, the need for supporting technology is lowest, commitment is highest, technology life cycle is earliest and potential application is narrowest.

Besides the criteria presented above, another set of popular criteria are complementary assets, dominant design and appropriability regime (Teece, 1986, 2006), which are further discussed in Chapter 7. A successful innovation consists not only of technical knowledge but also other capabilities and activities such as marketing, competitive manufacturing and after-sales support, referred to as 'complementary assets'. Dominant design is an agreement on the basic features of a product or service, showing standardization. Appropriability regime refers to the regulatory system for intellectual assets that makes protection possible (see Chapter 7).

Commercialization is directly related to earning revenue from sales, derived from a set of processes, particularly marketing, since successfully introducing a new product or service into the market requires advertising, distribution and selling of a product or service. The company's exploitation task involves selling the products that are based on technologies developed in-house or acquired externally. This is why the marketing of technological products and services is highly critical. This chapter focuses on marketing in the context of understanding the commercialization process as a whole.

Marketing theory and practice are justified in the belief that customers use a product or service because they have a need or it provides a perceived benefit (Kotler and Keller, 2006). Thus, marketing is concerned with anticipating customers' future needs and wants, often through market research and creative imagination. Two major factors of marketing are the recruitment of new customers and the retention and expansion of relationships with existing customers. Once a marketer has converted the prospective buyer, base management marketing takes over. The process for base management shifts the marketer to building a relationship, nurturing the links, enhancing the benefits that interested the buyer in the first place and continuously improving the product/service to protect the business from competition.

For a marketing plan to be successful, the mix of the four Ps (product, price, promotion and place) should reflect the wants and desires of consumers in the target market (Dibb et al., 2001). Marketers depend on market research, formal and informal, to determine their markets, competitors, customer wants and needs. Market research aims to supply information to what, where, when, how and why questions about a company's business. Marketers use different methods to acquire data. Appropriate techniques used to capture the voice of the customer will depend on the nature of the customer relationship, as shown in Table 3.1. Direct tools in forming relationships with customers include customer meetings, while indirect methods range from surveys to focus groups.

Besides data on customers, the marketing department needs to gather data on competitors and the market/business environment such as regulations. The majority of information comes from the type of analysis discussed in Chapter 4. There are different techniques used to identify markets. For example, 'Porter's diamond' (an analysis of firm strategy, factor conditions, demand conditions and related supporting industries) is a typical tool used to make a complete economic and commercial analysis for marketing that will help to segment the market and develop the marketing plan (Porter, 1985).

Table 3.1   Methods of direct and indirect relationships with customers

Direct relationship	Indirect relationship
Direct business relationship could be development through methods such as: • Requirements specification • Contract or order • Customer meetings • Warranty and repair data • Customer representatives	Distributors and retailers interface with customers and try to capture requirements by applying methods such as: • Surveys • Focus groups • Market research • Interviews • Customer service feedback

Marketing focuses on basic concepts like the four Ps as well as on the psychological and sociological aspects of marketing. Competitive advantage is created by directly appealing, better than the competition, to the needs, wants and behaviours of customers. Successful marketing involves creating brands and building relationships (such as one-to-one marketing and customer relations management) and offering business models that other companies cannot offer.

Marketing technology is distinct from any other product or service marketing (Navens et al., 1990; Easingwood and Koustelos, 2000). The distinctive characteristic of technology is its innovativeness. The history of technological advancements shows that the time-lag from invention to innovation is very high; for example it took 58 years for the ballpoint pen to become a sellable product after it was invented in 1888. But once the innovation is diffused, it might prevail for a long time. A famous example is the use of the QWERTY keyboard, invented in 1873 to reduce the speed of typists but which has persisted ever since (Rogers, 1995).

There might be many reasons why the time-lag exists between invention and innovation: non-existent complementary technologies, existence of low-cost alternatives, standards and government regulations (Shapiro and Varian, 1999). In the 20th century, the choice between gas, electric and steam technologies for automobile engines was not driven by technical criteria. Instead, assessment was based on different dimensions such as cost, safety, range, noise and power (David, 1990).

The diffusion process is related to five main elements (Rogers, 1995):

1 The characteristics of an innovation that may influence its adoption.
2 The decision-making process that occurs when individuals consider adopting a new idea, product or practice.
3 The characteristics of individuals that make them likely to adopt an innovation.
4 The consequences for individuals and society of adopting an innovation.
5 The communication channels used in the adoption process.

3.3   Marketing processes

Among the elements of the diffusion of innovation, the adopter categories have a specific importance for marketing activities. Their role in marketing is discussed on the basis of four major marketing processes (Easingwood and Koustelos, 2000; Jobber, 2001):

1 Market preparation.
2 Targeting.

3 Positioning.
4 Execution.

These are now discussed in more detail.

Market preparation

Preparing the market refers to readying customers and other companies for the change by educating the market on a product or service. This stage might take place while the product is still in development. In the case of technology marketing, getting the market ready involves building awareness of the new technology as well as forming relationships with customers and suppliers. As technology products are complex and expensive, educating customers beforehand may improve the perception of the product. A good example is the reaction to biotechnology-based foods in Europe, where producers have neglected to educate the public.

For many technology products, standards play a role in influencing the commitment of customers. Hence, alliances and licensing arrangements with other companies and even with competitors might help the adoption of technological standards. For example, Nokia, Sony and NTT DoCoMo formed a consortium called Symbian to develop an open source operating system for mobile devices (Easingwood and Koustelos, 2000). Another possible alliance mechanism is to share the new technology with original equipment manufacturers (OEMs) so that they get used to the technology and contribute to the development and promotion of standards, becoming partners. Besides setting standards, alliances might also help to supply the complementary technologies needed for the success of an innovation. For example, the success of IBM's personal computer compared to Apple in the 1980s was due to a wide variety of software offerings from suppliers that IBM outsourced. Software was a critical complementary technology for the success of the hardware.

Targeting

Targeting refers to finding the right customers and learning their characteristics in order to decide on the marketing features to direct to the varying customer segments, for which it is important to understand adopter types. The innovation adoption curve is a model that classifies innovation adopters into various categories, based on the idea that certain individuals are inevitably more open to new products than others (Rogers, 1995):

- *Innovators* lead the change and are important for communicating the benefits of a new innovation.
- *Early adopters* are willing to try out new ideas.
- *Early majority adopters* are willing to accept change more quickly than the average.
- *Late majority adopters* will only use new ideas or products when the majority are using them.
- *Laggards* tend to be critical of new ideas until the new idea has become mainstream or is in common use.

The innovation adoption curve highlights the fact that trying to quickly convince the mass market of a new controversial idea might be a waste of time and money. In these circumstances, it makes more sense to first convince the innovators and early adopters.

Also the categories and percentages can be used as indicators to estimate target groups for communication purposes.

Positioning

Positioning can be based on tangible or intangible characteristics such as image that will distinguish the firm from its competitors. The typical strategies for positioning are low cost, niche and product differentiation. But for technology marketing, a blue-ocean strategy is an option, aiming to develop a new market space that makes the competition irrelevant (Kim and Mauborgne, 2005). Many new products, such as mobile phones, created a completely new industry.

In the case of technology, customers need to feel secure that their move to a new technology is low risk. This is possible by offering a product that is standard or going to be standard. Another way of making the customer feel secure about technology is using technological superiority as the key distinguishing element/value proposition for customers (Kotler and Keller, 2006).

Technology marketing builds its positioning according to the adopter type. While innovators might be interested in technological superiority, the early-majority type is likely to be motivated by a well-functioning, low-cost version of the new technology. In fact, the main difficulty in marketing technology happens in the interval of going from early adopters to the early majority. This is often termed 'crossing the chasm', since the early adopter and majority types have completely different concerns and new technology firms can struggle to satisfy their concerns with their limited resources (Moore, 1991). This is why crossing the chasm requires a clear-cut positioning strategy based on developing a completely working product/application rather than diversification. Once the product/application works, marketing to the early majority type is a matter of:

- Attending industry conferences and trade shows.
- Frequent mentions in industry magazines.
- Being installed in other companies in the same industry.
- Developing industry-specific applications.
- Alliances with other key suppliers to the industry.

Execution

The way across the chasm is to target the company's resources to one or two specific niche markets where it can dominate rapidly and force out competitors. It can then use the dominance of the first niche to attack the surrounding niches and eventually reach the broader early majority group (Easingwood and Koustelos, 2000). This progressive approach will ultimately build a winning image and develop the trust of customers in the company. Customer trust and company image reduce the risk of adoption, but technology firms need to do more than that. There is a risk associated with learning new technology and there may be substantial assets committed to old/different technology. For example, changing a computer hardware platform may require changes in software and peripherals. Another dimension of risk of adoption in the eyes of customers is network externalities. Customers build relationships around their technologies, such as trusted suppliers and service providers. Network externality is built over time and might become binding. To reduce the risk of adoption, technology companies might consider offering a trial version, training customers in using the new technology and making the application as compatible as possible. Thus technology producers need to focus on strategic alliances as a critical marketing tool.

3.4   Technology transfer

Definition

Technology transfer is the process by which the technology, knowledge and information developed by a creator is applied and utilized by an applier (Khalil, 2000). Creators might be an individual, an R&D department within a company, another commercial developer company, a partner company doing collaborative R&D, a non-profit organization or a government agency. The applier might be a manufacturing department of the company where technology is developed internally or cooperatively, it might be a commercial company, a competitor or the government. If either the creator or applier is from a different country, technology transfer takes place at the international level.

As Steele (1989) highlights:

> [The] term technology transfer is a misnomer because it implies that something is moved, more or less untouched, from one place or one organisation to another.

The process is more complicated than that because the technology itself is changed as a part of its movement from one organization to another. This is because technology incorporates not only equipment but also know-how and skills, which in turn necessitates the transfer of tacit knowledge. Moreover, technology transfer becomes complicated due to the feelings and attitudes required in both organizations/units in order for two sets of people with different skills, values and priorities to become successful in passing the capability from one to the other.

The transfer of technology from creator to applier is frequently the point at which the system breaks down (Williams and Gibson, 1990). It therefore needs to be managed well. The following factors affect the success of technology transfer (Burgelman et al., 2004):

- High level of technical understanding where transfer is done.
- Feasibility findings of the technology are high.
- Advanced development activities overlap with the new technology.
- Growth potential of the application is high.
- The existence of an advocate of the transferred technology.
- The existence of advanced technology activities in a development laboratory to complement the transferred technology.
- External pressures from competitors and markets enforcing quick adoption.
- Joint programmes between technology developer and technology buyer.

Technology transfer has been one of the most important technology policy issues for developing countries importing their technologies. In recent years, it has become a popular policy item for developed countries. Considering that the majority of research in many countries is performed by state-owned research units and non-profit organizations such as universities, transferring knowledge from these organizations might benefit the economy in a larger context. Research institutions are experts in developing technologies but they do not apply them in production, so governments have put a high priority on the transfer of knowledge generated in research organizations to firms that will utilize it and create economic value. This is why the technology transfer activity has become an important dimension of industrial and technological policies in many countries. In practice, governments have set up many institutions to initiate and support technology transfer between research organizations and companies. For example, the USA has developed national technology transfer centres across the country that have special budgets to help SMEs to access technologies developed in government research organizations and universities. Similarly, the European Technology Transfer Initiative has developed special technology transfer programmes operating at the European level, including innovation relay centres, technology transfer funds, the European Centre for Innovation and Spin-Offs and the European Technology Transfer Network.

Technology transfer processes

Transferring a technology can be considered as a stand-alone project, so project management steps are the usual activities that need to be carried out. However, four specific managerial tasks are considered here in some detail (Beruvides and Khalil, 1990):

1 Determining the transfer method, actors and timing.
2 Pre-transfer activities.
3 Transfer activities.
4 Evaluations and improvements.

Determining the transfer method, actors and timing

Before a technology transfer decision is made, the maturity of evolving technologies needs to be assessed prior to incorporating the technology of interest into a system or sub-system. Generally speaking, when a new technology is first invented or conceptualized, it is not suitable for immediate application. Instead, new technologies are usually subjected to experimentation, refinement and increasingly realistic testing. Once the technology is sufficiently proven, it can be incorporated into a system/sub-system. However, this is easier said than done. One measure for assessing the maturity of technology is the 'technology readiness level scale', used by some US government agencies and many international companies/agencies (Graettinger et al., 2002).

Once the decision is made to transfer a technology, there are a number of possible methods that can be used, informal and formal. Informal processes include technical information exchange through published material, in the form of printed or electronic media, meetings, symposia, individual exchanges or reverse engineering. The process of training scientists in academic research institutions or acquiring critical technical personnel might also be considered as informal methods of technology transfer. The case of BICC Cables Ltd at the end of the chapter presents an example of the use of informal and formal transfers.

Formal technology transfer approaches are based on legal arrangements between the participants in the transfer process. The major methods of external technology transfer are:

- OEMs.
- Turnkey plants.
- Licensing (in and out).

- Acquisition.
- Collaborative R&D.

Once the method is decided, potential partners need to be identified and selected. Here the process is similar to finding technology suppliers for acquisition, discussed in Chapter 2.

Deciding which staff members should be involved in the transfer process is an element of the technology transfer process. Forming multifunctional teams and establishing communication among them improves the overall process and facilitates learning, as discussed in Chapter 7 (Selection). But the staffing decision should include not only the receiving organization's/unit's staff but also the developer's staff. All parties involved in the technology transfer process should assign staff who will participate in the whole process to make it smooth and consistent.

The technology transfer method puts limits on the structure of technology transfer. Some modes of technology transfer are (Williams and Gibson, 1990):

- *Over-the-wall mode*: Receivers have no close contact with developers. Examples are licensing and turnkey plants.
- *Receivers-as-consultants mode*: Developers have the main responsibility but they consult frequently with receivers. Some licensing and collaborative R&D might be performed in this mode.
- *Team mode*: Receivers and developers work together to develop and transfer technology, for example through collaborative R&D.
- *Apprenticeship mode*: Receivers become developers under the direction of the main technology or knowledge owner, for example OEM.

After determining the technology transfer method, timing issues need to be decided, such as when the technology is ready to move from R&D to production and finally to market. Timing depends on the degree to which the technology satisfies customer needs and ensures efficient and repeatable production.

Pre-transfer activities

Formal technology transfer relies on legal documentation, a contract including binding conditions on what will be transferred, between whom, when, how and for what price. Depending on the actors involved in the agreement, the type and extent of the contract might change. For reliable partners, the contract might be more flexible, while for developers who are not trusted, it might need to be more detailed. The contract preparation is even more complicated when the technology transfer is international, since the contract should be structured according to international regulations. After the contract is prepared either by the developer or the receiver, it is jointly negotiated and a final form is reached.

Before the technology transfer starts, there might be a number of adjustments to physical facilities and workforce. Depending on the location of the technology transfer, in an existing or new portion of the enterprise, there might be new installations or changes needed for the incoming technology to function. The new technology might work with special inputs that might not be available in the premises of the receiver organization and it might take time to acquire them. So the pre-transfer phase should consider all inputs and make a procurement plan accordingly.

Preparing the workforce is a multifaceted issue (Khalil, 2000). The receiving organization must be capable of and interested in receiving the information. The members of the organizations involved in the technology transfer must, to some extent, have some over-lapping training, skills and experience. Without some common base, those in the recipient organization will lack assurance that they truly understand what is being transmitted. So training might be an integral part of the recipient organization's role to ensure that its employees reach a comparable level. Another way of matching two organizations' skills can be through transfer of people from the original R&D group. Temporary assignments of people to the other organization, from operations to the R&D group or vice versa, can be useful. Alternatively, hiring or transferring the requisite skills from other organizations may be a solution. In fact, before technology transfer is achieved, management needs to assess staffing needs for the operation of the new technology, possibly leading to recruitment of new staff with the right skills and knowledge.

In some cases, developers and receivers/appliers might come together in the develop-ment phase before the project ends and the transfer starts. The process is an iterative one between developer and receiver that requires easy and frequently intense interactions. As a development progresses, the skills and equipment available in operations become valuable in performing tests and measurements (Steele, 1989). Consequently, the programme can become a joint development well before it officially transfers to operations.

Transfer activities

Physical installations and adjustments take place mainly before the transfer process starts, although further changes may be needed after technology is transferred in-house, depend-ing on whether problems arise and to accommodate unforeseen application needs. These installations may necessitate additional site arrangements such as updating electricity and transport infrastructure.

After physical installation, tests are carried out at different levels and, depending on the results, new sets of arrangements are undertaken. Other actions are needed during the actual start-up of the new technology, involving migration from the old process to the new (ICS UNIDO, 2008). If the company has the luxury of setting up the new equipment in a new area, it can keep material flowing to the old process until the new one is run-ning smoothly. If the new process has to be conducted in the same space as the old, there might be a hectic shutdown of the old process and last-minute installation and start-up of the new one. If this is the case, careful planning will be required to make the transition as smooth as possible. Timing of the start-up depends on many factors, including physical utilities, employee training, new process measurement systems and the processing of the data from those systems.

In technology collaborations, the risk of wasting outsourced R&D might be reduced by taking precautions. For example, the company might put in place a well-defined 'home' for the technology in the form of an in-house development project that builds on the results obtained but is more tightly focused on explicit commercial objectives (Steele, 1989). There is a need to set a handover period, in which the researchers stay in close contact with the R&D staff in the business so that they can communicate everything that was left unsaid in the reports. It is also important to minimize the time-lag between the outsourced emerg-ing technology project and the subsequent focused development project, to ensure that information is not lost or forgotten and to maintain momentum.

During the technology transfer, a critical management task is to secure learning and efficient communication. Transfer includes tangible as well as intangible knowledge. In addition, those creating a new technology rarely perceive with sufficient clarity what in fact they really do. They might not discern the truly critical information from other details. Thus skilled receivers are needed to pin down the information needed by them. In other words, receivers should pay special attention to capturing the intangible knowledge associated with the technology by actively putting learning as an item in the technology transfer process. In fact, it is not only the capturing and learning of knowledge, but also its diffusion across the company that makes it valuable, since some knowledge might be valid for some other units in the organization rather than the unit responsible for the transfer, increasing the opportunities for synergy. The details of learning and the learning organization will be further discussed in Chapter 5.

In terms of communication, culture-building activities involving manufacturing, marketing and R&D people should aim to establish a common language. For example, R&D people must recognize the enormous, overriding commitment that manufacturing people make to achieve uninterrupted output (Steele, 1989). Manufacturing is conservative with regard to incorporating new technology that is not yet proven. The factory environment poses much more severe constraints on adopting new manufacturing technology compared to new product technology. Thus it is better to start by working on carefully limited problems that only demand incremental changes. Another step is to establish credibility with manufacturing by showing the value of new technology to manufacturing people, the internal consumer of the new technology.

All these factors clearly indicate the importance of communication between the R&D, production and marketing departments of a company. Communication must be formal and informal and should deal with (Burgelman et al., 2004):

- Introducing new products from the development lab to the production floor.
- Providing the optimum level of documentation on existing products.
- Becoming multilingual, fluent in the language of customers, marketers, engineers and designers.
- Facilitating orderly and cost-effective changes to products now in production.

As technology transfer involves uncertainties in knowing what will work and what will not work, it is important to keep detailed records of the information produced, irrespective of its apparent significance at the time. These documents provide formal communication but, importantly, they might also help to understand what went right and wrong and to make adjustments, especially after technology transfer evaluations are carried out and improvements are planned.

Evaluations and improvements

When full production starts, feedback starts to flow either from internal production departments or from markets/customers, which creates another round of evaluation and improvement activity. This is why, in the days immediately following the start-up, a process of refinement and improvement of the new technology takes place in order to fine-tune the operations involved in the new technology. The process is monitored closely and any substandard performance is identified, the cause isolated and the problem rectified (ICS UNIDO, 2008). The cause could be technical or it could be due to inadequate training. Whatever the cause, it needs careful attention until the technology is producing products in line with the specifications in the contract with the technology supplier. The refinement and improvement process does not end there, however. The company needs to constantly work towards achieving an attitude of continuous improvement.

There are difficulties in measuring the success of technology transfer. The degree of technological innovation, the level of application and the purpose of transferring the technology play a role in determining the effectiveness of technology transfer. The evaluation might be carried out in any combination of the following effectiveness dimensions: benefits, system, availability, capacity and supply. The complexity is clearly observed in some of the measures used in technology transfer evaluations (Williams and Gibson, 1990) – licences, requests for help, competitive advantage gains, cost savings, site visits, technology briefs, jobs created, market share gains, technical presentations, new businesses started, new products, time spent, transfer budgets, new customers, new sales, transfer expenditures, productivity gains, royalties, return on investment (ROI), success stories, technical problems solved and user satisfaction.

Measures of the success of technology transfer are complicated and difficult to apply. Developers may understand the technology better, but operators have a greater understanding of the application environment. An effective approach might be to ask operations to take the lead in developing data and work closely with developers to ensure that the data reflect the special nature of the technology and are representative of cost and market factors (Steele, 1989).

Another critical issue with measurement is the degree of qualitative data to be employed. ROI can be a rudimentary measure to use since technologies contribute in many ways other than quantifiable dimensions, including quality enhancements. In evaluating an acquired technology, the situation may be complicated by the fact that products utilize many technologies and the technology may have a number of applications.

Once the evaluation is done, a plan for improvements may need to be designed. Besides the evaluation, all documentation in the technology transfer process can be screened to discover the best ways of finding out what needs to be done to improve the results, which might include factors other than those relating to technology transfer. Thus, improvement activities might be related to the general technology utilization tasks described below as the third sub-process of the exploitation activity.

An important aspect of improvements is change management. Transferring the commitment and enthusiasm of those who are creating a new technology to those who will develop and apply it can be challenging. Naturally, the degree of challenge depends on whether top management of the recipient firm of a new technology is supportive of transfer or not, as well as if the recipient firm is unclear about what it really wants from the company originating the new technology. The actions that need to be taken are the same in both cases, but the care and attention devoted to them will vary. This necessitates additional management mechanisms that are related to change.

3.5   Technology utilization

Definition

Although the technology transfer might have been successful, the results from the exploitation of technology might not be as expected or designed. Technology utilization might be considered in the lines of re-engineering and **total quality management** (TQM), since the goal is either maintenance or continuous improvement of the use of existing technologies. As the case of USG Corporation (see Chapter 5) shows, productivity gains in the commercialization of new technology platforms differ a lot, so by measuring performance and focusing on learning, firms might increase their returns from technologies.

3.6 Utilization processes

Utilization processes consist of three major steps:

1 Measure technology utilization/performance.
2 Identify priorities and develop a business case to improve utilization.
3 Implement changes.

Depending on the firm's structure and the aim of the utilization exercise, technology utilization might be carried out at the technology, plant or multi-plant level.

Measure technology utilization/performance

Most capital investments can be assessed quantitatively, helping to form an objective view on the worth of the investment. In contrast, technology investments may have a substantial but far less visible impact on the business, especially in the short term. In the long run, the firm may have a better product, with broader international application, based on shared new core technologies, providing the foundation for a new generation of profitable, standardized products.

Technology evaluation raises the following questions for technology managers: What is to be evaluated? Who is to be involved in evaluation? What roles do they play? What criteria are to be used in the evaluation? How they are weighted? How are the criteria to be measured?

Although there are no simple, directly quantifiable measures of the value of technology, a measurement approach that relies on an input-process-output evaluation framework is adopted here due to the difficulties of measuring technical work directly (Goffin and Mitchell, 2005). This method combines a balanced scorecard approach with operations management of the input-output model, offering a wide base for the evaluation of technology including the process. By doing so, it can help to include the qualitative advantages and intangible sides of technologies in the overall performance audit.

In the input-process-output model:

- *Input* measures are the time and resources required, such as people or information technology.
- *Process* measures are the indicators of efficiency of the innovation process within an organization, such as the time required to bring an innovation to market.
- *Output* measures are directly related to the commercial impact of innovations, such as revenues generated by a new service or product.

A list of potential measures developed for innovation management might also be valid for TM (Goffin and Mitchell, 2005). For example, financial input measures might be: percentage of revenues invested in product R&D; percentage of revenues invested in technology acquisition; and percentage of projects delayed or cancelled. Customer-related input measures could be the percentage mix of projects by their strategic drivers. Resource-related measures for input could be: percentage of total employees involved in innovation projects; number of ideas per source; and number of ideas considered per year for new products, services and processes.

TM involves an element of creativity, which should be reflected in the process measures used. Typical inputs and outputs are R&D personnel and the number of new products and patents, respectively. But managers should try to measure not only how creative the organization is but also how well it uses that creativity. Output process measures may include milestone hit rate, budget hit rate and time to commercialization.

Organizations need to choose measures in each of the categories based on their needs, while recognizing the danger of attempting to measure too much. Criteria for judging the importance of potential measures include strategic importance to firm, actionability, validity, appropriateness, clarity and cost-effectiveness.

Besides general measures, there might be specific micro-measures applied by operational managers to track a weakness and indicate progress in remedying it. Typically, only a few measures are used at a time, always linked to an internal customer need. Once an improvement has been made, the relevant measure can be dropped and replaced with another that tackles a different problem. The micro-measures chosen will depend on the desired improvement. For example, the number of unplanned changes might be tracked to understand how consistent the design is. Micro-measures are used predominantly to help local management in the drive for continuous improvement. They need to be simple, relevant and communicated widely. In addition, the organization needs to decide on the timeliness of performance evaluation. It might be a regular period or a variable one, depending on the life cycle of the technologies.

Performance measures alone do not mean much unless they are made in comparison to other companies' performance. Thus, the final activity in performance measurement is **benchmarking**. Benchmarking is the systematic comparison of organizational processes and performance to create new standards or to improve processes. Benchmarking models are used to determine how well a business unit, division, organization or corporation is performing compared with other similar organizations. A benchmark is often used for improving communication, professionalizing the organization/processes or for budgetary reasons.

Benchmarking is not just a comparative tool; it also stimulates questioning and learning. If the firm benchmarks widely within its own business, sharing objectives and pooling best practice understanding, the firm can achieve performance improvement without looking at other companies. With a good foundation of internal benchmarking, the firm can begin to look outside. Benchmarking against other companies can give the firm valuable insights into the structure and implementation of all the firm's technology development processes, from managing long-term research to product development and launch. Benchmarking can be at several different levels, starting with hard measures of output and moving towards process comparisons. The firm might look at how world-class companies across a range of industries manage their technology development and adopt the best elements.

Identify priorities and develop a business case to improve utilization

Performance evaluations can give conflicting results and prioritizing the improvements might be difficult, so criteria should be established for determining which measures are most appropriate and helpful.

One consideration is to understand the role of the external environment in utilizing the technology. If demand changes are the main reason for underutilization, there might not be enough room to make changes. A helpful mechanism for managing demand changes is increasing supplier and customer involvement at the early stages of technology development (Tushman and Andersen, 2004). For example, the lead user method might help to gain close contact with the main customers and integrate their views into the process. Another mechanism is diversification. As mentioned in Chapter 7, the core technology approach suggests focusing on core technologies that make it possible to diversify the product/market range based on the core capabilities developed. Thus, companies need to find ways of diversifying the use of technologies and to take appropriate actions.

Demand changes in the market can initiate a chain effect within the company. Besides technology adjustments for market needs, the company might need to make adjustments to match internal strengths, to eliminate weaknesses and to improve competitiveness in global markets.

Reliability concerns are also important when prioritizing improvement efforts. Potential direct and/or indirect losses due to the failure of a product may be detrimental to the reputation of a manufacturer. Special attention must be paid to the prevention or reduction of downtime and to the minimization of repair costs. To meet this long-term challenge, a technology manager needs to develop a process perspective on three interrelated features of a product in its life cycle: reliability, maintainability and availability (Gaynor, 1996):

- **Reliability** is centred on the frequency of breakdowns.
- **Maintainability** is focused on the time of breakdown.
- **Availability** is the consequence of reliability and maintainability. It is measured by the proportion of time during which a product is effectively available for operational use.

Although maintainability requirements are built into the product or system during the design and manufacturing stages, the causes of failure are realized during the operation or use of the product or system. During usage, the product or system generates information that can be systematically collected and analysed to initiate the required maintenance actions.

Another dimension in evaluating performance is to consider the characteristics of the technology itself. Due to technical limitations, utilization might not exceed a certain level. Bottlenecks and capacity limits are well-known problems causing underutilization and they are valid for technologies too. In some cases, brand new technologies might experience many technical problems that have a substantial impact on their application, opening the door for substitute technologies.

Technology integration and synergy are also critical aspects to consider, especially when a company uses multiple technologies for a similar purpose, leading to underutilization. The reasons why companies end up with different technologies include:

- The specialized needs of one line of products drive improvements in other lines.
- Partial investments/installations.
- Different standards of technologies.

Therefore, firms need to integrate and standardize manufacturing and process developments so that the harmonious contribution of different technologies can be achieved. This will bring many advantages, including synergies, and will prevent a misfit between technologies.

Another type of performance problem can arise from a misfit between technological innovation and organizational structure. If the organization cannot adapt itself to use a technology efficiently, the benefits significantly drop. As discussed in Chapter 2 (the section New product/service development), some managerial practices might become unsuitable for the technologies developed. Technological innovations do not exist alone; they influence organizational innovations and demand a fit between hardware and software parts of technologies. For example, computer-aided design, computer-aided manufacturing and flexible manufacturing systems are widely used, but have different implications in terms of organizational structures and processes. If there is a poor fit between the technological infrastructure and the business process, there will be problems. Hence, strategy makers need to consider the implications of their technology decisions on their organizational techniques and develop strategies to manage the fit by developing special structures and organizational innovations.

Another problem causing underutilization is the limited set of competencies the company might have. New technologies and changes in technologies might necessitate changes in the set of available competencies. This can be done through human resource adjustments.

After considering all the factors of underutilization, a priority list might be developed for improvement activities. This should include all suggested performance improvement plans and the reasons why they should be carried out. Senior management should undertake an evaluation using technology assessment techniques and draw up a final list. The improvement list should initiate projects for the R&D department where TQM techniques are applied.

Implement changes

Improvement projects are similar to new product or process projects and need to be implemented following approaches similar to those for R&D management (Chapter 2). Improving performance requires the management of a wide range of issues, including ideas, technologies, culture and organizational change. Therefore learning and change management become indispensable parts of the implementation process discussed in Chapter 5.

3.7   Reverse innovation

Emerging markets/rapidly growing developing countries such as China are becoming centres of attention for many businesses around the globe (Khanna and Palepu, 2010). This is because emerging markets offer many business opportunities to aspiring firms who wish to grow their businesses and do so rapidly: these are markets with high population and economic growth, revolution in consumers' rising expectations, urbanization, increasing numbers of middle and upper-middle-income segments composed of consumers who are hungry for goods and services, expanding distributor and telecommunication networks and exploding market demand. Further, many emerging market firms themselves are becoming highly successful abroad, exemplified by Haier of China, Tata of India, SAB Miller of South Africa, Embraer of Brazil, Arcelik of Turkey and Teva Pharmaceuticals of Israel. Many of these firms are growing into global champions carrying their local market success based on unique firm-specific and country-specific competitive advantages into international expansion (Ramamurti and Singh, 2009).

Reverse innovation is a set of innovations targeted for emerging/developing country populations. Reverse innovation attempts to understand the customer problem and come up with a solution that will take into consideration a variety of factors: availability of electricity, portability, durability and price. This type of innovation is not limited to disruptive innovations. The goal is to fill five gaps in a developing country that lead to reverse innovation: the performance gap, the infrastructure gap, the sustainability gap, the preference gap and the regulatory gap (Govindarajan and Euchner, 2012). For example, an Indian cardiac hospital offers cardiac surgery for $2,000 whose American equivalent would cost up to $20,000. It is important to note that the difference in price doesn't mean it is bad quality. This cardiac hospital has built a facility in the Cayman Islands to attract customers from advanced countries, because they create solutions that are affordable and of good quality.

Reverse innovation is a new wave of innovation that might bring variety into business making. In addition, a large subset of reverse innovation is based on social innovations that are human-centred and give opportunity to question the meaning of products and services produced for the sake of social and environmental concerns discussed in Chapter 13. By exploiting technologies in new geographies, the democratization of innovation tends to become more realistic (Green, 2007).

Suzlon: India's major wind power provider

Suzlon has become the world's fifth largest wind turbine manufacturer with a market share of 6%. Suzlon's founder Mr Tanti was unhappy with the erratic power supplies and rising energy costs at his textile mill in Gujarat, India. Therefore, he set up two windmills in 1990 with turbines imported from the German company Suedwind. He soon discovered that the windmills provided a reliable source of cheap energy, much cheaper than conventional energy and they were also environmentally friendly. Mr Tanti exited his textile business and set up Suzlon Energy in 1995 with a strategy of capitalizing on India's low manufacturing costs and providing end-to-end customized solutions at affordable prices to its Indian industrial clients.

When Suzlon's initial turbine supplier failed in 1997, Suzlon bought it and kept its R&D centres and turbine manufacturing facilities in Germany. Suzlon also acquired a rotor-blade manufacturer in the Netherlands; the acquisitions broadened Suzlon's reach, bringing a product range that now includes wind turbine generators in capacities from 350 KW to 2.1 MW with customized versions suitable for a variety of climates. Although Suzlon's products are not suitable for conventional power generation in urban areas, they were welcomed by customers with large manufacturing or other operations in rural areas that had poor or costly access to conventional power supplies.

Soon, Suzlon discovered that its products could find markets globally, including in developed countries seeking greener energy sources to supplement conventional power plants. Suzlon's business grew rapidly and has captured more than a 50% share of the wind power market in recent years. While its Indian business continues to grow steadily, its overseas sales have seen even greater growth, rising from 8% of total revenues in 2004 to over 70% in 2006. Orders have come in from Australia, China, South

(Continued)

Korea, Brazil, Italy, Portugal and Spain. Its global revenue in 2007 exceeded $900 million. Suzlon has a bright future as the global wind power market is expected to grow at an annual rate of over 25% during the next five years.

Suzlon succeeded where Suedwind had failed because it understood the market position of its products. Tanti perceived the potential of the wind turbine generators as disruptive products in the energy market and pursued a market strategy to exploit that potential. Understanding and developing the disruptive potential of a product is a key component of a disruptive innovation strategy.

Source: Summary from Hang, C-C., Jin, C. and Subramian, A. M. (2010) 'Developing Disruptive Products for Emerging Markets: lessons from Asian cases', *Research-Technology Management*, **53**(4), 21–26.

 Case study

Managers cannot relax once technology is in place, since technological exploitation depends on how efficiently and effectively managers handle commercialization, transfer and utilization. The case of BICC Cables Ltd, the UK's largest cable manufacturing company in the 1990s, with annual revenues of approximately £1.3bn and employing about 10,000 people, illustrates how technology transfer and utilization activities are carried out for an internal R&D invention.

BICC Cables Ltd

BICC developed a new process technology in-house through its R&D unit, which was the process plant machinery used to manufacture a particular type of optical fibre cable known as 'tight buffered fibre cable'. BICC had wanted to produce this type of cable in volume and thereby satisfy demand from the UK and European markets.

The process plant technology was designed as a flexible plant that could work in stand-alone mode to manufacture single optical fibres or multi-element optical fibre ribbon and in tandem with an existing cable extrusion line to manufacture tight buffered fibre cables. The latter operation enabled the extrusion line to apply the plastic coatings over the fibres (like a skin covering) after they had been produced in the first stage of the operation.

The process technology was designed and developed at BICC Cable's Helsby Technology Centre (HTC). The technology-receiving factory, BICC Brand-Rex, was based at the same site. Two reasons motivated the choice of in-house production: high demand and the high cost of bought-in fibre.

HTC had designed and specified the requirements for the tight buffered fibre process plant for a UK-based engineering firm, from which it purchased the initial plant. The plant was then successfully run and tested by HTC, producing the tight buffered cable in its lab for the internal customer Brand-Rex, which could sell this initial cable production to its end customers. Hence, a unique situation had arisen, an R&D unit running a three-shift operation not only to test the process plant but to meet the initial production demands placed on it by the internal customer's market demands.

After these tests and pre-production runs were completed at the prototype plant, the technology was transferred to the Brand-Rex manufacturing factory. In addition to the physical plant, this technology transfer process also included a set of process instructions, training procedures and plant operation and maintenance manuals.

During the tests and pre-production runs at HTC, some manufacturing engineers from Brand-Rex had been seconded to HTC for short periods to receive training on the plant technology under the supervision of HTC staff. Since there is tacit knowledge embodied in most cable production processes, which the HTC development team had accumulated over a period of 18 months, much of this knowledge was transferred to the Brand-Rex engineers training at the plant. The tacit knowledge related to fault-finding and problem-solving skills, process optimization and start-up procedures that could not be fully codified into a specification format.

The success of this technology transfer process could be traced to the technology sender and receiver serving a common mission that was compatible with a TQM philosophy. BICC employees were acting towards other internal customers in the supply chain as if they were dealing with external customers, by striving to deliver excellence. The receiving organization (Brand-Rex) did not have problems associated with quality control, operation or maintainability, since these had been dealt with in the test and pre-production phases.

The involvement of Brand-Rex senior management in this project was seen as a major catalyst for promoting successful technology transfer. The marketing information was consistent in outlining sales forecasts for the months ahead. The technology transfer process was driven by external market signals and the R&D department was aware of the wider business implications for tight buffered fibre cable development. This ensured that everyone involved in developing and transferring this technology within BICC was also aware of the wider business implications. This meant, in turn, that everybody involved realized that this was not just a speculative R&D project but had real goals and targets to achieve.

Source: Malik, K. (2001) 'How BICC Cables Transferred a New Process Technology from R&D to Manufacturing', *Research-Technology Management*, **44**(4), 55–60.

Summary

The exploitation activity consists of a number of critical sub-processes, the three major ones being commercialization/marketing, technology transfer and utilization. All these sub-processes help to find the right business models for commercialization, transferring technology in an effective and efficient manner and achieving incremental improvements continuously in order to achieve day-to-day operational efficiency. If exploitation capabilities are not developed, returns on technologies are low.

Key Questions

1 What are the key features of exploitation?
2 What are the types of commercialization?
3 What is the process of commercialization/marketing in TM?
4 What is the process of technology transfer in exploitation?
5 What is the process of technology utilization in exploitation?

Further reading

Bigwood, M. P. (2004) 'Managing the New Technology Exploitation Process', *Research-Technology Management*, **47**(6), 38–42.

Enkel, E. and Gassmann, O. (2010) 'Creative Imitation: Exploring the Case of Cross-industry Innovation', *R&D Management*, **40**(3), 256–270.

Govindarajan, V. and Euchner, J. (2012) 'Reverse Innovation', *Research-Technology Management*, **55**(6), 13–17.

Hang, C-C., Jin, C. and Subramian, A. M. (2010) 'Developing Disruptive Products for Emerging Markets: Lessons from Asian cases', *Research-Technology Management*, **53**(4), 21–26.

Khanna, T. and Palepu, K. G. (2010) *Winning in Emerging Markets: A Roadmap for Strategy and Execution* (Cambridge, MA: Harvard Business Press).

Lancaster, G. and Massingham, L. (1999) *Essentials of Marketing*, 3rd edn (London: McGraw-Hill).

Ramamurti, R. and Singh, J. V. (2009) *Emerging Multinationals in Emerging Markets* (Cambridge: Cambridge University Press).

Spivey, W. A., Munson, J. M., Flannery, W. T. and Tsai, F.-S. (2009) 'Improve Tech Transfer with this Alliance Scorecard', *Research-Technology Management*, **52**(1), 10–18.

4

IDENTIFICATION

Learning objectives

After studying this chapter, you should be able to:

1 Understand the identification capability.
2 Understand differences between intelligence and forecasting capacities.
3 List the advantages and disadvantages of forecasting.
4 Identify the key features of technology auditing.
5 Identify the key features of forecasting.
6 Analyse organizational capabilities.

4.1 Introduction

This chapter will focus on the technological capability dedicated to identifying technological opportunities and threats. The identification capability comprises forecasting, which aims to predict the future by conducting audits and collecting data internally and externally about technologies, capabilities and markets. **Technology intelligence** is a recent term that describes the technology forecasting activity, with the addition of all sorts of information on capturing and delivering capacities, which are relevant to identify future opportunities for and threats to firms. Based on the identification activity, firms might reduce the uncertainties surrounding technological decisions. However, technology identification not only requires the development of new technologies but also draws attention to identification of the existing technologies used in the environment as well as the evaluation of the technology being used in the organization to determine whether new application areas exist or not. This technological capability interacts with the strategic decision-making process mentioned in Chapter 7.

4.2 Definition

The goal of identification is to sense/spot technologies and their applications that are (or may be) of importance to the business. In order to identify opportunities, enterprises must constantly scan, search and explore technologies and markets. But accessing information is not enough to build an identification capability; the ability to recognize, sense and shape developments is needed. This requires specific knowledge, creative activity, the ability to understand user/customer decision making and practical wisdom (Teece, 2007).

The literature on identification activities is vast and the terminology is used interchangeably for overlapping activities, such as technology intelligence, technological forecasting, technology foresight, technology scouting, technology exploration, strategic foresight, technology monitoring and technology scanning. This chapter considers the identification capability to be developed through activities encompassing technology forecasting and technology intelligence.

Forecasting means predicting the future. Historically, technology forecasting has been considered to be forecasting the future characteristics of useful technological machines, procedures or techniques (Schnaars et al., 1993). When technological forecasting was used in the 1940s and 1950s, its main purpose was to forecast defence-industry-related technologies. In the 1960s, new forecasting methods were developed, but forecasting activities lost their popularity in the 1970s until a revival in the 1990s. The studies in the 1990s pointed out that the main problem with technology forecasting was its technical orientation, ignoring other factors that are critical in the determination of technological development, such as political, economic, social and environmental factors. This is why the recent forecasting activities conducted in so many countries have expanded the scope of forecasting in order to understand future trends in these factors (Linstone and Grupp, 2000).

By doing so, the new forecasting approach contributes to the data-gathering activity by adding a new dimension to consider: technology forecasting cannot be limited to an individual assessment of technologies but to a wider perception of assessing the long-term impact of technologies (Braun, 2000). So the forecasting activity needs to perform an **assessment** that is the systematic identification, analysis and evaluation of the potential secondary consequences (whether beneficial or detrimental) of technology in terms of its impacts on social, cultural, political and environmental systems and processes. In other words, technology assessment seeks to bridge the promotion and control of technology, such that the latter is no longer merely an after-the-fact consideration, and insight about potential development options and their impact is acquired ex ante (Genus and Coles, 2005). The aim is to find ways of experimenting with technology in society in order to avoid or learn about possible harmful impacts.

The process of predicting the future is in fact a bundle of systematic efforts to look ahead in order to choose more effectively, because there is not a single future. The process of technological forecasting aims to sketch a number of future visions by trying to be as inclusive as possible in collecting the opinions of different stakeholders of the available technology.

Although time and cost factors are considered the major hindrances to conducting a forecasting study, there are many advantages (Khalil, 2000; Reger, 2001):

- Observing the total environment to identify developments.
- Estimating the timescale for important events.
- Identifying and evaluating market opportunities or threats.
- Reducing uncertainty.
- Major reorientation of a company policy.
- Improving operational decision making.
- Developing plans, strategies and policies.
- Assisting R&D management.
- Evaluating new products or processes.

Data and information gathering for forecasting purposes is not a simple activity. Technology intelligence is intended to capture and deliver technological information as part of the process whereby an organization develops an awareness of technology threats and opportunities (Kerr et al., 2006). The value of intelligence lies not merely in the information but in the process of generating it. This process might lead to an enhanced capacity and commitment to understanding, anticipating and responding to external changes on the part of a firm's key strategic managers. This is particularly important, since there are many filters such as surveillance and power filters that data go through before managers take action on them (Ehrnberg and Jacobsson, 1996). Technology intelligence is a systematic way of organizing the forecasting activity within a firm in order to reduce the impact of filters stopping the relevant data/information reaching decision makers.

4.3 Identification processes

To adapt organizational skills and resources to the changing environment, a major step that should be taken is the identification of alternatives. Firms should analyse the requirements of the environment and compare them with the capabilities and resources of the firm, including labour skills, technology and know-how within the organization. In order to achieve this, a comprehensive analysis of the environment and an internal audit should be performed so that the gap between the expectancy of the market and the current situation of the company is determined. However, it should be remembered that the current capabilities and technology directly affect the technologies that can be developed in the future. The key steps involved in mapping the technology and its surrounding environment might be classified under four categories:

1 Technology auditing.
2 Forecasting technology, markets and external environment.
3 Identification of organizational capabilities.
4 Documenting and disseminating the information.

These steps are now discussed in detail.

Technology auditing

Auditing should be a detailed evaluation of the available in-house technologies and their status. It requires finding who needs information and what they want to know, followed with questions such as where and how to look for the information. Depending on what is requested by whom, the level of auditing will change.

The main objectives of the technology auditing process are identifying and evaluating the firm's technological resources and capabilities as well as assessing and ranking technologies (Khalil, 2000; Lindsay, 2000). The process is as follows. After the technologies have been identified and listed, they are assessed and ranked on the basis of different criteria, ranging from categories of technologies, maturity of technologies, competitive position, location in the supply chain, levels of competencies through to impact of technologies (Gagnon and Haldar, 1995; Braun, 2000).

The technologies embodied in a product can be identified using a mapping technique called the 'product/technology matrix'. The products are listed on one leg of the matrix and the technologies in the form of skills and knowledge on the other. An extension of this might be a 'technology/product/market diagnostic matrix'. These kinds of matrices help to list the technologies important for the company and show their link with particular products and markets.

However, the list of technologies can be achieved in various ways. For example, a company might start with a list of its markets and then identify the products in each market; the technologies used in producing the products are then listed. If there are many products, a classification might be needed. Product families might be used to summarize all products into key products. Another method might be first putting processes into groups either by analysing process flow diagrams and checking the basic operations or by linking process technologies with technology strategy and finding a key technology that helps the firm to execute any process.

The list of technologies in a company might be meaningless if technologies are very broad, so they need to be disaggregated to make a meaningful and manageable set of technologies to work with. For example, NASA's technology of sending people to the moon might be unbundled by identifying technologies such as rocket motor technology, life support system technology, solid rocket booster technology, guidance systems, re-entry shield technology and so on (Lindsay, 2000).

Technologies can be classified according to their competitive potential (Lindsay, 2000):

- **Base/enabling technologies** are essential to be in business and are widely exploited by competitors, so their competitive impact is low.
- **Critical/key technologies** are well embodied in products and processes and their competitive impact is high.
- **Pacing technologies** might be under experimentation by some competitors, and if a technology succeeds, its competitive impact is likely to be high.
- **Emerging technologies** are at an early research stage or emerging in other industries and their competitive impact is unknown, although they are expected to be tomorrow's pacing technologies.

Even though this classification implicitly considers technology maturity to some degree, the idea of assessing the maturity of a technology refers to its position in the S-curve or life cycle. As the S-curve is a powerful tool in understanding technologies and their development, it is described at length in Chapter 11. In general, the evolution of a company's technologies follows an S-shape distribution over time (see Figure 11.1), with the following phases in the life cycle:

- *Embryonic*: the direction of technological advance is not clear.
- *Growth*: major technological advance can be expected with regular efforts.
- *Mature*: minor technological advance would require very high efforts.
- *Ageing*: no technological advance can be expected.

After the maturity of technologies is listed, another useful assessment is to find the competitive position of the firm with respect to its technologies. The technological competitive position of a firm shows its strength compared to its competitors. A dominant position would mean that the company is the technological leader; if its position lacks any competitors, it is a follower. Then the competitive position of a company might be linked with maturity information by preparing a 'technological competitive position/technology maturity matrix' that describes the context for innovation activities. This matrix allows the portfolio of technologies within the business to be assessed in terms of their competitive position and maturity (such as emerging, growing, maturing and declining), enabling the 'balance' of the portfolio to be assessed (Dussauge et al., 1992; Lindsay, 2000).

The task of technology assessment might take many forms if its broad definition is considered, namely the systematic identification, analysis and evaluation of the potential primary as well as secondary consequences of technology in terms of its impacts on social, cultural, political and environmental processes. There is a wide range of techniques to be used in technology assessment, as shown in Appendix Table A.2 (Henriksen, 1997). These techniques include risk analysis, brainstorming, cost-benefit analysis, decision analysis, life cycle analysis and analytical hierarchy process. For example, cost-benefit analysis weighs the total expected costs against the total expected benefits of one or more actions in order to choose the best or most profitable option. Benefits and costs are often expressed in money terms and are adjusted for the time value of money, so that all flows of benefits and flows of project costs over time are expressed on a common basis in terms of their present value. Some of these techniques are briefly given in Chapter 9. The resulting output of these assessments presents rich data on various aspects of the technologies in which the company is interested.

Auditing needs to consider the competence level of technologies as well, since competencies are a critical technology resource. The competence level might range from low/obsolete competence to high, cutting-edge competence. The resulting technological competence list is an important input for strategy making. For example, the auditing exercise might develop a 'market/technology matrix for analysing technical and product competence', which can be used to analyse the technical and marketing competencies necessary to support strategic decision making in product innovation (Holt, 1992). This matrix could be even more detailed by including local and global market distinctions in the comparison.

Some comparisons may require further detailed information for technological competencies. So a competence list might be generated for each technology category, where levels might refer to the following characteristics (Floyd, 1998):

- *Clear leader*: sets the pace and direction of technological development and is recognized for being leader in the industry.
- *Strong*: able to express independent technical actions and set new directions.
- *Favourable*: able to sustain technological competitiveness in general and/or leadership in technical niches.
- *Tenable*: unable to set independent course, continually in catch-up mode.
- *Weak*: unable to sustain quality of technical outputs versus competitors; short-term fire-fighting focus.

Another assessment method for capabilities suggests the use of the assessment of a firm's capabilities in comparison to its competitors along five major dimensions (Lindsay, 2000):

1 Magnitude of internal technological resources, such as personnel.
2 Relevant external resources, such as alliances.
3 Production/operating experience, such as commercial application of technologies.
4 Proprietary position, such as patents.
5 Innovation record, such as the number of new products.

Forecasting technology, market and external environment

The unit of analysis for forecasting might be technologies or markets, as well as the social, economic and political environment in which the company is operating. Even though the unit of analysis varies, forecasting techniques remain more or less the same in predicting the future. Many forecasting techniques have been developed over the years (Martino, 1983; Porter et al., 1991; Makridakis et al., 1998) and they can be categorized on the basis of the type of forecast parameters. For example, the direct forecasting technique consists of methods such as expert opinion (the Delphi technique, surveys, nominal group); naive time series analysis; and trend extrapolation (growth curves, life cycle substitution). An alternative categorization might be to group techniques according to the use of computer models or other analytic tools, such as modelling, or the degree of human participation in the forecasting process, such as expert opinion, scenario building and the Delphi technique.

As there are many forecasting methods and they are not the core topic of this book, four major methods of technology forecasting (patent analysis, value analysis, roadmapping and S-curves) are described in Part II.

The search for the potential developments in technologies is not the only activity in the identification process; it also comprises the future trends in markets so that the linkages between existing technologies, products and markets and their future potential uses can be established. By listing the currently available products of a firm and showing their links with the technologies the firm currently owns and the markets in which these products are sold, a general overview of today can be sketched. But more importantly, in the same analysis, it is also possible to show the links of these products with the potential technologies and new markets where they can be sold. By doing so, one simple table/matrix can highlight a dynamic analysis.

Many forms of matrices linking technologies, products and markets might be developed through technology roadmapping (Phaal et al., 2004b). There are many forms of technology roadmapping; however, the main idea is to highlight the linkages among markets, products and technology (current and potential). The expected future business/market drivers are identified and then their impact on product features is made. Based on these future product characteristics to be achieved, the list of technologies that will be needed to realize these characteristics is decided.

Besides forecasting technologies and markets, it is necessary to expand the analysis to the context in which the technologies are developed and used, since many environmental factors determine the future of technologies. For example, at the turn of the century, the choice between gas, electric and steam technologies for automobile engines could not be driven by technical criteria, since each technology dominated on different dimensions of merit such as cost and safety (David, 1990).

More importantly, within the dynamic capabilities framework, the environmental context recognized for analytical purposes is the business 'ecosystem' – the community of organizations, institutions and individuals that impact the enterprise and the enterprise's customers and supplies (Teece, 2007). In other words, not only do environmental factors affect the company's search of opportunities, but by understanding the business ecosystem, the company itself might shape the opportunity in collaboration with its partners/stakeholders in the wider community. The identification capability expands to the capability of combining the know-how within the firm with organizations external to it, for example, that exist in the ecosystem, such as other enterprises, universities and so on. This is different from the absorptive capacity that relates to an internal capability of understanding the value of external opportunities, since identification includes skill in putting things together to capture co-specialization benefits from various assets or resources residing in the ecosystem.

In general, forecasting techniques might be applicable to social, economic and political developments. However, there are some simple and widely used tools such as scenario analysis that is used in the case at the end of this Chapter. The strategic management field is full of simple but powerful tools such as STEP, PEST, PESTEL, PESTLE, STEEPLE, SWOT and five-forces analysis (Thomson and Martin, 2010; Rothaermel, 2013; Johnson et al., 2014). We will shortly mention two such tools in this chapter: **STEEPA** (social, technological, economic, environmental, political and aesthetic) and PESTEL (political, economic, social, technological, environmental and legal) analysis. STEEPA is used by business leaders worldwide to build their vision of the future. Using the tool is a three-stage process (Norburn, 2005):

1 Managers brainstorm the relevant factors that apply to the context of the firm.
2 The information that applies to these factors is identified.
3 Managers draw conclusions from this information.

The following STEEPA factors may help as a starting point for brainstorming:

- *Social*: population growth rate and age profile, population health, education and social mobility, and attitudes towards these, population employment patterns and attitudes towards work and sociocultural changes.
- *Technological environment*: impact of emerging technologies, the Internet and technology transfer and R&D activity.
- *Economic*: stage of business cycle, current and projected economic growth, inflation and interest rates, unemployment and labour supply and labour costs.
- *Environment*: environmental laws and costs of pollution.
- *Political*: government type and stability, freedom of press, rule of law and levels of bureaucracy and corruption, tax policy and trade and tariff controls.
- *Aesthetic*: design and colour.

There is another version of STEEPA that is titled PESTEL. This analysis is a framework or tool used by marketers to analyse and monitor the macro-environmental (external marketing environment) factors that have an impact on an organization. The result of this is used to identify threats and weaknesses which are used in a SWOT analysis.

There are a number of software tools developed for forecasting purposes. Some examples are specialized programs such as Soritec, Autobox, Forecast Pro and SmartForecasts, as well as Microsoft Excel and many statistical software packages such as Minitab, SAS and SPSS. However, these examples cannot easily capture the multidimensional need of technological identification. There are a few exceptions, for example the IPTS-TIM software, which aims to combine market, society and technological information in forecasting future developments, created by the Institute for Prospective Technological Studies (IPTS), one of the EC's joint research centres in Seville (Moncada-Paterno-Castello et al., 2000).

Forecasting might be carried out through 'information or prediction markets' – virtual financial market games that are used as prediction tools. Some of the most popular are the Iowa Electronic Markets, Hollywood Stock Exchange and the Foresight Exchange Prediction Market. With these tools, a large number of people can collectively predict the next election outcomes, expected returns at the box office or the likelihood of future events. Similar tools may be developed and used within a specific company, for example General Electric established an 'imagination market' as an idea generation and group decision tool.

Besides forecasting technologies, it is necessary to forecast the impact of technologies as well. Impact assessment is the process of identifying the future consequences of a current or proposed action. Impact assessment is used to:

- Provide support for a technological development.
- Defer or stop the implementation of a technology.
- Stimulate research or development to remedy the adverse effects of a technology.
- Provide a reliable base of information for use by any parties concerned with the development of the technology (Khalil, 2000).

The impact assessment might be carried out either for an individual technology or a set of competing technologies. The key in impact assessment is to analyse the likely effects of a technology, and technology forecasting concerns the impacts on a technology from other forces. Among these impact analyses, the environmental assessment can be considered as the most advanced and standardized procedure in many countries. The most common approach for the assessment of potential environmental impacts is life cycle analysis:

> [An] objective process to evaluate the environmental burdens associated with a product, process or activity by identifying energy and materials used and wastes released to the environment and to evaluate and implement opportunities to affect environmental improvements. (Fleisher and Grunwald, 2008)

In the case of comparing technologies, comparisons consider current technologies while assessing impacts focused on future possibilities. While comparisons focus narrowly on assessing how well technologies fulfil a specific mission, assessing impacts addresses a broader set of effects concerning technological, economic, institutional, social, cultural, political, international, environmental and health-related impacts. There are many techniques used to assess technologies, ranging from economic tools such as net present value (NPV) to qualitative tools such as ethics analysis (Henriksen, 1997; Braun, 2000). Impact assessment tasks, by and large, involve the following steps (Khalil, 2000):

- Problem definition.
- Technology description.
- Technology forecast.
- Societal context description.
- Societal context forecast.
- Impact identification.
- Impact analysis.
- Impact evaluation.
- Policy analysis.
- Communication of results.

Identification of organizational capabilities

Technology auditing cannot be completed without preparing the technology resource base inventory that constitutes human resources, IP, project portfolio, libraries and databases and papers and publications. In other words, such a knowledge repository is a strong base for using and developing technologies (Chiesa et al., 1999).

In addition to analysing the technology resource base, searching the organizational capabilities of a firm might be a broader exercise to discover the strengths and weaknesses of the internal TM infrastructure. A study in identifying a capability profile indicates four major dimensions of an organizational capability (Lindsay, 2000): facilities and equipment, personnel skills, organizational capabilities and management capabilities. Exemplar organizational capabilities for R&D might be product and systems development capabilities, while management capabilities for R&D might be the utilization of advanced state-of-the-art technology, application of current state-of-the-art technology and cost-performance optimization. Recent studies in knowledge management suggest a number of new techniques to map the internal company knowledge base such as knowledge mapping and technology mining (EC, 2004; Porter and Cunningham, 2005).

Intelligence literature also offers useful models in linking people and organizational capabilities/knowledge with TM infrastructure. According to Kerr et al. (2006), the organizational knowledge matrix is formed on the basis of two dimensions, intelligence provision (being external or internal) versus awareness of information needed for the company. If the organization is aware of a gap in its knowledge and it has the information readily accessible, then it can mine the material to extract the necessary information, but if the organization is not aware of a gap in its knowledge, it needs to trawl in order to formalize knowledge not yet utilized. In the case of external knowledge, a firm can either scan for the knowledge it is not aware of or target its search by focusing on knowledge it identifies as critical for the future.

In order to gain different knowledge, the possible people and infrastructure combinations vary. For example, in the case of trawl-type of knowledge (meaning internal but not known knowledge), firms can rely on knowledge intermediaries and internal gatekeepers who utilize internal social networks as infrastructure.

Concerning the organization of technology forecasting/intelligence, it is important to remember that forecasting is not only difficult technically, but also that there are many organizational problems such as difficulties in opportunity identification, risk perception and surprise anticipation. For example, Ken Olsen, co-founder of Digital Equipment Corporation said in 1977: 'there is no reason for any individual to have a computer in their home' (Bowonder et al., 1999). So overcoming the main problems in forecasting requires a set of selection capabilities, learning capabilities and adaptation capabilities (Teece, 2007). In other words, any forecasting and intelligence activity requires multidimensional and multiple-perspective-oriented surprise anticipation models. This highlights the need for having people with the appropriate mindset and visualization capabilities.

Documenting and disseminating the information

Even though the importance of forecasting and intelligence activities is seen in the process of these activities, it is important to remember that the goal of identification is to:

> [Help] firms identify, understand and adapt to technological changes that most often occur externally; to anticipate the consequences of technology trends; and to develop well-thought-out plans and policies. (Mortara et al., 2007)

This is why the documentation and dissemination of findings help to filter and present data that result in developing a good 'sensing' capability (Teece, 2007). The sensing capability becomes a part of learning and should be managed accordingly, in order to ensure that the knowledge observed, analysed and produced and the experience gained are not lost (Levitt and March, 1988). A learning organization will be able to identify new technologies easily and efficiently (see **Chapter 5**).

It is important to have specific formats for presenting the findings of forecasting/intelligence to those requiring the information so that they can make use of it in their decision making. The documentation might be an Excel spreadsheet or intranet database, depending on the best way of disseminating the information. The tools mentioned in Chapter 5 indicate some further forms to be used for documentation such as technology *Yellow Pages*. P&G provide an interesting example in dissemination; it used the latest in webcasting and satellite technology to create an internal innovation news network (see Chapter 2) (Sakkab, 2002).

 Case studies

The importance given to identification, the strategic use of identification and the reasons for developing the identification capability will all influence how the process is structured. Whatever format is chosen, firms eventually conduct activities around auditing and forecasting that help them to identify opportunities. As the case studies of Clorox (a fast-moving consumer product producer) and Baxter Healthcare (a high-tech company in the medical instruments sector) clearly show, the identification processes within a company might take many different shapes.

Clorox

Identifying technology opportunities is an integral function of the technology acquisitions group at Clorox. The group actively pursues opportunities from a number of sources. For Clorox, acquisition agreements provide ways for the company to obtain access to IP that can be used to produce a product. Access can be secured through licensing agreements or arrangements for exclusive supply or manufacturing. The company actively searches for new technologies that fit into its existing businesses and/or enable it to move into new areas. Sources include universities, technical meetings, trade shows, online databases and personal contacts.

For example, the company's Kingsford 'Grill Cleaner' evolved from a technology and a small company that Clorox discovered at a janitorial trade show. Initially, the company hoped to use the finding in a new cleaning product, but follow-up efforts were not successful in that application. However, several Clorox employees felt that the technology had underlying value that could eventually be useful in a number of other applications, so they worked at developing a continuing relationship with the other company. They recognized the importance of establishing ties that could be maintained over long periods, withstanding changes in personnel. Eventually, the fit was found with the development of the successful grill cleaner, and this in turn has led to other partnering projects.

In Clorox's experience, identifying a technology with potential is not enough. Employees must have a clear understanding of just what the technology might be able to do, how it fits broadly with many other business applications and how a sustained relationship with the original supplier is critical in the effort.

Baxter Healthcare

The corporate technology sourcing (CTS) unit at Baxter operates in an innovative and creative atmosphere, seeking a broad, diverse range of inputs. The mission of the CTS unit is to monitor new external technological developments and channel this information to the appropriate experts. The actual sourcing process is quite standard; the company networks with contacts in companies, associations, universities and search services. CTS staff look for the unexpected and pass information on to the technical and marketing communities. Often, the technical and marketing people can see different opportunities in the same information. The services of the CTS unit include responding to specific requests, focused technology sourcing, acting as a resource for general technology scanning and generating unsolicited ideas.

The CTS unit considers that every specialist is doing a competent job in sourcing technology in their specialty, but looks beyond these specific contributions to areas that complement normal research efforts. This work requires people who love being creative and who do not have a compelling need to be right all the time.

Baxter's technology sourcing tries to find unusual contacts. For example, the company discovered that Leatherhead Food Research in Leatherhead, England, specialists in food technology and food products, had developed a technology for measuring the temperature of the raspberry filling inside angel cakes as they travel through a 100-ft-long continuous oven. Baxter took this technology, modified it somewhat and now uses it for continuous sterilization processes within the company.

Baxter's most dramatic success came in the 1980s and involved the transfer of Japanese vending machine technology to hospital pharmacy automation. The company knew that hospital pharmacies were looking for a way to dispense regularly prescribed medications accurately, without asking a full-time pharmacist to do such a repetitive task. Using high-quality Japanese vending technology, Baxter was able to develop automatic pharmacy machines that dispense customized medications according to doctors' instructions. Manufactured by Sanyo and sold by Baxter, these machines are now central to a division that has netted Baxter almost $1bn in total sales.

The CTS unit at Baxter does not have a problem with being wrong, since it is wrong 98% of the time. With a budget of only $1m, it is able to identify some 5,000 new ideas and technologies each year. About 100 of these are followed up within the company and 5–10% of projects become commercially successful. This provides a return of $30–40m in new revenue each year – a good return on Baxter's investment in competitive intelligence.

Baxter finds that a company with an open culture, with employees who are open-minded, willing to speculate and willing to share, gains great benefits from its competitive intelligence.

The experiences of these two firms provide important lessons for seeking technology opportunities. A successful use of technology intelligence might include some of the following simple considerations:

- The process should be structured and organized.
- R&D leadership should provide direction and define specific intelligence needs.

(Continued)

- Tools need to be developed for accessing and analysing intelligence.
- The effort should be staffed with individuals who have the experience, intelligence, skills and the right temperament.
- R&D leadership should be motivated to understand the implications of the findings and act upon the technology intelligence.

Source: Norling et al. (2000) 'Putting Competitive Technology Intelligence to Work', *Research-Technology Management*, **43**(5), 23–29.

Summary

Technology investments are risky and long term, thus the identification activity reduces the uncertainties surrounding technological decisions by forecasting the future. Forecasting markets and technologies provides a rich database in identifying technological opportunities and threats. Technology identification not only requires the development of new technologies but also draws attention to identification of the existing technologies used in the environment as well as the evaluation of the technology being used in the organization to determine whether new application areas exist or not.

In sum, the identification capability of a firm helps to understand the processes, asset position and paths of a firm by conducting audits and searching the future trends with forecasting techniques. This, in turn, helps to build the complementary/interactive TM actions such as selecting from strategic alternatives.

? Key Questions

1 What capabilities support identification?
2 What are the advantages and disadvantages of forecasting?
3 What needs to be done for technology auditing?
4 What tasks are undertaken during the process of forecasting?
5 How do organizational capabilities help TM?

Further reading

Braun, E. (2000) *Technology in Context: Technology Assessment for Managers* (New York: Walter de Gruyter).

Johnson, G., Whittington, R., Scholes, K., Angwin, D. and Regnér, P. (2014) *Exploring Strategy Text & Cases*, 10th edn (Harlow: Pearson Education).

Phaal, R., O'Sullivan, E., Routley, M., Ford, S. and Probert, D. (2011) 'A Framework for Mapping Industrial Emergence', *Technological Forecasting and Social Change*, **78**(2), 217–230.

Porter, A. L., Roper, A. T., Mason, T. W. et al. (1991) *Forecasting and Management of Technology* (New York: Wiley).

Roussel, P. A., Saad, K. N. and Erickson, T. J. (1991) *Third Generation R&D: Managing the Link to Corporate Strategy* (Boston, MA: Harvard Business School Press).

Routley, M., Phaal, R., Athanassopoulou, N. and Probert, D. (2013) 'Mapping Experience in Organisations: A Learning Process for Strategic Technology Planning', *Engineering Management Journal*, **25**(1), 35–47.

Rothaermel, F. T. (2013) *Strategic Management: Concepts* (Columbus, OH: McGraw-Hill/Irwin).

Thompson, J. and Martin, F. (2010) *Strategic Management: Awareness and Change*, 6th edn (Singapore: Cengage Learning).

5

LEARNING

Learning objectives

After studying this chapter, you should be able to:

1 Understand what learning is.
2 Describe the role of the learning capability in TM.
3 Understand learning processes as a part of KM.
4 Understand different types of learning.
5 Understand organizational learning.
6 Observe the role of IT in facilitating learning.

5.1 Introduction

The true sources of sustainable competitive advantage are organizational capabilities that enable firms to innovate at a faster rate. In other words, the focus is not the stock of technological capabilities but the flow of technological capabilities. Thus, the key source of competitive advantage is the rate at which firms develop or acquire new technological capabilities, not the technologies they can currently access. In addition, all capabilities, whether dynamic or non-dynamic, have the potential to accommodate change, so, like products, capabilities evolve over the phases of a life cycle, such as growth, maturity and decline. Therefore, the ability to learn and continually improve the organization's technological capability are important capabilities for TM, demanding management's continuous attention.

Learning takes place at all levels in a firm; it might be generated from the development and exploitation of technologies internally as well as externally. Thus, learning forms a critical part of technological competencies; it involves reflections on technology projects and processes carried out within or outside the firm. Learning processes might include various degrees of formality that are linked with processes derived from KM and the learning organization. Continuous alignment and realignment of specific tangible and intangible assets require effective KM, where learning, knowledge transfer, know-how integration and know-how protection are core activities. While knowledge protection is discussed in Chapter 6 and knowledge transfer and integration are topics mentioned in Chapter 3, this chapter focuses on KM practices oriented towards learning.

5.2 Definition

Learning is defined as the acquisition and use of existing knowledge and/or the creation of new knowledge with the purpose of improving economic performance (Boerner et al., 2001). Learning can occur at individual and organizational levels. The latter is the capability of a firm to facilitate knowledge creation or acquisition, disseminate it throughout the organization and embody it in products, services and systems (Nonaka and Takeuchi, 1995). The types of learning involve four basic categories: learning-by-doing, learning-by-searching, scientific learning, learning-by-using and spillover learning (Boerner et al., 2001).

Learning is a dynamic process, which helps tasks to be performed more effectively via repetition and experimentation. It also brings new production opportunities to light. To understand the importance of learning, the dynamic capability competence-based view can be useful where the main assumption is that a firm continues to exist if it leverages and develops capabilities sooner or better than the competition by creating revenue streams that are earned by innovators and occur between the introduction of an innovation and its successful diffusion until it is imitated (Korhohen and Niemela, 2005).

The concept of dynamic capabilities as a management process opens the door to the potential for inter-organizational learning as well (Teece et al., 1997). Companies can make collaborations and assign partnerships to share their knowledge with each other, which would make them both stronger in the competitive environment. The knowledge and experience of both firms can enable them to correct mistakes, saving time by gathering the experience the other has. Whether it is individual, organizational or inter-organizational, knowledge is a key component in responding to rapid technological changes in dynamically changing environments, so it is appropriate to include learning as a dynamic capability.

As the definition of learning is based on knowledge, this chapter draws substantially on the KM literature. KM aims to add and create value by more actively leveraging the know-how, experience and judgement within and outside an organization (Easterby-Smith and Lyles, 2003). It comprises a range of practices used by organizations to identify, create, represent and distribute knowledge for reuse, awareness and learning.

Data are recorded symbols and signal reading. The main purpose of data is to record activities or situations, to attempt to capture the true picture or real event. Therefore, all data are historical, unless used for illustrative purposes, such as forecasting. Information is a message that contains relevant meaning, implication or input for a decision and/or action. Information comes from current and historical sources. **Knowledge** constitutes not only the cognition or recognition (know-what) but also capacity to act (know-how) as well as understanding (know-why) that resides or is contained within the mind (Liew, 2007). In the context of business, the purpose of knowledge is to create or increase value for the enterprise and all its stakeholders (EC, 2004).

There are two types of knowledge: explicit knowledge, which can be expressed in words and numbers, and tacit knowledge, which is hard to formalize and highly personal (Nonaka and Takeuchi, 1995). On the one hand, structured or explicit knowledge takes the form of tangible assets, such as plant and information systems and equipment. Tacit knowledge, on the other hand, has two types: the first is the technical dimension, which encompasses the kinds of informal personal skills often referred to as 'know-how', while the second dimension is cognitive. The cognitive dimension comprises beliefs, ideals, values and mental models, which are generally taken for granted (Nonaka and Konno, 1998). One goal of KM is to capture this tacit knowledge and turn it into value by developing processes. KM also tries to develop policies, values, mechanisms and techniques so that tacit knowledge will stay in the company even after people have left the organization (Easterby-Smith and Lyles, 2003).

The interactions between explicit and tacit knowledge and how they lead to the creation of new knowledge are introduced by the SECI model – socialization, externalization, combination and internalization (Nonaka and Takeuchi, 1995). The SECI model describes the dynamic process through which explicit and tacit knowledge are exchanged and transformed:

- *Socialization*: the sharing of tacit knowledge between individuals, that is, capturing knowledge through physical proximity.
- *Externalization*: the articulation of tacit knowledge, that is, the conversion of tacit knowledge into explicit knowledge.
- *Combination*: the conversion of explicit knowledge into more complex sets of explicit knowledge.
- *Internalization*: the conversion of explicit knowledge into the organization's tacit knowledge (Nonaka and Konno, 1998).

Managers should be aware of this process when developing an environment for knowledge sharing in their organization. Knowledge is manageable only if leaders embrace and foster the dynamism of knowledge creation.

5.3   Learning processes

The ability of an organization to learn, adapt, change and renew itself over time is shaped by three main factors (Boerner et al., 2001):

1 Managerial and organizational processes – essentially, how things are done in firms.
2 The strategic position of a firm – its current technology and IP endowments, its customer base and upstream relations with suppliers.
3 Paths available to a firm.

Path dependencies and established technological trajectories shape the productive and technological opportunities faced by firms and the attractiveness of these opportunities. This chapter deals with the managerial and organizational processes that will help to create an environment where SECI can take place. The selected processes offer three major activity categories that can help to build routines within an organization to keep its learning capability alive:

1 Building learning/KM enablers.
2 Building and utilizing networks.
3 Becoming a learning organization.

These three activities are discussed in detail.

Building learning/KM enablers

The main goal of enablers is to complete a learning cycle, whose elements are concept, experiment, experience and reflection (Kolb and Fry, 1975). Learning is seen as following a pattern of reflecting on experience, building up conceptual models and then testing out their validity by experiment. Learning only takes place when the cycle is completed. Many organizations are strong in terms of the experimentation and resulting experience; what they often lack is the time and space in which to reflect and the conceptual models and frameworks with which to make sense of the things they are trying out.

In terms of learning in TM, it is necessary to consider enablers for:

- Structured and challenging reflection on the process – what happened, what worked well, what went wrong and so on.
- Conceptualizing, capturing and codifying the lessons learned into frameworks and eventually procedures to build on lessons learned.
- Experimentation – the willingness to try to manage things differently next time, to see if the lessons learned are valid.
- Honest capture of experience, even if this has been a costly failure, in order to have raw material to reflect on.

Effective learning from and about technology management depends on establishing a learning cycle around these themes. A variety of tools and mechanisms are suggested to help with the process (ICS UNIDO, 2008):

- *For reflection purposes*, post-project reviews, benchmarking, structured audits, project evaluation and measurement need to be done.
- *For conceptualization*, managers can use new structures and product designs, formal planning reviews, pilot projects and training and development.
- *Experimentation* is based on testing, prototyping, R&D activities, designed experiments and simulations. The importance of prototypes is well recognized in learning rapidly by minimizing mistakes and successfully integrating the work of the many functions and support groups involved in the project (Leonard-Barton et al., 1994).
- *Experience* can be captured through measurement, documentation, display and sharing, such as on video, via diaries, project records and photographs.

A study of KM best practices (Armbrecht et al., 2001) clearly indicates the importance of IT tools such as search and retrieval tools. This kind of infrastructure makes it possible to establish a learning culture and promote creativity across company units.

There is no doubt that KM benefits a lot from IT because of its role in facilitating knowledge creation, capture, transfer and reuse (Easterby-Smith and Lyles, 2003). Historically, there have been a number of technologies enabling KM practices in the organization, including expert systems, databases, knowledge bases, various types of information management, software help desk tools, document management systems and other IT systems supporting organizational knowledge flows. All these technologies have evolved and developed further with advances in the IT field. Examples include on-the-job peer discussions, formal apprenticeships, discussion forums, corporate libraries, professional training and mentoring programmes. However, with computers becoming more widespread, specific adaptations of technology such as expert systems and knowledge repositories have been introduced to further simplify the knowledge transfer process. Additionally, the Internet brought with it further enabling technologies, including e-learning, web conferencing, collaborative software, content management systems, corporate *Yellow Pages* directories, email lists, wikis, blogs and other technologies. Each enabling technology can expand the level of inquiry available to an employee, while providing a platform to achieve specific goals or actions.

The practice of KM will continue to evolve with the growth of collaboration applications, visual tools and other technologies. The majority of tools are, for the most part, still based on text, and thus represent explicit knowledge transfer. These tools face challenges in distilling meaningful reusable knowledge from their content. Data mining is an example of such distillation practices.

Tools and technologies can facilitate the implementation of knowledge processes and in some cases they may be able to automate some kinds of knowledge work in these areas. Still, they must be taken in context and implemented as a part of the overall effort to leverage organizational knowledge through integration with the business strategy, the culture, the current processes and the existing technologies.

Building and utilizing networks

As knowledge is created by individual people in interaction with others, there are two main sources: internal and external. In that regard, building networks within the company across different units and geographies is a starting point but it is not enough; it needs to be complemented with the establishment of networks with external sources such as suppliers and customers that contribute to two specific types of learning: learning-by-using and spillover learning (Boerner et al., 2001).

The task of building and utilizing a network needs to start with a knowledge auditing or mapping activity. Knowledge mapping generates a graphic picture of the explicit (codified) information and tacit knowledge, showing the importance of and relationships between knowledge stores and dynamics (Pelc, 1996; EC, 2004). Such a knowledge map is expected to portray the sources, flows, constraints and losses or stopping points of knowledge within the organization. Knowledge mapping comprises survey, audit and synthesis, and aims to track the acquisition and loss of information.

Further, an important set of KM practices relate to the coordination of internal and external R&D capabilities, inter-firm relationships and market requirements (Teece, 2007). This often requires spanning disciplinary, organizational and company boundaries using 'capability maps', which identify the locations within a company of formal knowledge bases, skills and supporting equipment and services (Cotec, 1998). In addition to internal capability maps, it is important to map the relationships between external sources/partners and internal human resources (HR) involved in knowledge creation and sharing. A map/audit exercise helps to explore personal and group competencies, and illustrates or maps how knowledge flows throughout an organization internally and externally. This mapping exercise could be done while the identification activity is carried out (Chapter 4). Guidelines for knowledge mapping include (EC, 2004):

- Finding knowledge in processes, relationships, policies, people, documents, conversations, suppliers, competitors and customers.
- Recognizing and locating knowledge in a wide variety of forms: tacit and explicit, formal and informal, codified and personalized, internal and external.
- Being familiar with organizational levels and aggregation, cultural issues and reward systems, legal process and protection such as patents and trademarks.

The resulting knowledge maps might be effectively used for human resources management (HRM), R&D management and IPR management (Hull et al., 2000). Further, their existence support innovation in many ways but particularly in facilitating team management in networks, since projects and innovations are managed by teams. There are four major team types in the literature: functional, cross-functional, autonomous project and virtual teams (Tushman and Andersen, 2004). The two extreme team types for in-house teams are the functional and autonomous team structures. The functional team passes the project in sequence from one department to another, each manager taking responsibility for their own phase and then passing it to the next one in the chain. The latter is set up to do the job with its own management and resources and full powers to do whatever is necessary to achieve the agreed result. The projects allocated to autonomous teams are normally challenging and risky. Consequently, these teams require an entrepreneurial style of management. In cross-functional teams, each functional area assigns people to the project so that the team combines experience from every function. A virtual team is drawn from a mixture of organizations and managed by the organization that launches the project. The advantages of such teams are that they can bring together expertise, which is not available in a single firm, and can be fast and entrepreneurial in nature. Disadvantages include the fact that team members are not co-located, communication can be difficult and the cost of external resources can be high. Whatever the team structure, team managers should have good communication, negotiation, consensus-building and conflict resolution skills.

Team structure changes when the project is collaborative and includes external partners. Collaboration in innovation projects is difficult (Chiesa and Manzini, 1998). Clear contractual relationships are important in managing collaborations but there are limits to what can be written into a contract to ensure success, especially when there is an element of discovery/innovation in the work. There should be a climate of trust and confidence between the partners and communication should be open (Powells, 1998). Thus, the sharing of data, information and knowledge among members of a supply chain is critical to the success of an alliance. Overall, the successful integration of a supply chain requires careful linking of internal processes with external suppliers and customers.

Mechanisms for integrating teams may take various forms, as mentioned earlier: electronic linkages, personnel flows, use of common systems such as computer-aided design or reports, manuals, project teams and written or oral channels of communication. The Internet has led to an increase in creative collaboration, learning and research, e-commerce and instant information that facilitate networks. There are also a variety of organizational enablers for KM programmes, including communities of practice, before-, during- and after-action reviews, peer assists, information taxonomies, coaching and mentoring. In addition, portfolio management processes offer an opportunity to share and learn within and across teams and projects. That is why project management tools are valuable in tapping into knowledge dispersed in teams internally and externally (Dyer and Nobeoka, 2000). For example, team debriefings allow cross-functional learning and ideation. Debriefing at the conclusion of projects brings out and captures lessons learned about project content and process. Documentation is a necessity to transfer the tacit knowledge into explicit/codified knowledge.

In addition to setting an IT infrastructure, collaborations require a clear strategy on learning. In other words, networking companies need to consider how to manage skills learning and capability transfer from partners. Some important elements of a learning strategy should include (Doz and Hamel, 1997; Dyer and Nobeoka, 2000):

- The learning agenda.
- The level of openness to learn.
- The nature of the capabilities to be developed.

- The operationalization of the learning process.
- The establishment of boundaries between the partners to allow observation and co-practice.
- Learning through practice.
- Measuring the compatibility of skills learning.
- Internalization with the continuation of the alliance.
- Thinking benefits from the learning investment.

These and related critical strategic questions should be answered on an interactive basis with business and technology strategy.

Becoming a learning organization

A **learning organization** is skilled at creating, acquiring and transferring knowledge, as well as modifying its behaviour to reflect new knowledge and insight (Argyris and Schön, 1978; Garvin, 1993). In other words, the learning organization is defined as the one that learns continuously and can transform itself. A learning organization (Baiyin et al., 2004):

- Is not just a collection of individuals who are learning.
- Demonstrates organizational capacity for change.
- Accelerates individual learning capacity but also redefines organizational structure, culture, job design and assumptions about the way things are.
- Involves widespread participation of employees in decision making and information sharing.
- Promotes systemic thinking and building an organizational memory.

According to Senge (1990: 1), learning organizations are places:

> [Where] people continually expand their capacity to create the results they truly desire, where new and expansive patterns of thinking are nurtured, where collective aspiration is set free, and where people are continually learning how to learn together.

A learning organization is not simply the sum of the absorptive capacities of its employees, but also the structure of communication between the external environment and the organization and among the sub-units of the organization.

Learning organizations are built on culture and hence it is not an overnight process. Management needs to foster an environment/culture that is conducive to learning, opens up boundaries and stimulates the exchange of ideas. Opening boundaries is particularly important for collaborating companies in open innovation systems. In general, a learning organization:

- Empowers its people.
- Encourages collaboration and team learning.
- Promotes open dialogue.
- Supports systematic problem solving and experimentation with new approaches.
- Acknowledges the interdependence of individuals, the organization and the communities in which they reside (Garvin, 2003; Teece, 2007).
- Recognizes different types of learning, such as learning-by-doing, as well as learning from the company's own experiences and from the experiences and best practices of others.

Processes need to be in place to transfer learning quickly and efficiently to where it is needed.

Organizational learning is closely related to **continuous improvement** and TQM activities. Rather than looking for a single leap forward followed by a period of stability, continuously improving organizations keep stretching the boundaries of their knowledge. They operate a learning cycle that never stops, and as a result they develop the capacity to cope with and lead in an uncertain environment (Bessant and Caffyn, 1996). Continuous improvement is not limited to a handful of technical specialists, rather it depends on finding ways to involve everybody in the process of identifying and solving problems. Most innovation is about small-scale problem solving, getting the bugs out, tightening up performance, adding and refining features and so on. Firms need to train and develop their employees, develop a continuous improvement process, experiment with alternative approaches, measure the results, document the overall process and display and reflect on the results (ICS UNIDO, 2008).

At the macro-level, for the effective development of a learning organization, the 'three Ms' – meaning, management and measurement – need to be clarified (Garvin, 1993). Firms need to be clear what they mean with regard to learning and indicate clear operational guidelines for practice. Task breakdown enables learning objectives to be identified and the resulting learning agenda to be disaggregated into specific achievable steps. Measurement tools can then be used to assess an organization's rate and level of learning. Using this framework, Garvin (1993, 2003) defines learning organizations as capable of:

- Systematic problem solving.
- Experimentation with new approaches.
- Learning from past experiences.
- Learning from best practices of others.
- Transferring knowledge quickly and efficiently throughout the organization.

Learning curves are widely used as a measurement framework, indicating the reduction of costs with increases in cumulative volume. These increases are viewed as proxies for greater manufacturing knowledge. Typically, learning rates are calculated in the 80–85% range (meaning that with a doubling of cumulative production, costs fall to 80–85% of their previous level), although there is wide variation among industries (Garvin, 1993). Drawing on the logic of learning curves, industries as a whole face experience curves – costs and prices that fall by predictable amounts as industries grow and their total production increases. Both learning and experience curves are still widely used, as shown in the case study on USG at the end of this chapter. However, these measures are incomplete, since they only focus on a single measure of output (cost or price) and ignore learning that affects other competitive variables, such as quality, delivery and new product introduction.

The half-life curve responds to these concerns, since it measures the time it takes to achieve a 50% improvement in a specified performance measure (Garvin, 1993). A graph is created by plotting the performance measure of interest, such as defect rate, on the vertical axis (using a logarithmic scale) against time on the horizontal axis. Steeper slopes then represent faster learning. The 50% target is a measure of convenience, which typically has the disadvantage of a long gestation period, so is unlikely to capture any short-run learning that has occurred. A more comprehensive framework is needed to track progress.

Organizational learning can usually be traced through three overlapping stages (Garvin, 1993, 2003):

1 *Cognitive*: organization members are exposed to new ideas, expand their knowledge and begin to think differently.
2 *Behavioural*: employees begin to internalize new insights and alter their behaviour.
3 *Performance improvement*: changes in behaviour lead to measurable improvements in results, such as superior quality or other tangible gains.

Because cognitive and behavioural changes typically pave the way for improvements in performance, a complete learning audit should include all three. Measures might be collected through surveys, questionnaires, interviews and direct observation. Performance measures are essential for ensuring that cognitive and behavioural changes have actually produced results (Bontis et al., 1999). For example, a **balanced scorecard** – an accounting model combining financial and non-financial performance criteria – could be used to measure intangibles in a company by offering a set of metrics tied to an organization's critical business processes against which it openly and regularly measures progress, usually at corporate and business levels, and occasionally by group or function. In particular, the format of a balanced scorecard has a 'learning and growth' section, where all the measures relating to employees and systems the company has in place to facilitate learning and knowledge diffusion are included (Kaplan and Norton, 1996). Without these types of measure, companies would lack a rationale for investing in learning and the assurance that learning was serving their ends.

Organizational learning requires the ability to manage change (Hargadon and Sutton, 2000). In order to build a learning organization, managers might redesign the organization to address inadequacies and build new, more appropriate capabilities and processes, including organizational self-design and learning. Employees might become anxious and fear that they will lose their power and control (Hatch and Dyer, 2004). Consequently, the changes are not easily digested by employees. To enable a smooth transition to the new organizational design, managers need to give support and allow a reasonable time so that the change is diffused and then accepted (Weinzimer, 1998).

Supporting people at the operational level can be an effective mechanism for building commitment to change. They can make important contributions from an early stage of a project. A second mechanism is to use financial resources as a motivating force. The money helps to reduce the budget limitations and also presents tangible evidence of R&D's belief in the opportunity. Effective nurturing of change must address anxieties as well as seek to stimulate vision. It must systematically emphasize areas of continuity, skills and experience that will be valuable and capital investment that will help to ensure success. Coping with anxiety also means responding to the dynamics of technological change.

In addition, knowledge and change management require support from HR departments. As people are a firm's source of intellect, HRM plays a crucial role in managing knowledge. Thus, HR managers are expected to (Hatch and Dyer, 2004):

- Recruit the right people.
- Stimulate them to internalize the information, knowledge, skills and attitudes needed for success.
- Create systematic technological and organizational structures to capture, focus and leverage intellect.

- Create an incentive system not only to provide the organization with knowledge but also to manage and handle staff ideas.
- Increase employee involvement by engaging personnel to identify issues, propose solutions and become partners in implementing the changes needed to succeed in present and future environments.
- Demand and reward top performance from all employees.
- Develop each employee through training and other opportunities.

A further consideration for the learning organization is the structural dilemma of how to set free the creativity that promotes growth and change while controlling innovation (Tushman and Andersen, 2004). One potential solution to this dilemma is to manage different parts of the firm differently – some units for innovation, others for efficiency – so that exploitation-based learning can take place where efficient production within well-defined and routine parts of the business is carried out, while exploration-based learning takes place in a less tangible environment with a loose organizational structure (Crossan and Beldrow, 2003). Another solution is to develop different management approaches at different times in the evolutionary cycle of the firm.

5.4 Improving learning environment

A study of nearly 6,000 organizations across 15 countries shows that learning organizations exhibit higher performance than their less learning-inclined counterparts (Shipton et al., 2013). In that study, a learning organization is considered to be capable of achieving ongoing strategic renewal. By observing different technological learning environments, the study finds out four of the most common HRM practices, which are rewarding, problem solving, top-down management and decentralization. The study concludes HRM forms an essential part of the technological learning structure of firms.

Another HRM element is building learning capabilities. Capability implies an ability to do something, and the most significant concept in relation to this is that of absorptive capacity, which, according to Cohen and Levinthal (1990: 128), is 'an ability to recognize the value of new, external knowledge, assimilate it, and apply it to commercial ends'. It is, therefore, to be found in the underlying knowledge and experience base of the firm. Capabilities might be observed through maturity models, which can be used to benchmark an organization's competence in some particular activity against a body of knowledge. Such models tend to show generic levels of capability development from a low base up to one level of excellence. For example, Rush et al. (2007, 2014) propose a maturity model for technology management, and their model measures learning capability according to the following three key questions: (1) Does your company have systems for assessing technology projects? If so, please elaborate; (2) Does your company learn effectively from one technology project to another? If so, how?; (3) Does your firm carry out post-project reviews? Please describe. Depending on the responses, they evaluate a firm's learning capability from a scale of 1 to 4, where 1 stands for unaware, weak capability; 2 refers to reactive, weak to average capability; 3 means strategic, strong capability; and 4 signals creative, very strong capability.

Besides HRM and a capability maturity scale, another study proposes a practical tool of experience maps to initiate, develop and institutionalize learning at the organizational level. Maps are derived from roadmapping activities and called 'Experience Scan' (Routley et al., 2013). Organizational learning requires collecting retrospective information. Thus, structured workshops have been shown to be a useful technique for generating and capturing information, and promoting an active component of learning for those present as they combine and recombine the information presented. Project reviews have also been used as a mechanism for facilitating KM across the multiple perspectives of project team members. Group storytelling has been used to capture participants' innovation experience for application to future projects.

Therefore, roadmapping could contribute to the collective-learning process as well as to the knowledge-creation process. Roadmapping workshops might enable diverse personnel to engage in collective problem solving. Through intuition and interpretation, individual learning can feed group learning, and then with interpretation and integration group learning, it can feed organizational learning. Finally plans and procedures are developed, and they can institutionalize the learning (Mintzberg et al., 1998).

The generic roadmapping approach and architecture is used to investigate the emergence of technology-based industries at the sector level and the firm level (Phaal et al., 2011). As lessons could be learned from generic enablers and barriers seen at the industry level, firms may also be able to use similar mapping mechanisms to identify key learning points. This experience scan aims to capture multiple organizational perspectives as narratives that form information to be used for strategic purposes (Figure 5.1).

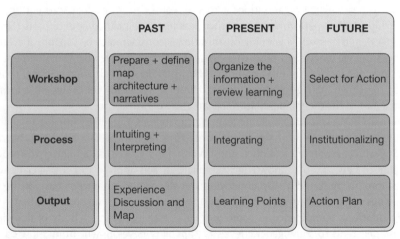

Figure 5.1   Experience scan process
Source: Adapted from Routley et al., 2013 with permission.

The experience scan process help the organization to collect, capture and integrate individual and group learning into organizational learning. It also provides an efficient dissemination mechanism so that different perspectives within the organization can 'start from the same page' for strategic future discussions. The output is a map and a set of learning points that can be used for an action plan to address the current or future situation. By implementing the knowledge captured through the workshop, the company can learn from the benefits of hindsight, reduced time to market for new products, capturing greater value through maximizing opportunities, reducing risk and cost through better navigation of barriers and improved communication between the functional areas involved in the workshop.

Case study

Learning is not easy to quantify or keep track of, so managers search for measures that will fit their own context. The case of USG Corporation, which manufactures and distributes building materials to the construction industry in the USA, shows how traditional learning curves help the firm to observe its productivity gains. In addition, the log-linear productivity model used by USG can be used to benchmark past projects in an effort to identify best learning practices within the organization to apply to future projects. Naturally, it would be expected that rates of learning vary by organization and industry.

USG: Learning from productivity learning curves

USG, a Fortune 500 company, operates continuous, high-volume production lines that serve domestic and international markets. It has a centralized R&D organization located outside Chicago, Illinois. This unit provides applied research services to USG's operating businesses. These services include new product and processes development, product value engineering and manufacturing support. Typically, USG researchers are actively involved in all phases of new technologies from conception to post-commercialization support.

Since the early 1980s, USG has started 13 new major production lines representing first- and later-generation panel technologies. Products made on these lines include drywall panels, fibre-reinforced gypsum boards, cement panels and ceiling tiles. These products included three new-to-the-world technology platforms developed by USG's Research & Technology Center.

A study of USG's commercialization of new technology platforms was initiated to evaluate productivity gains through learning-by-doing (LBD) or experience-based learning. Specific goals of the work were to address the following questions:

1 How do LBD concepts apply to USG production lines?
2 Are there common rates of learning across panel technology platforms?
3 Can historical results be used to predict future process performance?
4 Can LBD analysis be used as a tool to identify processes performing below their potential?

Productivity performance at new USG operations was found to be consistent with the log-linear learning curve model. However, three distinct productivity periods were identified, as illustrated in Figure 5.2:

1 *Stagnant period*: This is the first 1,000 net hours of operation immediately following commencement of production, which typically lasts less than six months. During this time, productivity performance is relatively flat. This period is characterized by low process efficiency and reliability due to product quality problems and frequent equipment failures. Worker knowledge is low and response times to process upsets are slow. The primary focus of the production team is to keep the process running. Although worker learning occurs throughout this period, there are few measurable performance gains.

(Continued)

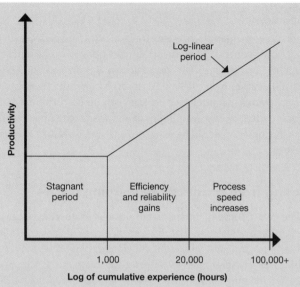

Figure 5.2 Learning curve

The R&D organization is heavily involved in this early period:

- Product chemistries are adjusted to resolve product quality and process issues.
- Process engineering support is provided to assist in addressing process reliability problems.
- Training is provided to quality control personnel.
- Product certifications through independent third parties are obtained.
- Field sales and quality support are rendered.

2 *Efficiency and reliability gains*: The 'process hardening' period extends from 1,000 to roughly 20,000 net hours of production, which can last between one and three years, depending on sales levels and resultant production demands. During this time, process reliability and product quality improve. Workers gain key operating knowledge. Process hardening results from the resolution of chronic equipment problems. At the end of this period, the process achieves its full efficiency and reliability potential.

R&D personnel are less involved during this phase. Ownership of the new technology transfers from R&D to manufacturing and support is provided on a requested basis. By the end of the period, process knowledge within the manufacturing staff has reached or surpassed that of the R&D personnel.

3 *Process speed increases*: The final, or mature, period extends beyond 20,000 net hours of operation. During this phase, productivity gains are almost exclusively attributed to process speed-ups. Process efficiency and reliability factors are at or near their peak potential. Worker knowledge is high. For USG, this period extends indefinitely without notable signs of productivity plateaus.

The R&D organization provides ongoing, sustaining-type support at this stage. Research initiatives include product line proliferation, cost optimizations of raw material systems and assisting with in-place capacity expansions. A strong partnership exists between R&D and manufacturing during this phase.

The commercial deployment of new technology platforms is challenging. Initially, expectations among researchers, business leaders and manufacturing personnel are high. Often, this initial enthusiasm decreases as problems with the new technology and low operating experience result in lower than expected initial financial returns.

The log-linear learning-curve model appears to have value as a tool for predicting early productivity performance of first-generation product platforms. Researchers can study prior technology commercialization to characterize productivity progress ratios of first- versus later-generation platforms for forecasting purposes. More realistic process performance and financial projections would help to set proper expectations.

There are steps that can be taken to enhance learning rates and resultant productivity:

- Processes need to be engineered for uniformity and reliability.
- R&D and engineering staff involved in process design and development should include reliability analyses in pilot-scale work.
- Initial product lines should be kept simple, particularly through the second steep learning phase.
- Product line proliferation should be deferred to the third period where feasible. This often creates a dilemma in that product line breadth is required to accumulate the production hours required to push through the early learning periods.
- The manufacturing team should be kept in place until full process potential is reached.

Source: Blancett, R. S. (2002) 'Learning from Productivity Learning Curves', *Research-Technology Management*, **45**(3), 54–58.

Summary

Learning is a key part in creating technological competencies and is part of all other technological management activities. It involves learning from successes and failures, keeping the knowledge and experience, reflecting these findings in new research and reviewing all activities of technological management. Learning is an unconscious process for organizations and individuals, but informal ways are not as effective as codified learning methods. The firms that want to strive for better dynamic capabilities should try to make their learning processes conscious and formal. The methods developed will record internal knowledge produced and experience gained in various activities such as internal R&D and identification. The learning activity is not just internal but also involves capturing knowledge from outside sources such as training or watching the competition. Considering external R&D activities and exploitation activities, external learning should also be seen as part of the dynamic capabilities associated with TM activities.

Furthermore, building competitive advantage requires the development of unique and difficult to imitate resources, including knowledge. Innovation is about learning new ways to understand or configure the world around us. It is concerned with creating new knowledge or using current knowledge in ways that create new forms

(Continued)

of thinking or new products, which requires effective learning. Thus, the focus should be not only on what is learned but also how learning takes place and evolves in the organization.

Through learning, firms adapt to the changing and evolving environment by upgrading their capabilities, leading to new insights and concepts. Therefore, to enhance its capability to learn, an organization should establish a system where individual learning can be shared among members.

 Key Questions

1   How does 'learning capability' relate to KM?
2   What are the learning processes?
3   What are capability maps and how are they used?
4   What is a learning organization?
5   What is the role of IT in facilitating learning?

 Further reading

Amara, N., Landry, R., Becheikh, N. and Ouimet, M. (2008) 'Learning and Novelty of Innovation in Established Manufacturing SMEs', *Technovation*, **28**(7), 450–463.

Berghman, L., Matthyssens, P. and Vandenbempt, K. (2012) 'Value Innovation, Deliberate Learning Mechanisms and Information from Supply Chain Partners', *Industrial Marketing Management*, **41**(1), 27–39.

Cohen, W. M. and D. A. Levinthal (1990) 'Absorptive Capacity: A New Perspective on Learning and Innovation', *Administrative Science Quarterly*, **35**(1), 128–152.

Horibe, F. (1999) *Managing Knowledge Workers: New Skills and Attitudes to Unlock the Intellectual Capital in Your Organisation* (New York: John Wiley & Sons).

Krogh, G., Takeuchi, H., Kase, C. and Canton, C. G. (2013) *Towards Organizational Knowledge* (Basingstoke: Palgrave Macmillan).

Malerba, F. (1992) 'Learning by Firms and Incremental Change', *Economic Journal*, **102**(413), 845–859.

Mintzberg, H., Ahlstrand, B. and Lampel, J. (1998) *Strategy Safari: A Guided Tour through the Wilds of Strategic Management* (New York: Free Press).

Phaal, R. and Palmer, P. J. (2010) 'Technology Management – Structuring the Strategic Dialogue', *Engineering Management Journal*, **22**(1), 64–74.

Phaal, R., O'Sullivan, E., Routley, M., Ford, S. and Probert, D. (2011) 'A Framework for Mapping Industrial Emergence', *Technological Forecasting and Social Change*, **78**(2), 217–230.

Routley, M., Phaal, R., Athanassopoulou, N. and Probert, D. (2013) 'Mapping Experience in Organisations: A Learning Process for Strategic Technology Planning', *Engineering Management Journal*, **25**(1), 35–47.

Rush, H., Bessant, J. and Hobday, M. (2007) 'Assessing the Technological Capabilities of Firms: Developing a Policy Tool', *R&D Management*, **37**(3), 221–236.

Rush, H., Bessant, J., Hobday, M., Hanrahan, E. and Medeiros, M. Z. (2014) 'The Evolution and Use of a Policy and Research Tool: Assessing the Technological Capabilities of Firms', *Technology Analysis & Strategic Management*, **26**(3), 353–365.

Shipton, H., Zhou, Q. and Mooi, E. (2013) 'Is there a Global Model of Learning Organizations? An Empirical, Cross-nation Study', *International Journal of Human Resource Management*, **24**(12), 2278–2298.

Teece, D. J. and Pisano, G. (1994) 'The Dynamic Capabilities of Firms: An Introduction', *Industrial and Corporate Change*, **3**(3), 537–556.

6

PROTECTION

Learning objectives

After studying this chapter, you should be able to:

1 Recognize the different protection methods.
2 Understand the difference between tangible and intangible assets.
3 Recognize the advantages and disadvantages of IPR.
4 Understand the difficulties of measuring the value of intellectual assets.
5 Describe the processes of how to protect a firm's intellectual assets.
6 Understand the links between protection and business models.

6.1 Introduction

Protection refers to protecting the knowledge and expertise embedded in products, services and manufacturing systems. In broad terms, intellectual capital/assets include competencies, technologies and brands. Most companies recognize that technology assets are a crucial part of their intellectual capital and that their challenge is to generate more value from these assets by efficient acquisition, utilization and protection. The ability to visualize, measure and effectively manage intellectual capital is thus a prerequisite for effective TM.

Knowledge and developed products and processes can provide competitive advantage and generate revenue only if they are based on a collection of routines, skills and complementary assets that are difficult to imitate. If they can be replicated, imitated or emulated by competitors, they can lose their value. Therefore a firm must protect its IPR, such as trademarks, and new technologies through **patents** and staff retention. This chapter will focus on the protection activity where the goal is to manage a portfolio of intellectual capital/assets residing in a company.

6.2 Definition

In the S&P 500, the market to book value of technology-based companies is often greater than six, meaning that the balance sheet number traditionally used to measure and report the performance of these companies represents only 10–15% of the company's value (Giordan and Kossovsky, 2004). This is not due to overvaluation, rather the missing variable in the traditional value equation is the value of intangible assets.

Intellectual capital or assets are intangible and fundamentally different from tangible assets such as capital, equipment and buildings. **Intellectual assets** consist of two sub-groups of assets (Tao et al., 2005): legally protected assets (such as patents) and intangible assets (such as know-how) that are closely held in the minds of individuals and groups.

A different definition of intellectual capital considers intangible as any factor that contributes to the value-generating processes of the company and is, more or less directly, under the control of the company itself (Bontis et al., 1999). Thus, intangible assets might be of three main types:

1 Competencies, including skills and know-how, attitude, such as the motivation and leadership qualities of top management and intellectual agility, such as the ability of organizational members to be 'quick on their intellectual feet'.
2 Innovation and entrepreneurship.
3 The ability to adapt and cross-fertilize.

Regardless of the method of commercialization, all technologies developed or utilized within the company are subject to IP rules or rights if they can be codified or reduced to paper. In law, IP is an umbrella term for various legal entitlements that attach to certain names, written and recorded media and inventions. The holders of these legal entitlements may exercise various exclusive rights in relation to the subject matter of the IP. The term IP reflects the idea that this subject matter is the product of the mind or the intellect.

IP laws and enforcement vary widely from country to country and there are inter-governmental efforts to harmonize them through international treaties such as the 1994 World Trade Organization (WTO) Agreement on Trade-Related Aspects of Intellectual Property Rights (TRIPs). Disagreements over medical and software patents and the difficulty of copyright enforcement have so far prevented consensus on a cohesive international system.

Besides government and international regulations, culture is another element determining IP laws and their enforcement across countries. Cultures that value collaboration, such as Germany, tend to place less emphasis on complex legal arrangements. Cultures that value implementation rather than invention tend to have a wider view of what should be patentable, such as Japan. Developed countries such as the USA and the UK tend to use IP to create market-entry barriers, and are tougher on enforcement. Less developed countries such as China tend to use IP to enable growth and innovation, and are more relaxed about enforcement or require arbitration.

There are various types of IP protection:

- *Copyright* may subsist in creative and artistic works, for example books, movies, music, paintings, photographs and software, and gives a copyright holder the exclusive right to control the reproduction or adaptation of such works for a certain period of time – historically, 10–30 years depending on the jurisdiction, and more recently, the life of the author plus several decades.
- A *patent* may be granted for a new, useful and non-obvious invention, and gives the patent holder a right to prevent others from practising the invention without a licence from the inventor for a certain period of time – typically 20 years from the filing date of a patent application.
- A *trademark* is a distinctive sign that is used to distinguish the products or services of different businesses.
- A *domain name* is a distinctive Internet address designated for a firm/product/service.

- An *industrial design right* protects the form of appearance, style or design of an industrial object, for example spare parts, furniture or textiles.

Although IP protection is important, it is not enough, since there are a wide range of assets that cannot be codified and these intangibles might form a critical resource for value creation in a company. The problem of intangibles is even worse for intangibles that cannot be isolated. Isolatable assets can be subjected much more readily to protection, but those that are not isolatable are difficult to protect on their own. For example, it is difficult to isolate individual improvements in software and therefore the asset created by iterative development is difficult to protect even if it can be codified or reduced to paper.

Although IP laws and rules help to protect the IP of a firm, in some cases, such as the existence of intangible assets, protection might come from secrecy (Cohen et al., 2000). A trade secret, which is sometimes either equated with, or is a subset of, 'confidential information', is secret, non-public information concerning the commercial practices or proprietary knowledge of a business, public disclosure of which may sometimes be illegal. Secrecy can be used in product and process innovation. In the former case, there are two techniques that can be adopted (Lu, 2007): home-base or host-base integration. In home-base integration, R&D units define product specifications, devise system structures and develop the system core, then the host R&D units implement the submodules. In host-base integration, the home R&D units define the product specifications, architect the system structures and develop the system core. Once these are encrypted, the system core is delivered to the host R&D units. Generally what is seen in the business is that a company starts from the home-base integration mode and after its engineers become capable, the host-base integration mode is phased in. This is because the latter needs a more complete organization function and more capable engineers in the host R&D units.

The secrecy in process innovation is achieved by the distribution of various production processes among facilities in order not to reveal fully the underlying know-how. This could also be done by assigning several engineers to a process and having each one learn a part of the process. After this secrecy operation, if competitors want to imitate the process by recruiting the engineers, they need to recruit the whole team. It is much more difficult to recruit a whole team than a single key engineer, and the cost is much higher.

A protection strategy should consider all intellectual assets. So this chapter will focus on a broader capability that will protect the intellectual assets of a firm. Thus the capability is not a legal capability alone but a creative and managerial process of understanding and extracting the value of the overall intellectual assets of a firm.

6.3   Protection processes

To achieve a protection capability, four core processes need to be in place:

1 Identifying and measuring technology assets (internal and external).
2 IP portfolio management.
3 Managing knowledge workers and their IP.
4 Managing IP in open innovation/technology collaborations.

These four processes are now discussed.

Identifying and measuring technology assets

The identification activity is the main input for the auditing needed to lay down the base of intellectual assets of a company. The main difference from the general identification activity given in Chapter 4 is the inclusion of intangible assets in the analysis. Needless to say, any identification activity regarding IP includes a detailed patent search. This is why patent analysis is considered as one of the key TM tools (see Chapter 8).

By identifying and then assessing the existing intellectual assets in a firm and its competitors and relevant third parties, it is possible to understand:

- A firm's legal ability to practise its technology without infringing the intellectual assets of others.
- The acquisition of intellectual assets.
- The methods of extracting value from the intellectual asset portfolio (Tao et al., 2005).

The case of Microsoft (at the end of this chapter) illustrates how firms proactively search for ways to utilize their R&D investments.

The intangible character of intellectual assets requires a definition of the context of their use. Its value can only be understood within the context it will be used. Experts assert that intangibles count for more than half the value of many companies, for example Microsoft is the largest intangible knowledge asset holder at \$211bn, with Intel at \$170bn (Giordan and Kossovsky, 2004). These examples show clearly the importance of intangibles, including patents, brands and, to some degree, market position/penetration. National accounting bodies are trying to integrate new methods to account for intangibles, including IP. For example, as a result of recent accounting rule changes and the enforcement implications of the 2002 Sarbanes-Oxley Act in the USA, the fair market value of IP is now reported in greater detail on corporate ledgers (Kossovsky et al., 2004).

The standard methods for delivering fair value for a potential licence or IP donation usually include one of three approaches: market reference, cost or income (Goldheim et al., 2005):

1 The market reference method assumes that the value of a particular asset or portfolio of assets is determined by comparison with sales or licences of similar IP or technologies.

2 In the case of cost-based evaluations, a buyer values an asset at the cost of producing the asset, the cost of obtaining a substitute or the benefit of introducing the product to the marketplace sooner.

3 The income method calculates the value from the Net Present Value (NPV) of future cash flows associated with the asset.

In addition to these three general methods, there are also hybrid and advanced methods that consider additional factors to arrive at a more insightful valuation, for example the 25% rule, options, relief from royalty, the Black-Scholes model (option pricing method) and Monte Carlo simulations (Goldheim et al., 2005). Each method has its own set of operating assumptions and data requirements.

In the case of open innovation, assessment is complicated. However, there are different methods developed to overcome the problems. For example, to maximize the possibility of finding interesting technology, GSK Consumer Health (www.innovation.gsk.com) posts its wants online and P&G Bioscience (www.pgbiosciences.com) places its want list in the public domain (Slowinski et al., 2009). After technologies are found, both parties make negotiations and decide on the price of technology together.

IP portfolio management

Companies need to manage their intellectual assets as a portfolio, since IP forms one of the most significant parts of their intangible assets, which cannot be seen, touched or physically measured and is created through time and/or effort (Pisano and Teece, 2007). Legal intangibles generate legal property rights defensible in a court of law. IP can generate revenue and result in competitive advantage for a firm if the country in which it is operating has a legal enforcement capacity. If gaining a patent is troublesome and expensive, and the laws cannot be enforced for individuals/companies, then patenting does not protect the IP rights of firms.

Besides the legal system, the importance of protection activity will depend on a number of factors such as company size and commercialization strategy. For example, small firms might consider either licensing out so that the set of complementary assets might be reached, or try to generate some revenues, knowing that the firm itself cannot exploit its technologies.

Commercialization strategy is a crucial decision factor in how to extract value from intellectual assets. This strategy is driven from processes mentioned in Chapter 7, where strategic choices for technology are developed. Companies focused on internal exploitation may not give the protection process a high priority, since for them the protection of technology is not the major determinant of competitive position. But a significant number of (mostly large) companies file patents to protect their 'freedom to operate' (or act). It is not that they believe that others could operate in their marketplace, it is just that others, by taking a patent, could block them from operating in that marketplace. Companies that favour trade secrets over patents for protection tend not to develop formal protection processes, since they think that trade secrets are more difficult to identify and measure. Companies who are active in collaborations and frequently perform technology transfers tend to consider patenting and protection more important than other companies.

One of the commercialization methods is selling technology. Selling technology might take the form of licensing, cross-licensing, donations and royalties. Different externally oriented methods for extracting value from a firm's intellectual assets indicate that managers need to consider the time frame when value will be extracted from a particular intellectual asset as well as the potential of opportunities. In other words, if it will take a long time to achieve the value and the costs are high, managers might prefer equity investments or spin-out. In another situation where there is low value combined with almost no future prospects for a particular intellectual asset, managers might abandon IP to save patent maintenance fees.

Many companies focus on selling products once a technology is developed, but an alternative choice in commercialization is to sell technology before the development is completed. The reasons for this choice may include:

- Ever-increasing costs and risks of R&D.
- Poor fit with a company's overall strategy.
- Limited patent protection.
- Fear of competition.
- Financial and other problems preventing market exploitation.
- Lack of production facilities.
- Antitrust legislation (Burgelman et al., 2004).

If it is decided to sell a technology, then technology managers need to be aware of the following concerns: the selling decision should fit into the strategy for a full portfolio of technologies, and the value of the technology might be underestimated, since without full development, assessing the value is difficult.

When a decision is made to sell a technology, management needs to handle the following processes, which are similar to those of buying technologies, as discussed in Chapter 2: finding technology buyers, choosing the selling method, contract preparation and negotiation and technology transfer. Some selling options may depend on collaboration, for which the following processes are relevant: finding partners, contract preparation and negotiation, technology transfer and managing long-term collaborations. Donation is another possibility in extracting value from an intellectual asset, because of tax advantages, less time and resources required compared to licensing or developing relationships with universities (Goldheim et al., 2005).

Although it might seem obvious, selling technology is not an easy task. For example, P&G is a successful company in IP management, but it utilizes only 10% of its technologies in its own products (Sakkab, 2002). Thus, for P&G and many companies, there is a lot of value to be had in the remaining 90%. However, these technologies sit on the shelf because the process of identifying the patents, copyrights, trademarks and trade secrets requires extensive technical and market insight. It is important to remember that IP portfolio management is not a licensing/legal problem alone. Extracting the value of intellectual assets takes flexibility and the ability to combine networked IP development, asset management and financing, market intimacy and commercialization skills (Giordan and Kossovsky, 2004).

Besides IP laws, another way of protecting technology is through setting standards for the technology developed. In the early stages of a technology, there is no single generally accepted conceptual treatment of the phenomenon in a field of study, but in later stages, a body of theory appears and sufficient evidence has accumulated that a design has been delivered (Shapiro and Varian, 1999). The rise of dominant design leads to standards being set in the industry for that particular technology, with alternative technologies failing to receive wide acceptance. An example is the case of open source software where the core IP is protected even though it is open to be used on a no-fee basis. The goal in open source is to stimulate innovation through the use of IP and to generate new technologies in a wider sphere and at a lower cost. The resulting impact is payback through market position, service provision and so on.

Managing knowledge workers and their IP

Intellect means the capacity for understanding, knowing and reasoning, the rational or highly developed use of intelligence. Hence, the intellect of an organization covers:

- Cognitive knowledge – know-what.
- Advanced skills – know-how.
- System understanding and trained intuition – know-why.
- Self-motivated creativity – care-why (Tushman and Andersen, 2004).

A firm's intellect resides with its people, making HRM the critical dimension of managing knowledge. This is why, in protection, the goal of managing knowledge workers is keeping their knowledge protected and keeping them innovative.

Employee agreements are supplementary legal mechanisms to patenting and copyrighting (Lu, 2007). Firms try to use anti-disclosure clauses in contracts with key personnel to cope with the claiming problem. Putting typical statements that impose constraints in confidential information is one way to do this. The confidential information stated here includes methods of doing business, R&D, know-how, customers, trade secrets, manufacturing methods, computer programs, algorithms, finances and other proprietary information. However, this process is not as easy as it seems. Employee turnover and a lack of loyalty are great concerns in this issue.

One approach for keeping knowledge workers innovative in an organization is to establish **corporate entrepreneurship** within the firm. Corporate entrepreneurship means venturing, innovativeness and self-renewal through employees becoming entrepreneurs or owners of intra-corporate ventures (Zahra, 1996). It requires:

- Norms to promote innovation and change.
- Norms that promote creativity.
- Support for risk taking and change.
- Rewards and recognition for innovation.
- Positive attitudes and role models for change.
- Tolerance of mistakes.

These goals can be achieved with a combination of HRM and an organizational structure that supports and provides mechanisms for idea generation, evaluation, selection and implementation. For example, Whirlpool has institutionalized I-mentor roles for all areas of the company and encourages employees to be trained to become formal I-mentors. In addition, Whirlpool supports I-heroes in the company by providing tools, time and structure to the creativity process (Snyder and Duarte, 2008).

After innovative and entrepreneurial initiatives are finalized, depending on the strategic and operational importance of the initiatives, a number of organizational designs might arise (Tushman and Andersen, 2004):

- Direct integration.
- New product department.
- Special business units.
- Micro new ventures department.
- New venture division.
- Independent business units.
- Nurturing plus contracting.
- Contracting.
- Complete spin-off.

For example, in 1995, Xerox created technology ventures to solely invest in unique technology start-ups through spin-offs, which are new businesses outside the core business (Loutfy and Belkhir, 2001). In 1999, Xerox's technology ventures evolved into two major organizations: Xerox Intellectual Property Operations and Xerox Venture Lab. For six years, Xerox Venture Lab created over a dozen companies where Xerox kept 51%-plus ownership.

Handling corporate entrepreneurship within an organization is not easy since there are many IP rights involved. Corporate and divisional managements must be made aware of long-term growth and benefits. Senior management needs to develop a venture charter specifying the functions and procedures of venture management. There should be uniform formats for business plans within determined time frames. At any given time, a limited number of ventures with independent budgets must be sponsored. To support variety, multiple sources of internal sponsorship should be maintained. As an incentive, product champions must always be selected to manage such ventures. The rewards and IP rights need to be settled at the initiation of projects to prevent any conflict between employees and the firm.

Managing IP in open innovation

By adapting open innovation, managers aim to achieve two goals:

1 Harnessing outside ideas to advance their own businesses.
2 Leveraging their internal ideas outside their current operations.

Thus, managers are involved with many forms of collaborations ranging from spin-in and out, licensing in and out, buyouts and alliances to joint ventures (Chesbrough, 2003). Open innovation provides a platform, a springboard for private profits, therefore firms have incentives to preserve and feed the common platform, as in the creative industries and video game industry (Cohendet and Simon, 2007). Yet, knowledge is not available to all companies; rather it flows within a closed circuit of parties involved in the open innovation exercise, and even within that circuit, different IP rights might hold.

For example, two Internet sites where open innovation practices are carried out show how their open innovation models are limited when it comes to IP issues (Tao and Magnotta, 2006). They are:

1 InnoCentive (www.innocentive.com), where 'seeker' companies post a problem on their website. They also post the 'bounty' for receiving a solution that meets their criteria. 'Solvers' propose solutions through the website. Seekers receive IP ownership for paid solutions. The website hosts scientists from over 170 countries around the world.
2 NineSigma (www.ninesigma.com), which is building global innovation networks that identify and connect the talents in order to create the next generation of products and opportunities of interest to their clients. The process works as follows: project proposals are provided to the client; the client makes an independent decision to fund a proposal and negotiate a business arrangement appropriate to the situation; NineSigma charges the client firms a small upfront fee in order to conduct a search for talents and when the client firm chooses to work with one talent, an additional fee is charged.

In general, the collaboration should start with an initial non-disclosure or confidentiality agreement to cover early negotiations (Utunen, 2003; Fröhling, 2007). Sometimes, if the parties are going to collaborate on more than one project, or if the project is large, it might be appropriate to create a framing agreement to cover overall goals. Further agreements can support each phase of the collaboration, such as feasibility studies, development, prototyping, production and commercial exploitation. The agreement for each phase should include a clearly defined exit strategy for the partners, in case the collaboration fails or is not continued as originally planned.

Protecting IP is important and working through the issues refines everybody's understanding of their collaboration. It is a learning process that the parties, used to closed innovation processes, must go through if they want to participate successfully in open innovation.

6.4 Recent challenges

Strategies for the protection of IP are under pressure due to four major challenges: patent pools, patent trolls, open innovation and the rise of digital manufacturing. Managers need to develop a dynamic IP strategy depending on the density of problems they face in their industry.

Many high technologies involve blocking patents owned by multiple patent owners such as the competition between three prominent smart phone operating systems: iOS, Android and Windows Mobile (Uijl et al., 2013). These operating system developers use patents to make the other platforms more expensive and spread uncertainty among application developers. When a technological field develops through the contributions of many entities, negotiating the number of requisite patent licences may become inefficient and too costly for users. The result is a 'patent thicket' that is an overlapping set of patent rights requiring those that seek to commercialize new technology to obtain licences from multiple patentees. To solve this issue, companies such as CD, DVD, Blu-ray and MP3 producers employ a patent pool licensing model. A **patent pool** aggregates IPR for the purpose of joint licensing. It is an innovative business model to enhance technology adoption and IPR monetization by facilitating the interaction of multiple licensors with many licensees.

Even though patent pools offer a solution to complicated patents, patent trolls might be problematic. **Patent trolls** are companies or individuals that buy up patents in bulk and block these patents' application in new innovations (Petrick et al., 2014). Patent trolls and the rise of patent litigations put pressure on companies. This act results in the underuse of technologies.

As the complexity of technology increases and open innovation spreads, it is becoming increasingly rare for a single company to have all the expertise and capabilities to fully create a technology platform or solution (Granstrand and Holgersson, 2014). Moreover, innovation happens at companies of all sizes. There are different forms of open innovation offering special IP solutions. For example, Quirky (www.quirky.com) offers inventors a platform to post their ideas and receive feedback from potential customers to guide the refinement of the invention. The most popular ideas then become products that are sold through the site. The influencers, while often an important source of ideas, don't own any rights to the resulting IP. But this is not the case in many collaborative open innovation cases. Collaboration between organizations solves a technical problem by sharing core technical knowledge across organizational boundaries, but then they also jointly hold patents or copyrights. After collaborations end or when partners conflict, managers need to negotiate ownership of IP assets. Thus, companies start to plan for potential IP asset distribution even before such assets are created.

The final challenge is the developments in digital manufacturing. The roles of designers, producers and customers have been well understood in the traditional supply chain (Petrick et al., 2014). However, the digital revolution in design and manufacturing such as the rise of 3D printing, also called additive manufacturing, is blurring the roles of supply chain actors. An interesting example is Shapeways (www.shapeways.com), that enables individuals to design, prototype and buy or sell products online. At Shapeways, individuals can download a product design and then customize it, reload it to the Shapeways website, and have it produced by the company's 3D printers. Shapeways then ships the finished product to the customer. In such a business model, IP issues get confusing since it is hard to find out who the designer is. Is it the primary designer or the individual who downloaded and customized the design, or both?

Shapeways is just an example that shows how firms might create physical products from digital files. The integration of products and services are further challenged with Smartphone applications that enable a user to create digital design files from photographs of physical objects. How does the owner of the IP embedded in the original physical object even track how it is used after a digital file is created? We have seen similar problems in the entertainment sector, where digital rights management was a critical enabler of the eventual protection of IP. There is no such standard established in the design and manufacturing space yet. In short, digitalization of products and services is reshaping the conceptualization of patents and copyrights, while redefining the party who holds the rights to use them.

Due to all these challenges, IP strategies are not limited to particular patents and standards but they have become highly sophisticated managerial tools at the strategic level. For example, a very interesting case took place between Sony's Blu-ray and Toshiba's HD-DVD in blue laser DVDs (Gallagher, 2012). Analysis of the battles between these standards suggests two interesting findings. First, corporate strategy provided a decisive advantage to the Blu-ray alliance led by Sony. However, Sony appears to have 'won' the battle in the USA by exploiting a superior corporate strategy to not only provide complementary products as called for by the traditional model, but also by utilizing its technology as a component in an ancillary product, its PlayStation 3. Second, indirect network effects seem to complement 'Metcalf's Law' for direct network effects. 'Metcalf's Law' means the potential value of a network is proportional to the square of its users. In short, the widened community generated results in higher network benefits for users.

The past decade has shown the stories of companies that have either reinvented themselves or withered such as IBM or Kodak. Downes and Nunes (2014) describe these new dynamics of competition where digital technologies enter traditional sectors. In their view, competitive advantage in this emerging world comes through experimentation, rapid failure and more experimentation. Since long-term IP protection does not guarantee market success anymore, managers need to employ a good strategy of IP, standards and flexibility (McGrath, 2013).

 Case study

Even though the company names are not given, the following story is an actual case of collaboration for joint technology development and commercialization between a large European multinational corporation and a small US R&D firm. The brief description of the case is given below (see for details, Granstrand and Holgersson, 2014).

The two companies involved were engaged in R&D and commercialization collaboration in the heavy inorganic chemical industry. This industry is typically characterized by raw material extraction, standardized bulk products and cost-cutting process technologies. It is dominated by globalized oligopolies, and there are significant entry barriers, retaliation capacity and imitation risks. The two firms involved in this case were LF, a large, multinational European technology firm with over 60,000 employees working in more than 100 countries, and SF, a small US innovation firm with just a few employees working mainly in R&D. SF was a non-producing entity, but not a typical patent troll.

(Continued)

In the 1990s, LF needed a new cost-saving purification and separation process technology. SF provided a process technology that was at a small pilot-plant stage, not yet developed to the commercial demonstrator stage. They decided to collaborate in order to develop the technology and scale it up. The two firms officially entered into an exclusive two-year technology collaboration agreement, which was extendable and terminable. The agreement included a set of terms governing IP assembly at the inbound acquisition phase, and IP disassembly at the outbound exploitation and termination phases of the collaboration. Some highlights from the agreement are as follows:

Inbound acquisition

- SF specified and provided all its know-how (including patents and trade secrets), and LF provided some (but not all) of its know-how as cleared background technology.
- Each party owned its background technology and was obliged to obtain, maintain, and defend its background patents at its own cost.
- SF granted LF an exclusive, worldwide licence on its background technology. LF paid SF a background-technology user fee based on a specific licence-pricing model, which they agreed.
- All foreground technology was owned, managed and paid for by LF, which compensated SF for the engineering work.

Outbound exploitation and termination

- If both parties agreed that the joint development work had been successful, the companies would collaborate for joint commercialization. Otherwise, they agreed to do the following. LF would grant SF a non-exclusive, irrevocable, royalty-free licence to the foreground technology with unrestricted sublicensing after five years. SF would grant LF a non-exclusive, irrevocable and restricted licence of such background technology as was necessary for LF to exploit the foreground technology, and then pay SF the background-technology user fee. These licences should also include a non-exclusive right to any written reports relating to background or foreground technology.
- The agreement could be terminated in the case of collaboration performance default, financial default, third-party acquisition or key persons leaving SF. In this case, mutual licensing would become non-compulsory.
- All of the materials received from each other should be treated as confidential, and its disclosure should be prevented for ten years after the termination of the agreement unless it had become common knowledge.

Change of control

- If SF received an acquisition offer, LF had the right of first refusal to purchase all or part of the shares in SF or all or parts of the background technology. LF retained this purchase right for five years after the agreement ends.

When collaborative work failed to scale the process technology sufficiently for a commercial demonstration plant, the two companies developed technological and economic disagreements. LF chose to terminate the agreement and continue with in-house R&D under the premise that enough knowledge had been developed and gathered to enable it to continue the project on its own. SF asked LF for access to the demonstration plant (run by LF) for a new customer partner from Asia. LF denied access, whereupon SF sued for damages of roughly $150 million for breach of post-contractual loyalty, patent infringement and misappropriation of trade secrets in the form of breach of a confidential relationship and unrightful use of IP.

An important issue in this case was the valuation of and determination of damages for SF's lost profits due to LF's termination of the collaboration project. In this case, SF invoked the '25 percent rule,' which stipulates a licence royalty amounting to 25% of a profit-related royalty base, such as the licensee's EBITDA (earnings before interest, taxes, depreciation and amortization). However, this determination was opposed by LF, which challenged the fairness of the 25% rule. LF also claimed that the 25% rule did not reflect the large difference in R&D and commercialization investments between the two companies in this case.

The court decided that LF had indeed engaged in breach of post-contractual duty of loyalty and IP infringement. LF appealed, and the case ended with SF being awarded about $1 million in damages for some minor misappropriation of its trade secret rights.

Source: Summarized from: Granstrand, O. and Holgersson, M. (2014) 'The Challenge of Closing Open Innovation', *Research-Technology Management*, **57**(5), 19–25.

Summary

During the whole life cycle of technological management, all findings, knowledge and expertise should be protected from competition. This process not only includes physical or legal ways of preserving knowledge and experience but also uses the technology creation cycle to generate additional technologies in order to render reverse engineering attempts useless. So, the protection cycle not only involves learning, but may also incorporate all TM activities. However, IP protection strength is not the same in all technological fields, so patent protection should only be seen as an additional barrier on top of other guarantees on core competencies.

Whereas products or technologies can be replicated or imitated with or without protection laws, the dynamic capabilities of an organization, consisting of organizational processes, procedures, culture and tacit knowledge, are not easy to replicate. So a company should focus on the protection capability as well as improving its dynamic capabilities in technology management to stay competitive.

 ## Key Questions

1 What are the major means of protection?
2 What is the difference between tangible and intangible assets?
3 What are the advantages and disadvantages of IPR?
4 How is the value of intellectual assets measured?
5 What are the processes for protecting a firm's intellectual assets?

📖 Further reading

Downes, L. and Nunes, P. (2014) *Big Bang Disruption: Strategy in the Age of Devastating Innovation* (New York: Penguin-Portfolio).

Gallagher, S. R. (2012) 'The Battle of the Blue Laser DVDs: The Significance of Corporate Strategy in Standards Battles', *Technovation*, **32**(2), 90–98.

Granstrand, O. and Holgersson, M. (2014) 'The Challenge of Closing Open Innovation', *Research-Technology Management*, **57**(5), 19–25.

Lichtenthaler, U. (2011) 'Implementation Steps for Successful Out-Licensing', *Research-Technology Management*, **54**(5), 47–53.

McGrath, R. G. (2013) *The End of Competitive Advantage: How to Keep Your Strategy Moving as Fast as Your Business* (Boston, MA: Harvard Business Review Press).

Mortara, L. and Ford, S. (2012) *Technology Acquisitions: A Guided Approach to Technology Acquisition and Protection Decisions* (Cambridge: University of Cambridge).

Petrick, I., Rayna, T. and Striukova, L. (2014) 'The Challenges of Intellectual Property', *Research-Technology Management*, **57**(5), 9–11.

Pisano, G. P. and Teece, D. J. (2007) 'How to Capture Value from Innovation: Shaping Intellectual Property and Industry Architecture', *California Management Review*, **50**(1), 278–296.

Ritala, P. and Hurmelinna-Laukkanen, P. (2013) 'Incremental and Radical Innovation in Coopetition – the Role of Absorptive Capacity and Appropriability', *Journal of Product Innovation Management*, **30**(1), 154–169.

Slowinski, G. and Zerby, K. W. (2008) 'Protecting IP in Collaborative Research', *Research-Technology Management*, **51**(6), 58–65.

Uijl, S. D., Bekkers, R. and Vries, H. J. D. (2013) 'Managing Intellectual Property Using Patent Pools: Lessons from three Generations of Pools in the Optical Disc Industry', *California Management Review*, **55**(4), 31–50.

Note: A rich source for a wide variety of research papers on intellectual property is the journal entitled "Queen Mary Journal of Intellectual Property" published by Edward Elgar Publishing.

7

SELECTION

Learning objectives

After studying this chapter, you should be able to:

1 Understand the transformation of the identification activity into strategic decisions.
2 Understand the complexity of decisions involved in selecting technologies and related business models.
3 Understand technological core competencies and their role in strategy making.
4 Identify strategies based on core competencies.
5 Recognize the dimensions of strategic decisions involved in the selection capability, particularly the key make-buy-collaborate decision.
6 Identify key processes in selecting technologies among alternatives.

7.1   Introduction

Selection requires important decisions to be made for technologies and business models that should be supported by the organization. In other words, the selection capability is a strategy-making capability. In essence, strategy involves selecting and developing technologies and business models that build competitive advantage through assembling and orchestrating internally or externally owned resources.

Even though the identification capability provides a large volume of information on different dimensions, including technologies, markets, environment and so on, the decision is made through selection among alternative choices based on a number of major strategic analyses. This chapter will present some of these critical strategic analyses and then show how some key strategic choices are made; the focus being selecting technological core competencies and deciding on the make-buy-collaborate alternatives.

7.2   Definition

In the dynamic capabilities tradition, strategy involves selecting and developing technologies and business models that build competitive advantage through assembling and organizing difficult-to-replicate assets, thereby shaping competition itself (Teece, 2007).

Strategy making includes two integrated sub-processes – selection and implementation; this chapter focuses on the selection process, while development processes are discussed in Chapters 2 and 3. Following the dynamic capability perception, the selection capability comprises processes used in strategic decision making.

Selection requires important decisions to be made about the technologies that should be supported by the organization. These decisions require a strategic stance and, once made, they become the pillars of the technology planning at the company. Minzberg (1994) suggests that planning is one proposed approach to strategy making among several other possibilities. He argues that planning is a formalized procedure to produce an articulated result in the form of an integrated system of decisions. This formalization helps to deconstruct, articulate and rationalize the processes by which decisions are made and integrated in organizations. This is why technology planning and technology strategy activities are integrated.

In an age of technological innovations, a firm is not only a 'profit maker' but also an innovator. So it should have the profits and scale necessary to finance the overhead expenditures required to anticipate change and create 'future values', as IKEA, a global furniture company, did when it changed the furniture industry by introducing its modular furniture model (Normann and Ramirez, 1993; Kim and Mauborgne, 1997, 2005). Thus, the selection process should shape and calibrate opportunities so that it is possible to decide on how current and future technologies should be utilized as part of an organization's business strategy. Business and technology strategies need to be coupled for long-term success.

7.3   Selection processes

The selection capability does not have any meaning without a good assessment capacity, which requires a grasp of strategic objectives and priorities developed at the business-strategy level. Such an assessment capacity relies on rich data that is collected through an identification activity or driven from an acquisition activity. Then, selection uses a number of analyses and decision-making processes to generate the firm's technology strategy and align it with the business strategy.

As planning and strategy development are intertwined, eight steps in technology planning (Khalil, 2000) might be regrouped by using the terminology of the strategy triangle (Johnson and Scholes, 1999), as shown below:

1 Technology audit.
2 Forecast the technology.
3 Analyse and forecast the environment.   1 Strategic analysis.
4 Analyse and forecast the market/user.
5 Analyse the organization.
6 Develop the mission.
7 Design organizational actions.   2 Strategic choice.
8 Put the plan into operation.   3 Implementation.

The strategy triangle concept leaves out an important element for continuous improvement that constitutes the final step in strategy making – measurement and evaluation. This chapter will briefly discuss the strategic analysis process that is based on the data and information gathered in Chapter 4 and then the main focus will be the processes related to making strategic choices, in other words, making a selection. The final two processes, implementation and measurement and evaluation, are dealt with in Chapters 3, 5 and 6.

7.4   Strategic analysis

The strategic analysis takes the information gathered in the identification process (Chapter 4) one step further. The analysis aims to develop potential decision alternatives for senior executives based on information about the competencies, assets and capabilities of the organization, the environment it operates in and the goals and expectations of the people with power to guide it.

Before making any strategic choices, an assessment of technological gaps and opportunities in light of the business strategy needs to be carried out. In addition, firms need to make a value analysis in order to see the potential to break out from existing **value chains** (Kim and Mauborgne, 1997, 2005). Strategic analysis focuses on gap and value analyses, where different tools ranging from traditional SWOT to roadmapping techniques are used (details are given in Part II).

There are many ways of doing gap analysis. One might be the competitive position of the company with respect to its technology. While one leg of the matrix lists the company's competitiveness, the other leg shows the level of technology competitiveness. The values of both competitiveness types might be weak, viable or dominant. If the competitive position is dominant but technology competitiveness is weak, a firm might decide to invest in that particular technology to support its existing market dominance.

Rather than looking at the business competitiveness in isolation, companies might try to capture their technology position vis-à-vis the impact of technology on competitiveness. The technology position/impact map supports the competitive assessment of a company's technology, based on two key dimensions (Lindsay, 2000): technology position with respect to competitors and technology impact such as the potential competitive impact in the market. Each combination of technology position (dominant, superior, viable, tenable or untenable) and technology impact (base, key, pacing or emerging) indicates a threat or an opportunity. For example when technology position is dominant and technology impact is pacing, a firm has high potential future advantage.

Another gap analysis might attempt to measure strengths and weaknesses with respect to the fit between technological and organizational competencies. For each technology, it is necessary to ensure that the required organizational competencies are in place for effective exploitation of the technical knowledge.

Gap analysis is necessary but not sufficient to develop technology strategies, since it is rather static. This is why firms should take into consideration a dynamic approach and value analysis is a good tool for this, which is described in Chapter 13. All commercial activities are performed with the objective of providing value of some kind, where the value is a combination of the benefits gained from the activity and the cost of achieving these benefits (Melnyk and Denzler, 1996). Value analysis, sometimes called 'value engineering', is an intensive, interdisciplinary problem-solving activity that focuses on improving the value of the functions required to accomplish the goal or objective of any product, process, service or organization (Cooper and Slagmulder, 1997). So value analysis utilizes many tools such as business process re-engineering in order to identify activities that add no value and new ways of carrying out a particular process.

Value analysis applications are extended to integrate customer choice in order to go beyond the minimum essential product functions. **Quality function deployment**, a TQM tool used in designing products on the basis of customer feedback, extends value engineering in that it is not restricted to minimum essential product functions (Shillito and de Marle, 1992; Shillito, 1994). In that regard, the use of value analysis in TM requires the company to analyse its **value propositions** in a wider context. Value innovation fits well with the dynamic capabilities approach (Kim and Mauborgne, 1997, 2005). Value innovation is the simultaneous pursuit of radically superior value for buyers and lower costs for companies by analysing the value chain of a firm (Kim and Mauborgne, 1997).

Firms decide whether to perform some or all of these analyses before they make strategic decisions. This depends on contingency factors such as the level of complexity of technology involved and market conditions.

7.5   Strategic choices

After the strategic analysis is carried out, firms go through a process where they make decisions based on the available choices. Once managers receive an analysis of technologies and markets, they realize that there are a number of opportunities, of various magnitudes and urgencies, in different places. Managers must decide which gap to tackle, which innovation to carry out for the value set offered to customers and which opportunity to grasp based on general strategy goals and how to grasp them. The decision a firm faces is not just about when, where and how much to invest but particularly about whether 'to select or create a particular business model' (Teece, 2007). Business model issues range from investment priorities and incentives to enterprise boundary choices and their alignment with the physical technology. This includes the way commercialization will be carried out. For example, Motorola's $5 billion Iridium satellite telephone venture failed because it did not attract sufficient users to break even amid complaints of prohibitive costs and cumbersome handsets; in other words, its identification of a market need was incorrect (Carrol and Mui, 2008).

A positive example of the importance of strategic choices is Apple's iPhone, an Internet and multimedia-enabled smart phone, launched in 2008. Although Apple is a computer company, it identified an opportunity in the phone business and pooled together technological and organizational competencies embedded in different organizations and delivered a new product that challenged the existing phone industry.

Therefore, regardless of the purpose of a technology strategy, decision makers need to develop a list of criteria to shape the details of their technology strategy. These criteria are expected to help managers in making two main decisions:

1 Identifying the core technology competencies the company wants to develop.
2 Selecting a buy-make-collaborate option for each technology they have or plan to have.

These two decisions will influence the enterprise structure, procedures, designs and incentives for seizing technological opportunities.

Identifying core technology competencies

The strategy literature emphasizes the identification of core competencies for a firm in order to capitalize on the benefits of their competencies (Prahalad and Hamel, 1990). The idea of core competencies is finding competencies that might be applicable to a wide variety of products and business markets, as shown in Figure 7.1. This allows a company to leverage its investments in core competencies through a portfolio of applications by lessening the risks of failure in one product or market.

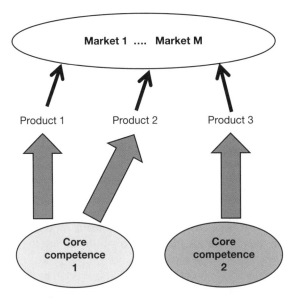

Figure 7.1 Core competencies

Core competencies are selected on the basis of three criteria (Prahalad and Hamel, 1990). A core competency should:

- Provide potential access to a wide variety of markets.
- Make a significant contribution to the perceived customer benefits of the end product.
- Be difficult for competitors to imitate.

Core competency might be in anything ranging from manufacturing to advertising. One example is Benetton, whose core competence is its colours. For core technology competencies, an example might be Sony's competency in miniaturization, which combines its competencies in mechanical, electronic and material technologies in designing and producing miniaturized electronic products.

The strategic choice of a firm's core technology competencies depends on a number of factors. The main factor is the list of core competencies selected for the business strategy. Core technology competencies must support the overall business strategy. For example, the Raytheon Company, a US defence company, launched a new business unit in homeland security in 2002, where core technologies are used in adjacent markets to gain more benefits from the skills, know-how and technologies (Meyer and Poza, 2009). Based on this business strategy, the company developed a new profit source, a business earning $2 billion in six years.

The business strategy might be passive or highly proactive, resulting in different sets of competencies. For example, if a firm has a 'blue-ocean strategy', that is, a highly proactive strategy based on the idea of the repeated creation over time of new market space, such a firm will apply value innovation thinking to the selection of its core competencies (Kim and Mauborgne, 1997, 2005). Instead of head-to-head competition, representing a 'red-ocean strategy', the blue-ocean strategy creates and executes strategic moves that unlock unchallenged market space, making competition irrelevant. Hence, a blue-ocean strategy shows companies not only how to create and capture blue oceans but also how to monitor when it is time to reach out for a new blue ocean. In this way, a blue-ocean strategy presents a dynamic iterative process to create new market space across time based on the value analysis carried out in the company (for details of value analysis, see Chapter 13).

From the core technologies perspective, managers should ask four questions that translate value innovation thinking into a new **value curve** for technologies (Kim and Mauborgne, 1997):

1 Which of the technology/competence factors that our industry take for granted should be eliminated?
2 Which technology/competence factors should be reduced well below the industry's standard?
3 Which should be raised well above the industry's standard?
4 Which technology/competence factors should be created that the industry has never offered?

Thus, there are important decisions that need to be made on the basis of a firm's value offerings. Once the answers are found, they help to determine the core technological competencies.

The selection of core technology competencies is also affected by the level of technology and organizational competencies available in the company. As shown above, gap analysis indicates the level of technological capabilities and the extent to which the technological capabilities under consideration are supported by the necessary organizational capabilities. This might affect the decision on core technological competencies.

After the core technology competencies are decided, possible technology strategies related to core competencies might be (Chiesa and Manzini, 1998):

- *Competence deepening*: investing in the skills/applications fundamental to the firm's current strategy.
- *Competence fertilizing*: using skills already available within the firm to create new applications.
- *Competence complementing*: acquiring new skills to be integrated with the current set of skills in order to open new market opportunities.
- *Competence refreshing*: acquiring new skills to generate a cluster of new applications in the future.
- *Competence destroying*: identifying certain skills that might erode the set of knowledge required for some current applications to be performed in the future.

Buy-make-collaborate decision

The main strategic decision to be addressed in terms of implementing a technology strategy is that of the resources needed to generate and carry out the innovations looked for in the plan. If they are available in-house, allocating budgets and responsibilities might initiate project management activities. If they are not available, it is important to decide how to acquire them. This is the make-buy-collaborate dilemma.

One proposed model for solving this dilemma is balancing the strategic impact of technology (base, key and pacing) with the anticipated cost of technology development (Floyd, 1998). If technologies are critical or just new and the cost of technology development is medium to high, forming an alliance/collaboration might be the best strategy to acquire technologies by reducing the cost burden.

In the case of technology, the make-buy-collaborate decision is complicated because of the dynamic nature of technological change. Rapid changes in technology necessitate technology strategy taking into consideration three additional factors:

1 The constituent technologies embodied in the product and the production process used to manufacture it.
2 Extending the technology analysis to the whole value chain in the industry involved.
3 The choice of how to commercialize the technology.

In dealing with these three factors, the dynamic capabilities and the value constellation views might be useful due to their systemic nature (Normann and Ramirez, 1993; Teece, 2007). Consequently, the focus of strategic analysis is not the company or even the industry but the value-creating system itself, within which different economic actors – suppliers, business partners, allies and customers – work together to co-produce value. The key strategic task in this view is the reconfiguration of roles and relationships among this constellation of actors in order to mobilize the creation of value in new forms and by new players. And their underlying strategic goal is to create an ever-improving fit between competencies and customers. In other words, successful companies consider strategy as a systematic social innovation: the continuous design and redesign of complex business systems. For example, when IKEA introduced its modular furniture model, it changed the roles of agents in the value chain; customers became transporters and assemblers of the products they had purchased. The characteristic of becoming a social innovator necessitates a reconfiguration capacity that not only enhances combinations for new value but also aligns co-specialized assets inside the enterprise and between and among enterprises or supporting institutions.

Value-adding activities are not necessarily linear; they may take place simultaneously or sequentially and may be performed by one party on one occasion and another party on another (Normann and Ramirez, 1993). So rather than having fixed boundaries between organizations, the boundaries and the organizations become flexible and fluid (Ashkenas et al., 1995). Information flows readily between different participants in the value constellation/ecosystem. As the actions of all parties become more transparent, tasks can be allocated more efficiently and there is less need to closely monitor performance and rely on traditional command and control to get things done.

When an organization develops its long-term strategy, managers need to grasp three main factors: the regime of appropriability, the role of dominant design and complementary assets (Teece, 1986, 2006). The regime of appropriability refers to the existing legal structure for IPR that protects innovations from being copied, while dominant design is about the standards set for particular technological innovation. The existence of IPR and the emergence of standards allow innovators to gain higher returns from their innovations, so they support the decision making.

Dominant design refers to an agreed standard upon which full-scale production will be carried out. Before dominant design appears, many alternative technologies compete and following a set of complex interactions of various stakeholders, one technology becomes widely accepted. At some point, the design becomes accepted as the industry standard. Dominant designs have the benchmark features to which subsequent designs are compared. Examples include Ford's Model T automobile and the IBM PC, while GSM (Global System for Mobile communications) is the most popular standard for mobile phones worldwide.

Complementary assets are related capabilities that the innovator needs to achieve in the market. They might be generic such as car/steel producers, co-specialized such as ships/

harbour services and specialized such as McKinsey's consultancy services (Teece, 1986). An example illustrating the importance of complementary assets is the commercialization story of EMI's computerized axial tomography (CAT) scanner. In the late 1960s, Godfrey Hounsfield (now Sir), a researcher at EMI, one of the world's leading music companies, came up with a method of examining body organs by scanning them with X-rays and using a computer to construct a series of cross-sectional scans along a single axis. In 1968, EMI patented the invention and invested in the CAT scanner. Initially, EMI was successful, but after six years, it lost market leadership to its large competitors in the health industry who bypassed the appropriability regime. After eight years, EMI dropped out of the business, mainly because of a lack of sales, marketing and after-sales service capabilities crucial in the medical industry.

The process behind the make-buy-collaborate decision might involve considerations related to complementary assets, the appropriability regime and dominant designs (Teece, 2006). For example, a profit-seeking innovator faced with weak IP protection and the need to access specialized complementary assets or capabilities is forced to expand through integration to prevail over imitators.

When a firm's technology strategy results in a decision to either acquire a technology or develop it collaboratively, the next step is implementation or commercialization. However, one final decision needs to be made: how to manage intra- and inter-firm management processes.

Managers need to analyse the internal processes that will handle the type of technological innovations called for by the technology strategy. For example, a company may have a well-developed new product development process and competent staff able to generate a string of new products. But this organizational strength might not allow the company to handle a series of acquisitions. A new form of organizational and managerial structure might be needed. In fact, the main organizational problems in the implementation stage include the challenge of balancing the use of pacing and emerging technologies together with the use of key and base technologies.

To be a leader in global manufacturing, a company must excel in two contradictory ways (Tushman and Andersen, 2004). On the one hand, a company must constantly build and refresh its individual areas of expertise or 'explorative' capabilities, so it has the critical capabilities needed to stay ahead of its competitors. On the other hand, a company must make sure its changing mix of disciplines work together to gain 'exploitative' capabilities. In other words, the company should encompass both explorative and exploitative capabilities within its organizational structures so that it can develop reconfiguration capabilities (Teece, 2007). This solution demands the establishment of an effective KM system and corporate entrepreneurship practices.

 Case study

Ferrofluidics was founded in October 1968 to develop and market magnetic fluid technology. The product, a fluid known as ferrofluid that can be magnetized, may have been the first commercial nano-engineered system. Through the application of a magnetic field, the ferrofluid can be precisely positioned and controlled. Over time it was discovered that the unique properties of ferrofluids were exceedingly valuable as lubricants, sealing agents, bearings and dampening agents.

The company developed numerous products based on ferrofluid technology, including: seals to isolate hazardous environments from ambient or normal conditions and near frictionless sealed bearing to allow disk drives to spin at incredible rates. In the early 1980s, Ferrofluidics' management spun off their Japanese operations and entered into the silicon crystal puller business through an acquisition. Ferrofluidics planned to improve the Varian silicon puller and its operation using their technical competencies and managerial capabilities.

The value provided from their existing operations was to improve the silicon puller by adding a few parts that involved Ferrofluidics technology. However, this was a small modification. In addition, the company did not have any experience in managing a product involving more than a handful of components. The company found it difficult to produce large subsystems like vacuum and furnace chambers and computer controls.

The use of 'the Strategy-Technology Firm Fit Audit' (originally developed by the authors and details are given in the article) to the case offers an assessment as shown in Table 7.1. Accordingly, there are only a few if any managerial capabilities and processes

Table 7.1 Strategy-technology firm fit audit

Managerial capabilities	Fluid	Bearing	Seals	Pullers
Tier I – General managerial capabilities				
Offering type				
Physical product	x	x	x	x
Service product				
After sales service				x
Physical products				
Materials	x	x	x	
Fabrication and assembly				x
Service products/after sales service				
Knowledge embedded				
Knowledge based				x
Knowledge extracted				
Tier II – Specific managerial capabilities				
Managerial emphasis				
Operations				x
Technology development	x	x	x	
Complexity				
Few components or processes	x	x	x	
Moderate number of components or processes				
Many components or processes				x
Technology maturity	L	L	L	M
Type of innovation				
Regular				x
Niche creation				
Revolutionary	x	x	x	
Architectural				
Technology push/market pull	Pull	Pull	Pull	Push

(Continued)

Table 7.1 Strategy-technology firm fit audit (*continued*)

Technological competencies	Fluld	Bearings	Seals	Pullers
Tier III – General technological competencies				
Generic engineering skills				
Biological				
Chemical	x	x	x	
Civil				
Computer science				x
Electrical				
Materials	x	x	x	
Mechanical		x		x
Nanotechnologies	x	x	x	
Tier IV – Specific technological competencies				
Engineering skills				
Inorganic chemistry	x	x	x	
Organic chemistry	x	x	x	
Systems engineering				x
Technologies				
Vacuum systems				x
Furnace systems				x
Automation				x

Source: Walsh and Linton (2011).

that are transferable from Ferrofluidics' existing product lines to silicon puller manufacturing, sales and support. While all of Ferrofluidics' offerings are products, the puller is the only product that requires after-sales support (Table 7.1, Tier I). The puller involved fabrication and assembly, while all of the other products focus only on materials. The Tier II Managerial capabilities are different between the puller and other Ferrofluidics products. For example, the puller is more operation focused as it focuses on the production of a large machine with a large number of parts and processes involved, but very little variation from unit to unit. This is a clear contrast from the few steps and processes for all their other products. Technology maturity is higher for silicon pullers than other Ferrofluidics products and the focus is on incremental innovation for pullers, while many of the other products are developed through radical innovation processes.

Even though a little overlap exists in technology competencies, Tier III Generic engineering skills, there is no overlap with either specific engineering skills or specific technologies (Tier IV). Thus the overall match between managerial capabilities and technological competencies between the silicon puller and other Ferrofluidics products is quite limited.

The entry of Ferrofluidics into the silicon puller business ended with a failure due to poor performance and the company ended up selling their entire business to their former Japanese subsidiary.

Note on the case: Nippon Ferrofluidics embarked on a path of expansion and product diversification, establishing locations in Japan and China. In 1995, the company changed its name to Ferrotec Corporation, and in 1999, Ferrotec purchased Ferrofluidics, unifying the business and establishing the company as a worldwide leader with a broad product portfolio. Over the years, Ferrotec's product offering has grown from ferrofluids and Ferrofluidic® seals to include critical components using advanced materials like silicon, quartz and ceramics for semiconductor manufacturing processes, thermoelectric components for temperature control and precision coating systems used to manufacture LEDs and smart phone components.

Source: https://www.ferrotec.com/company/about

Source: Excerpts from Walsh, S. and Linton, J. (2011) 'The Strategy-Technology Firm Fit Audit: A Guide to Opportunity Assessment and Selection', *Technological Forecasting and Social Change*, **78**(2), 199–216.

Summary

The main element of strategic planning, namely the selection of capabilities, is to identify the list of core technological competencies. Besides this, the selection capability requires evaluating markets and competitors in order to identify or develop a relevant business model. Thus, the reconfiguration and transformation process of organizational and managerial processes can also be addressed by the selection capability of technological capabilities, where the ability to sense the need to reconfigure a firm's asset structure and accomplish the necessary internal and external transformation take place.

In conventional strategic planning, the outcomes might be programmes and actions at various hierarchies. In other words, corporate strategies are transferred into lower level strategies, namely business unit strategies and functional strategies. The business strategies that indicate the positional standing of the company in that particular business line result in capital programmes. The functional strategies develop capital and operating programmes. At the operational level, all these capital and operating programmes are carried out if enough budget is allocated to them. The strategy implementation results in actual actions taken by the organization.

In a similar way, the final output of selection processes should contain a set of decisions that will become action plans. Choices about technology strategy become inputs to operational plans for functions such as marketing and finance. But more importantly, it ends up with choices about which technologies to make, which ones to buy, which ones to collaborate, which ones to utilize/divest and how to protect technologies. These outcomes influence other TM activities and vice versa.

? Key Questions

1 What is the selection capability?
2 What are technological core competencies and what is their role in strategy making?
3 What are gap and value analyses?
4 How can make-buy-collaborate decisions be addressed?
5 What technology strategies are driven by core competencies?

📖 **Further reading**

Canez, L., Platts, K. and Probert, D. (2001) *Make-or-Buy: A Practical Guide to Industrial Sourcing Decisions* (Cambridge: CTM University of Cambridge).

Maier, A. M., Moultrie, J. and Clarkson, P. J. (2012) 'Assessing Organizational Capabilities: Reviewing and Guiding the Development of Maturity Grids', *IEEE Transactions on Engineering Management*, **59**(1), 138–159.

Probert, D., Dissel, M., Farrukh, C., Mortara, L., Thorn, V. and Phaal, R. (2013) 'The Process of Making the Business Case for Technology: A Sales and Marketing Perspective for Technologists', *Technological Forecasting and Social Change*, **80**(6), 1129–1146.

Teece, D. J. (2006) 'Reflections on "Profiting from Technological Innovation"', *Research Policy*, **35**(8), 1131–1146.

Teece, D. J., Pisano, G. and Shuen, A. (1997) 'Dynamic Capabilities and Strategic Management', *Strategic Management Journal*, **18**(7), 509–533.

Tushman, M. L. and Andersen, P. (2004) *Managing Strategic Innovation and Change*, 2nd edn (Oxford: Oxford University Press).

Walsh, S. and Linton, J. (2011) 'The Strategy-Technology Firm Fit Audit: A Guide to Opportunity Assessment and Selection', *Technological Forecasting and Social Change*, **78**(2), 199–216.

Part II

TECHNOLOGY MANAGEMENT TOOLS

Man is a tool-using animal ... without tools he is nothing, with tools he is all. (Thomas Carlyle, essayist and historian, 1795–1881)

TM activities refer to the operations firms perform in their day-to-day routines. Therefore TM needs to offer some practical guidelines to apply and reinforce TM concepts within the business so that managers can incorporate TM into their daily routines. This book presents six tools specifically applicable for managing technology: patent analysis, portfolio management, roadmapping, S-curve, stage-gate and value analysis.

The core TM toolkit was decided on the basis of simplicity and flexibility of use, degree of availability and standardization level. In addition, we wanted to highlight tools that are dynamic in nature and applicable to all the dynamic technological capabilities described in the TM process model. So the chosen tools are the prevailing ones across all TM activities and capture internal and external dynamics.

As discussed in Chapter 1 (Introduction), the selection of a small set of tools to be used in TM activities was based on the analogy of a carpenter's toolbox. There are a large number of possible tools that a carpenter could have in their toolbox, but the carpenter typically carries around only a small set of the most commonly used tools, keeping a larger set of more specialized tools at their workbench. Even then, the carpenter pays an occasional trip to the hardware store for special jobs. So this book suggests a toolkit for TM; a number of tools that will be handy when managers are faced with decisions regarding TM.

In Part II, Chapters 8–13 are each devoted to a specific TM tool, while Chapter 14 presents challenges for technology managers. These selected TM tools are applicable in all activities, but each tool is associated with two activities to which it is more widely applied compared to the rest, as shown in Table II.1. Not all these tools have been uniquely developed for TM, for example the stage-gate process is a project management tool extensively used in the analysis of new product development. Similar to the format of Part I, TM tools are given in alphabetical order to avoid any hierarchy among them.

Chapters 8–13 follow the same format:

- Introduction.
- Where and why it is used.
- Process.
- Case study.

Table II.1 TM tools and their applications

Tools/ activities	Patent analysis	Portfolio management	Road-mapping	S-curve	Stage-gate	Value analysis
Acquisition	★					★
Exploitation			★	★		
Identification				★	★	
Learning		★	★			
Protection	★				★	
Selection		★				★

Case studies present real-life examples showing the different facets of each TM activity in varying detail. Almost all cases come from *Research-Technology Management*, a highly respected practice journal in the field of TM.

The website of the book holds a reference section for TM tools that are mentioned in the literature. Some tools are available publicly in some detail, such as the T-Catalogue, so providing references will allow the reader to obtain more detailed information on topics of interest to them. It is possible to have a long list of tools that might be used in individual TM activities such as decision-making tools or leadership tools. However, they are extremely broad tools that any manager would benefit from having awareness of, regardless of their interest in TM, so this list has been limited.

The appendix links TM activities with TM tools. Turning TM skills and knowledge into practice is as important as developing them, making TM activities and tools the two sides of the same coin. The value of management tools is occasionally brought into question, since most of the time they are seen as some form of automatic support mechanisms that managers deploy. This book ends by offering a list of tools that will satisfy the needs of each TM activity. This is a wider list than the six key tools discussed in this book in order to give a broader framework to understand how tools and activities can be matched. Clearly, real life is complicated and there are many tools which could be of benefit. However, managers need to start somewhere and the six TM activities and six tools discussed in this book provide a useful starting point.

8

PATENT ANALYSIS

8.1   Introduction

A patent is a set of rights granted by the government to a legal entity or a person who is the inventor or their assignee for a fixed period of time in exchange for a disclosure of the invention (Abraham and Moitra, 2001). The fixed period of time for the protection of the invention varies from country to country, but is generally around 20 years from the date of filing for patents and it must be renewed after five years or so. After the patent expires, the invention covered by the patent can be used by anyone.

Patent analysis is a tool to convert the statistical information related to patents into useful information for a specific need. Patent search and patent analysis are differentiated by the method of their use:

- A *patent search* is used to assess the patentability, novelty, clearance, infringement, validity and prior art of a technology.
- *Patent analysis* is often used by product managers, business managers and IP strategists in order to synthesize useful information about companies and/or sectors in terms of technological competitiveness and the particular trajectory of technology development (Breitzman and Mogee, 2002).

There are two potential drawbacks in using patent analysis (Cotec, 1998). First, in high-tech and fast-moving industries, the patent analysis might not work due to the time-lags involved in the patent process. Second, companies might treat patent information for legal purposes alone and outsource it to service firms. To prevent this limited use, patent analysis should become a core element in a company's technology competitor intelligence and it needs to be undertaken by top management. Retaining in-house expertise is recommended to ensure an effective and efficient patent search and to facilitate the transfer process of patent information into the long-term strategic planning process within the company.

8.2   Where and why it is used

Patent analysis has many different applications, but is particularly useful for building three main technological capabilities:

- Acquisition (both R&D management and M&A).
- Identification.
- Protection.

Patent analysis contributes to acquisition capabilities described in Chapter 2. In general, it is a key input for R&D managers since the number of patents is a major indicator of the technological output of a company. To illustrate the core competence of a company, or to assess the technology of a company, patent analysis might be used. However, technology trend analysis is a more detailed analysis of changes in the content of technical details and indicates the trajectory of a technology. In other words, the number of changes in the technical details of patents enables the drawing of a forecasted track that the technological development will follow. For instance, in relation to the S-curve of a product's life (discussed in Chapter 11), in the beginning, there are few companies with patents. Once it reaches the period of fast growth, many patents will have been filed and in the last stage of saturation, there are few companies still working in the field.

Patent analysis is widely used by technology companies engaging in M&A activities in order to discover the company with the best price to target from a technology perspective. By investigating the patents of the company, the strong points of the company will be revealed. Also, it is a significant matter whether the companies are compatible or complementary in terms of their technologies. Apart from the relations between the two companies, patent analysis will direct decisions on whether key employees will stay or leave after the M&A has taken place.

Identifying technologies is easy with a patent analysis, which supplies information on a number of dimensions. It helps to support a detailed competitive analysis by enabling assumptions to be made about the strength of a firm in terms of:

- The number of patents owned.
- The growth pattern of the technology.
- The significance of an innovation, that is, the number of times the patent is cited in R&D planning in comparison to competitors (Liu and Shyu, 1997).

Although the records of patent databases are publicly available, patents are not always easy to trace, as sometimes the patent has been sold or the owner has merged with another company. Professionals only search databases within the valid territory of the patent (Hunt et al., 2007). If, for example, the patent is only valid in the UK, research only needs to be conducted in UK patent databases. Another benefit of using such tools is that grouping patents under categories allows companies to identify their strengths and weaknesses by analysing their area of specialization. For example, if a company has a number of patents in a particular field, it would be considered as specialized in this area and therefore a strong competitor in the sector.

Protection is not possible without patent analysis. Firms have to be mindful of their IP management in order to benefit from their monopoly rights and to decide an accurate focus of interest for their own benefit (Goldheim et al., 2005). Most companies are unaware of their patent status, whether they are protected anymore and what they have. Therefore, it will be beneficial to generate a patent portfolio inventory. A patent portfolio makes it easier to track all the important information about a company's patent-related issues, such as their rights in different countries, expiry dates and amount of patent they grant (Mogee and Kolar, 1994). Moreover, patent analysis might be used to determine the strengths and weaknesses of a company, which in turn helps managers in shaping their IP strategy, as discussed in Chapter 6.

Related to protection, patent analysis is useful in licensing (Breitzman and Thomas, 2002). Patent citation analysis allows companies to filter patents that are not in their own specialization but in that of other companies. By so doing, these patents could be out-licensed, and any errors in out-licensing required patents would be avoided by being aware of the relationships between the patents held by a company (Goldheim et al., 2005; Tao et al., 2005). Firms can easily determine whether they should or should not in-license a group of patents in order to use an interesting technology. In some sectors such as IT, companies share their portfolios by cross-licensing. This enables both parties to use each other's patents in case of need, free of charge. Analysing patents could reveal some patents that are not used for any monetary benefit for a company; in such cases, firms should decide whether to renew or donate patents to non-commercial entities and gain a tax deduction. The donate-or-renew decision is based on how frequently a patent is cited or used in new production.

One other significant benefit of patent analysis is related to managing a firm's key HR in order to protect its intellectual assets (Breitzman and Mogee, 2002). Patent analysis generates documents that reveal the key inventors. Therefore identifying these highly skilled people and keeping them happy helps to protect a firm's HR in the long term. Moreover, the company will be alert to the potential retirements of key experts and the required set of talents that are missing in the company. This awareness helps the search for experts who will fulfil the future needs of expertise in a company.

In sum, patent analysis is a method with impact at the strategic, tactical and individual levels and provides a valuable means of planning technology development. Patent analysis offers a further insight into global competitors' technological performance in related technologies. This method increases the reliability of technological competitiveness in the long run.

8.3 Process

Patent analysis extends the patent search to a technological assessment. So, a patent analysis includes four main steps:

1 Patent search.
2 Categorization.
3 Visualization.
4 Integration of data into strategic decision making.

During a patent search, a company must establish a database of its own patents by creating a patent inventory. The expiry date of patents is critical. Moreover, reassignment of the patents must be searched. If there is a lack of information with respect to the patent inventory, the required search must be done to complete the data. The second step is to identify the patent data of all other companies in the industry.

A patent search should be based upon patent groups or classifications. The simplest form of classification is the US patent classification (USPC) or the International Patent Classification (IPC) (Breitzman and Mogee, 2002). The UK Patent Office has its own Patent Classification Key; however, all published UK patent specifications are also classified using the IPC system. Apart from these classifications, companies might use co-citation, co-word or co-classification analysis to put patents into groups. For example, the idea behind the co-citation is that if two patents have common citation patterns, they will be in the same cluster. These groups are labelled 'patent families'. The larger the patent family within a company, the more technology the company has. Similarly, an international patent family is the level of technological activity intended for international exploitation. It shows the intention to exploit a patent in the international arena.

Another grouping could be formed on the basis of the number of citations received for a patent. Such a grouping might show the technological quality and importance. A company with a large number of cited patents is likely to possess technology that is central to developments in its industry. Not all important patents are highly cited, nor is every highly cited patent important, but studies show a strong positive relationship between citations and technological importance (Breitzman and Thomas, 2002).

After the patent search is completed, managers have a rich set of information that could be visualized by using software such as Aureka (http://ip.thomsonreuters.com/training/aureka/). By adopting these tools, the patent analysis results are critical inputs for decision making related to:

1　The type of protection.
2　A number of strategic issues such as technology investments and acquisitions.

Based on the patent analysis, managers decide on the type of protection and the legal process starts. Most European countries' laws follow the European Patent Convention (EPC). In the first instance, one applies to the national patent office. Some countries offer different forms of patents depending on the level of inventiveness. Then, in line with the internationalization goal of a company, patent applications are made in countries where the company intends to do business.

Once the broad information is gathered for patents, they can be further analysed according to the company's needs and become sub-processes of the company strategy. Patent information is used with other company-specific information such as market attractiveness in order to enrich the analysis, depending on the reason for carrying out the patent analysis. For example, as Chapter 7 clearly describes, the selection of which technologies to invest in is related to the technological position of a company and the patent analysis that supplies critical information on the standing of a company in a particular technology. However, this needs to be combined with its potential impact. Similarly, the level of technological competence can be built on the patent analysis results and combined with the significance of technologies. Such a combination of data is another input for technology investment decisions.

The use of patent analysis in M&A decisions demonstrates how the overall process can be embedded in other strategy processes. Patent analysis can be an integral part of four major M&A activities: targeting, due diligence, technological capability and valuation (Breitzman and Thomas, 2002):

1　*Targeting* entails finding a partner company or acquisition that compensates for a particular technological shortage or need. This technique is conducted initially by several filters, groupings and diagrams followed by a metric analysis of patent portfolios, in terms of being highly cited, quantity of patents granted, recently filed patents, high impact patents and patents' links to scientific works (Breitzman and Mogee, 2002).
2　*Due diligence* involves testing the accuracy of known profile data of the target company.
3　*Technological capability* consists of dynamic and operational capabilities that are a collection of routines/activities to execute and coordinate the variety of tasks required to manage technology.
4　*Valuation* of technology firms is difficult, since there is a significant difference between the market and book value because of the intangible assets of this type of company

(Tao et al., 2005). The patents need to be included as intangible assets. In this way, an underpriced company will be found and invested in.

Overall, patent analysis enables managers to decide whether the candidate company is appropriate for M&A.

In order to use patent analysis for identification, patent information might be plotted as an S-curve as well. Patent analysis can indicate the growth pattern of a technology (emerging, maturing or declining) based on the number of patent applications in a specific technology (Cotec, 1998). It can also indicate which firms are about to enter or leave a technology, the age and type of each firm's technological base and the relative technological strengths of firms. The development of patent data over time helps companies to observe different technological development stages and take precautions accordingly. For example, the first substantial peak of patent applications has to be interpreted as a serious warning signal for a new technology. The company needs to be aware of the development at this point and needs to evaluate strategic responses in the market. Thus, to prevent a firm from becoming obsolete, it is necessary to continuously monitor the patenting activity of competitors in different technological areas in order to anticipate technological advances and subsequent market shifts.

 Case study

Patent analysis is applicable to a number of managerial problems. The Siemens-Acuson case shows how patent analysis helps to identify which company to acquire. Siemens is an international company with many business lines including medical products. Acuson Inc. was one of the leading companies in the ultrasound industry. By patenting, Acuson protected its technological knowledge while it built a company image that attracted Siemens, who was searching for a valuable source of technology for its own business. After the discussion on Siemens-Acuson, another example of patent analysis will be shown to highlight that patent analysis might help to get an industry-level perspective as well. The general analysis will show that electronic shopping has evolved over time. This might be valuable input for managerial decisions.

Siemens-Acuson

In 2000, Siemens acquired Acuson based on patent analysis. To evaluate Acuson compared to its competitors, managers in Siemens carried out a patent search in order to discover the technological strength of firms in the ultrasound industry. Figure 8.1 shows the results of this analysis for seven companies with 50+ ultrasound patents in the period 1995–1999. The 'current impact index' measures the influence of a company's patents, based on the frequency of citations from later patents to patents issued before them. This metric has an expected value of 1.0, so that Acuson's index value of 2.9 indicates that its patents are cited three times as often as average patents in the same technology and of the same age. A third metric shows a high degree of scientific referencing by Acuson, indicating that Acuson's inventors are familiar with, and are building directly on, scientific literature.

(Continued)

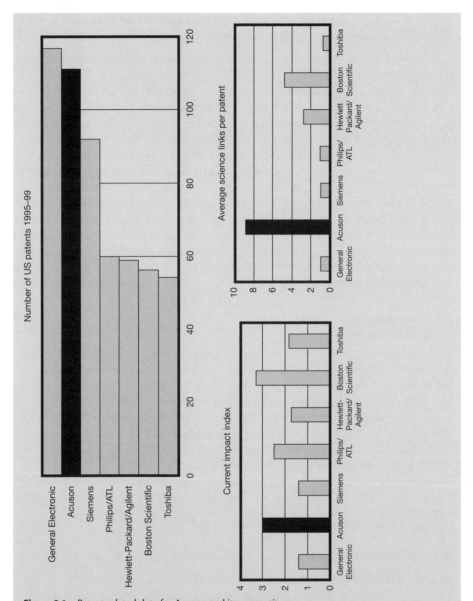

Figure 8.1   Patent-related data for Acuson and its competitors

Figure 8.2 shows citation patterns among peer companies in ultrasound technology. Thus, it provides further evidence of the impact of Acuson's patent portfolio. The arrows reveal companies whose patents receive the largest number of citations from other companies' patents. Acuson has arrows pointing to it from five leading ultrasound companies. From a peer perspective, this demonstrates that the ultrasound industry has built extensively on Acuson's technology.

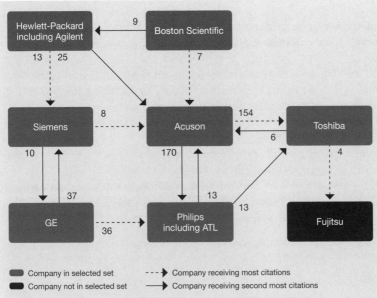

Figure 8.2 Patent citations for Acuson and its competitors

Acuson had been a company with a high-quality patent portfolio with many cited patents, indicating that this was a company worth acquiring. But, although the estimated book value of Acuson was low, taking its patents into account, its value was more than five times higher. As a result, Acuson was acquired at a low share price by Siemens.

Source: Breitzman, A. and Thomas, P. (2002) 'Using Patent Citation Analysis to Target/Value M&A Candidates', *Research-Technology Management*, **45**(5), 28–37.

Business Model Evolution: Electronic Shopping

A dynamic patent analysis could identify trends in technology-driven business model evolution. A study (Lee et al., 2013) used patents to observe technological changes in business models over time for electronic shopping. Business method patents represent a specific way of doing business and include technological configurations of business models at an operational level. Lee et al. (2013) used the patent class 705 that encompasses machines and corresponding methods for performing data processing or calculation operations, where the machine or method is utilized in (i) practice, administration or management of an enterprise, (ii) processing of financial data or (iii) determination of the charge for goods or services.

Based on the distribution of business method patents, the evolution of electronic shopping is divided into four phases: infancy, stagnancy, growth and expansion.

- The first era is the infancy of electronic shopping technology. It started in 1998 shortly after the patentability of business models was allowed by the US Patent Office in 1996. During this period, the secure and convenient electronic transaction

(*Continued*)

accelerated the evolution of electronic shopping. The transition of the payment method from offline to online especially supported the expansion of electronic shopping.

- The second era, stagnancy of electronic shopping technology, appeared as the dot-com bubble burst in the early 2000s. The number of patents issued dropped in this period compared with the previous period. Based on the technologies developed in the era of infancy, advanced technologies were developed and applied to different platforms in a more advanced way.
- The third era is called growth of electronic shopping technology, since after the 2000s portable devices were invented and widely spread.
- The last era, expansion of electronic shopping technology, was based on wireless Internet services such as Wireless Application Protocol (WAP), local area wireless technology (WiFi) and Wireless Broadband Internet (WiBro).

Source: Lee, C., Park, H. and Park, Y. (2013) 'Keeping Abreast of Technology-driven Business Model Evolution: A Dynamic Patent Analysis Approach', *Technology Analysis & Strategic Management*, **25**(5), 487–505.

 Key Questions

1 What is a patent?
2 What are the advantages and disadvantages of patent analysis?
3 What is the process of patent analysis?

Exercises

1. Adidas versus Nike

By using the US Patent Office data, please find the following numbers for the companies Adidas and Nike. Then, you should compare the numbers within the perspective of patent analysis and discuss implications for the managers of these two companies.

Patent Applications (PA):

PA   =   # patent applications at the Patent Office

Share of Granted Patents (Share of GP):

Granted Patent: Invention consists of new technology elements.

Share of GP   =   # granted patents / (PA-Patents under exam.)

Share of Valid Patents (Share of VP):

Valid Patent: Granted & Protection fee is still paid.

Share of VP   =   # valid patents / # granted patents

Share of US Patents (Share of USP):

Share of USP = # US Patents / # PA

Citation Ratio (Cit-Ratio):

Cit-Ratio   = # patent citations / # PA

Relative Patent Position:

In a particular technology field =
patents owned by the company / # patents of a competitor (with the largest
patents as the benchmark)

Technology Attractiveness:
Growth rates of PA at Patent Office in the respective IPC (International Patent
Classification) Classes:

1 RGR = Average growth of PA / Average growth of total PA
2 RDGR = RGR (2010–2015) / RGR (2010–2015) (that shows the growth trend)

Importance of a Technology Field (that indicates company priority within its R&D
activities) = # firm's patents in a technology field / total # firm's patents

2. Mobile phone application

Imagine that you are the CEO of a software company that developed a mobile phone
application that will add the mobile phone to the business directories. The business
model summary is given in Table 8.1.

Table 8.1   Business directory annotation mobile phone reminder

Business directory annotation mobile phone reminder				
Entity	Role	Benefits	Costs	Volume
End user	Prime beneficiary	Convenience timely	Per message received	High volume
Directory content provider	License and implement core system	Increase usage of directory	Licence fees plus network operator fees	One licence
Network operator	Location determination services	Network usage and messaging fees	Infrastructure and operating	High load volume

Based on the information given in the table regarding the users, suppliers and respective benefits for each category, try to find out the advantages and disadvantages of
following the options listed below for your IP strategies:

(Continued)

- Sell the whole patent/system to one directory 'Yellow Pages'.
- Sell the patent to different directories in different geographies e.g. Australia, Singapore, USA, UK.
- License the patent as above – to one global licensee or many e.g. Vodafone.
- A combination of the above plus assignment of partial rights to a third party to undertake similar (non-conflicting endeavours, e.g. the right to sell or license the system in Japan).

Source: ©2004 OpenTTO.org, walter.adamson@opentto.org

 **Further reading**

Breitzman, A. and Mogee, M. (2002) 'The Many Applications of Patent Analysis', *Journal of Information Science*, **28**(3), 187–205.

Chang, S.-B., Lai, K.-K. and Chang, S.-M. (2009) 'Exploring Technology Diffusion and Classification of Business Methods: Using the Patent Citation Network', *Technological Forecasting & Social Change*, **76**(1), 107–117.

Hitchcock, D. (2007) *Patent Searching Made Easy*, 4th edn (US: Lulu.com).

Lee, C., Park, H. and Park, Y. (2013) 'Keeping Abreast of Technology-driven Business Model Evolution: A Dynamic Patent Analysis Approach', *Technology Analysis & Strategic Management*, **25**(5), 487–505.

9

PORTFOLIO MANAGEMENT

9.1   Introduction

A portfolio is a bundle of projects and/or programmes that are grouped together to facilitate their effective management to meet strategic business objectives. A project has a definable objective, consumes resources and operates under three main constraints: time, cost and quality. This is why the components of a project can be measured, ranked and prioritized (Kerzner, 2003). Portfolio management is the centralized management of one or more portfolios, which has the steps of identifying, prioritizing, authorizing, managing and controlling projects and programmes to achieve the strategic goals of the business. The goals of a business vary as widely as the ambitions, competence, vision and culture of each business.

Portfolio management is generally used in the financial services industry to define decisions about investment mix and policy, matching investments to objectives, balancing risk against performance and asset allocation for individuals and institutions. However, portfolio management has also become a field of interest for TM, since increasing globalization forces companies to invest in many R&D activities. Portfolio management is especially important for high-tech firms since the uncertainty faced by these companies can vary greatly. Therefore, strategies should be formed to avoid threats and exploit advantages through forming appropriate project portfolios (Mikkola, 2001).

Cooper et al. (1999) define portfolio management as a dynamic decision process that includes a constant updating and revising of a company's active new technology projects. The process is dynamic since new projects are continually evaluated, selected and prioritized, whereas ongoing projects may be speeded up, closed or reprioritized, and resources may be reallocated among projects. Managers are also constrained by the constantly changing opportunities, goals and strategic plans of the company and the interdependence of projects. Further, managers face the problem of high uncertainty since their decisions concern the products, services and processes that will be launched in the future. All these constraints explain why the portfolio should be closely monitored periodically to make go/kill decisions using a stage-gate process, as described in Chapter 12.

9.2   Where and why it is used

Portfolio management is extensively used in project-based organizations. From the perspective of manufacturing or technology-providing firms that have R&D projects, this tool can be used to manage three main TM activities:

- Acquisition.
- Learning.
- Selection.

Internal acquisition (Chapter 2) and selection (Chapter 7) capabilities require good management of portfolios for a number of reasons:

1 Resources could be spent on unrewarding projects, causing potentially superior ones to fail if there is no portfolio management.
2 All projects related to product, service, technology and process development involve a high risk, so portfolio management can help to manage the risks of these projects by choosing appropriate numbers of high- and low-risk projects.
3 The lack of a systematic procedure to choose between projects can lead to choices based on politics, opinion and emotion (Cooper et al., 2001).
4 Portfolio management helps to prevent a short-term focus, which would result in too many small projects.

Portfolio management helps selection decisions not only at the formation of the portfolio but also during the realization of the individual projects chosen within the portfolio. In other words, portfolio management facilitates the formation of criteria for go/kill decisions in order to prevent carrying out unsuccessful projects at stage-gates that may cause long lead times to market and poor quality products. Having sound selection criteria results in efficient acquisition activities as well, since these criteria bring discipline to acquisition activities.

Portfolio management is based on the notion of evaluating all projects at the same time. This is particularly important for sharing experiences across projects and diffusing project results across the company. Thus, the learning capability (Chapter 5) finds a solid ground to exercise its influence.

Besides the numerous advantages, there are a few drawbacks to portfolio management when determining the technologies to invest in or managing them, such as managing R&D projects. According to Ernst (2003), the main disadvantages are:

- Portfolios are based on subjective assessments made by respondents.
- They fail to incorporate competition due to a lack of necessary information.
- They do not allow for the analysis of dynamic technological developments.

9.3   Process

The major process in portfolio management is selecting projects that form the portfolio. It would be beneficial to adopt the framework developed for portfolio selection (Archer and Ghasemzadeh, 1999), in which there are three major steps:

1 Individual project analysis.
2 Optimal portfolio selection.
3 Portfolio adjustment.

The individual project analysis stage includes activities such as pre-screening and screening. Pre-screening considers whether the project being considered for the portfolio is in line with the strategic focus developed. A feasibility analysis and estimation of parameters are also essential for a project to pass this stage. Mandatory projects such as improvements to certain products are also decided at this stage. Activities at this stage of the process include strategy development and methodology selection, which are the tools to be used for portfolio selection. Screening is the elimination stage for projects or interrelated families of projects that are not compatible with the expectations of the company, such as rate of return. The goal is to reduce the number of projects to be considered in the next stage.

The individual project analysis stage calculates parameters, such as project risk, NPV and ROI, with the estimation of uncertainties for each parameter. Ongoing projects can also be re-evaluated at this stage. The dominant models developed for project selection were from mathematical programming in the 1960s and 1970s. More recently, other methods are used to find the value of a project, such as financial models, probabilistic financial models, options pricing theory, strategic approaches, scoring models and checklists, analytical hierarchy approaches, behavioural approaches and bubble diagrams (Cooper et al., 1999). These groups of methods will be briefly mentioned below:

1 *Financial models* mainly depend on sorting and selecting the projects according to criteria such as NPV, internal rate of return (IRR) and payback methods (Cooper et al., 1999). The 'productivity index' is another measure that can be used to rank projects. It is simply calculated by dividing the difference between discounted and probability-weighted streams of cash flows from the project and R&D costs with R&D costs (Cooper and Edgett, 1997).

2 *Probabilistic financial models* include simulation methods such as Monte Carlo, which evaluates 'the outcome of alternative paths that have different payoffs with certain probabilities', and decision trees, which 'describe a problem as a series of decision nodes unfolding sequentially over time' (Canez and Garfias, 2006).

3 The Black-Scholes *options pricing theory*, where projects are treated as real options investments by facilitating decision making about an investment during different stages of the project (Whitney, 2007). The return on value allows management to make decisions about an investment during the different stages of the project, using multiple stages and considering a range of possible outcomes, including the financial consequence of failure.

4 *Strategic approaches* ensure that the projects selected are aligned with the overall business strategy. In the strategic buckets model, according to the strategy adopted, management decides on the resources to be allocated for each type of project, such as new product developments, process improvements, maintenance projects or fundamental research. The project portfolio is aligned with the strategy of the business with this top-down approach (Cooper and Edgett, 1997).

5 *Scoring models* are generally used to prioritize the projects in the portfolio selection process. In these models, evaluators rate each project according to certain criteria and then the scores are multiplied by their weights before summing up to reach the total score of the project (Cooper and Edgett, 1997).

6 *Analytical hierarchy approaches* determine the relative importance of each criterion by which projects will be evaluated and then compare each project alternative on these criteria to reach a ranking of alternatives.

7 *Behavioural approaches* are suitable for early stage-gates, since there is not much quantitative information available. Methods such as Delphi are used to reach a consensus between managers when choosing among projects (Cooper et al., 1999).

8 *Bubble diagrams* are used as graphical representations to visualize the balance of a portfolio. These maps typically illustrate the spread of portfolios on two-dimensional graphs, with axes showing risks versus profitability, marketplace fit versus product line coverage, financial return versus probability of success and so on. Figure 9.1 is an example of a bubble map that compares different projects in terms of their NPV and

probability of success. A third dimension is also added to the graph by representing the total revenue generated over the lifetime sales of the product with the size of the bubbles. The graph is a good representation of the risk–reward balance of the portfolio.

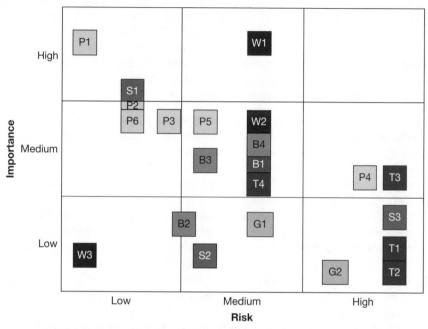

Figure 9.1 Technology assessment for *Scenario A*: 'Season in the Sun'

Code names of renewable energy technologies W1: On-shore wind energy; W2: Off-shore wind energy; W3: Small wind turbine; G1: Geothermal energy; G2: Incremental geothermal energy; P1: Crystal Si; P2: film of a-Si; P3: film of CIGS; P4: film of CdTe; P5: Organic dye; P6: Concentration photovoltaic; S1: ¼ Solar heating water boiler; S2: ¼ Solar heating air condition; S3: ¼ Solar heating energy; B1: Biomass energy; B2: Anaerobic ferment; B3: Biodiesel; B4: Bioethanol; T1: Wave energy; T2: Tide energy; T3: Ocean current energy; T4: Ocean Thermal Energy.

Source: Chen et al., 2009.

In optimal portfolio selection, three goals are used (Cooper and Edgett, 1997): maximizing the value of the portfolio, providing balance and supporting the strategy of the enterprise:

- Maximizing the commercial value of the portfolio involves allocating resources to the combination of projects so as to maximize its commercial value.
- A balanced portfolio involves balancing risk (high- and low-risk projects), types of projects (basic research and applied research), as well as target markets, among others.
- Linking the portfolio to the technology strategy of the business means making sure that the analysis takes the organization's technology strategy into account.

Although all the goals must be satisfied, the fit between the strategy of the enterprise and the R&D portfolio is particularly important for new product, service and process development (Cooper et al., 1997). Strategic planning for technology products was found to be the most important issue followed by organizational learning about technology (Scott, 2000). Therefore, firms need to define their R&D strategies and determine the areas in which they are planning to invest, such as new product development or maintenance projects. Then resources should be allocated to each of the project types. Bubble diagrams can be used to ensure the balance of the portfolio, whereas the productivity index or expected commercial value can be used to serve the goal of maximizing the value of the portfolio.

At the final portfolio adjustment stage, some of the project parameters are recalculated when changes are made to substantially change the portfolio from the original at the optimal portfolio selection stage. At the adjustment stage, it is also important to consider the balance of the projects in terms of their risk, size and short-term versus long-term orientation (Archer and Ghasemzadeh, 1999).

 Case study

The technology portfolio planning process provides a systematic procedure for the strategic decision of finding a coordinated set of resource allocations among available technologies. Because of the large uncertainty involved in forecasting the business environment and technical development of emerging technologies, the **scenario analysis** has been embedded into the technology portfolio planning process.

The study of Chen et al. (2009) presents an example to illustrate the comprehensive process. The exemplar case is about the portfolio planning carried out for renewable energy in Taiwan. The study uses all seven steps of technology portfolio planning with a scenario: (1) specify the decision value and focus, (2) identify key decision factors and major driving forces, (3) identify the axes of uncertainty, (4) develop and select scenarios, (5) generate technology alternatives, (6) assess the technology alternatives under different scenarios and (7) develop a robust technology portfolio plan.

1   The values for the resource allocation decision of the renewable energy technology portfolio were derived from a survey of 65 society leaders in Taiwan, including: technology experts, business executives, government officials, major educators, prominent artists and community leaders. The values indicate a 50% weight on economic growth; a 25% weight on social equity, such as reduction in the income gap and increase of the care of elderly and disadvantaged populations; and a 25% weight on the quality of life, including environmental quality and balance between work and leisure. These values formed the basis for assessing the overall importance of the technology alternatives.

A comprehensive list of alternative renewable energy technologies were collected by technical experts from research groups as well as from a broad literature search. The list includes 22 technologies from six major fields of renewable energy: photovoltaics, wind energy, bio-energy, solar heating, geothermal energy and ocean energy.

2   A Scenario Analysis Committee consisting of 14 experts in technology or other professional fields identified key decision factors and major driving forces in the future development of renewable energy technologies.

Key decision factors are identified as follows:

Political factors: government energy and industry policies and international environmental issues.

(Continued)

Technology factors: breakthroughs in renewable energy technology and the criteria for technology assessment.

Market factors: market demand of the renewable energy related industry, the development of domestic industry and the requirements of the international market.

Natural resource factors: availability of renewable energy in Taiwan and the supply costs of renewable energy.

Major driving forces are grouped as follows:

Policy driving forces: government industry policy and energy policy.

Technology driving forces: position of renewable energy technology and the developing cost of renewable energy.

International driving forces: international oil price, greenhouse gas reduction requirements, international eco-issues, the politics of foreign countries and the international demand for energy.

3 These major driving forces were then distributed into three axes of uncertainty: the situation of global warming, the breakthrough in renewable energy technology and the government's renewable energy policy.

4 Eight scenarios are constructed from combining various extremes of the three axes of uncertainty. After the elimination of internally inconsistent or similar scenarios, the Scenario Analysis Committee selected three different scenarios. Due to space limitations, this book will only introduce one of these scenarios titled *Scenario A*: 'Season in the Sun'. In this scenario, global temperature continues to climb resulting with high restrictions on the emission of carbon dioxide. However, the scenario is optimistic since it foresees significant progress in renewable energy technology as well as strong government support that will promote the renewable energy industry.

5 The Scenario Analysis Committee use the portfolio analysis approach to assess the 22 candidate technologies from six major fields of renewable energy: photovoltaics, wind energy, bio-energy, solar heating, geothermal energy and ocean energy. The assessment is carried out in two dimensions: risk and importance (as a representation of the decision values).

The risk of a technology from Taiwan's perspective was assessed on the basis of five indicators: technology position, manufacture capability, industrial supply chain, market entry barriers and lead time for commercialization. Here, the first three indicators focus on the risk in the manufacturing and the last two indicators focus on the risk in the markets.

The importance of a technology was assessed on the basis of the four indicators: market value in 2017, compound market growth rate from 2007 to 2017, cost ratio to traditional energy in 2017 and percentage reduction in energy cost from 2007 to 2017. The first two indicators focus on the market value of the technology and the last two indicators focus on the cost competitiveness of the technology.

6 Based on these indicators and their respective measures, the assessment results and the technology portfolio planning implications for each scenario are summarized graphically in Figure 9.1. For the *Scenario A*: 'Season in the Sun', the

importance-risk assessment indicates that crystal Si (P1) and solar heating water boiler (S1) both enjoy high importance and low risk and are ideal for private business development. Thus, government might invest in these two technologies in order to reduce risk and increase importance.

7 The case study concludes that a robust renewable energy technology portfolio plan appears to be one of the following four choices:

- Taiwan should promote private business investment in the mature technology of solar heating water boilers.
- Dependent on the evolving development of future business environment, Taiwan should either promote private business investment or provide public investment or develop international cooperation in crystal Si, film of a-Si, film of CIGS, concentration photovoltaic and possibly organic dye technologies.
- Taiwan should consider public investments to wind energy as well as selected bio-energy and ocean thermal energy developments.
- Taiwan should continuously monitor other renewable energy technologies for possible technological breakthroughs.

Source: Chen, T.-Y., Yu, O.-S., Hsu, G. J.-Y., Hsu, F-M. and Sung, W.-N. (2009) 'Renewable Energy Technology Portfolio Planning with Scenario Analysis: A Case Study for Taiwan', *Energy Policy*, **37**(8), 2900–2906.

(?) Key Questions

1 What is portfolio management?
2 What are the advantages and disadvantages of portfolio management?
3 What is the process of portfolio management?

1. Project on a page

The project manager must continually be aware of the status of the project. Is the project progressing to plan or is it behind schedule? Is the project likely to be over or under spent? Is the unit cost of the new product on target? Are project risks being managed proactively? Are the project objectives clear and agreed by all? Managing this complex data and providing meaningful reports can be a time consuming and laborious task. Furthermore, different project managers may report on these issues in different ways, depending on their experience and skills.

Also known as a project dashboard, the 'project on a page' document has a dual use, providing an accessible summary of objectives and status to the project team, while also forming a simple, high-level project-status report for senior management. It provides a consistent way of presenting project status which can be used by all project managers. It is expected that the summary will be supported by appropriate documentation to enable a more detailed analysis if required.

(Continued)

Method

Determine the critical information which requires tracking /communicating

To produce a 'project on a page', the organization must first decide the information and measures which are of interest to both the project team and also the senior management. Ask the different management and project stakeholders exactly what information they would like to see. The example below includes:

- Project objectives, project description, deliverables and business case.
- The core project team.
- Continuous tracking of unit cost, with a baseline comparison against an existing product.
- Continuous tracking of project spend – monitoring committed spend and accounting reports against plan.
- Project financials – indicating expected returns on investment.
- Risk management.
- Current position in the process and status – graphical indication of progress against plan.

Imagine your company produces ice cream. Please consider what might be the list of items you will need as a project manager in your 'project on a page'.

Design layout

Determine how the information of measure is to be presented. Can it be graphed, is a table appropriate or will some other visual suffice? Is all of the information included absolutely critical?

Source: Adapted from http://www2.ifm.eng.cam.ac.uk/dmg/tools/process/page2.html

2. Fast Car

Fast Car produces competitive consumer vehicles. In 2014, the company started a new programme of green vehicles with two projects in the portfolio: Lighter Metals for body and Alternative Fuel using Biofuel. You should collect information on the Internet about alternative metals and biofuel use in car production and try to develop a set of criteria for each project category that could be used in the evaluation of the alternatives for your company Fast Car. Prepare a number of charts to compare the projects according to the selected criteria to be used for the assessment.

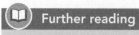 **Further reading**

Chen, T.-Y., Yu, O.-S., Hsu, G. J.-Y., Hsu, F.-M. and Sung, W.-N. (2009) 'Renewable Energy Technology Portfolio Planning with Scenario Analysis: A Case Study for Taiwan', *Energy Policy*, **37**(8), 2900–2906.

Chien, C. (2002) 'A Portfolio-evaluation Framework for Selecting R&D Projects', *R&D Management*, **32**(4), 359–368.

Dickinson, M. W., Thornton, A. C. and Graves, S. (2001) 'Technology Portfolio Management: Optimizing Interdependent Projects Over Multiple Time Periods', *IEEE Transactions on Engineering Management*, **48**(4), 518–527.

Eggers, J. P. (2012) 'All Experience is Not Created Equal: Learning, Adapting, and Focusing in Product Portfolio Management', *Strategic Management Journal*, **33**(3), 315–335.

Mathews, S. (2011) 'Innovation Portfolio Architecture, Part – 2: Attribute Selection and Valuation', *Research-Technology Management*, **54**(5), 37–46.

McDonough, E. F. and Spital, F. C. (2003) 'Managing Project Portfolios', *Research - Technology Management*, **46**(3), 40–46.

Sonnenblick, R. and Euchner, J. (2013) 'Addressing the Challenges of Portfolio Management', *Research-Technology Management*, **56**(5), 12–16.

Tritle, G. L., Scriven, E. F. and Rusfeld, A. E. (2000) 'Resolving Uncertainty in R&D Portfolios', *Research-Technology Management*, **43**(6), 47–55.

10

ROADMAPPING

10.1 Introduction

Roadmapping is extensively used in industry and government to support strategy, innovation and policy. Motorola is widely credited with the development of the roadmapping approach in the 1970s to support integrated product/technology strategic planning (Willyard and McClees, 1987). Since then, the method has been adopted by many organizations in a wide range of sectors and for many purposes.

Bob Galvin (1998), who was CEO of Motorola during the period when roadmapping was established, provides the following definition:

> A 'roadmap' is an extended look at the future of a chosen field of inquiry composed from the collective knowledge and imagination of the brightest drivers of change in that field.

At the heart of the method is the use of simple graphical charts that provide an overview of strategy, in particular how various aspects of strategy are aligned. This concept is illustrated in Figure 10.1 (Phaal et al., 2004b), which is adapted from the approach developed by Philips in the 1990s (EIRMA, 1997; Groenveld, 1997).

The roadmap provides an integrating framework that summarizes at a high level (on one page) the various strategic elements that must be aligned to achieve the overall organizational goals. The roadmap provides a structure (a common visual language) that enables key stakeholders to articulate their perspectives and identify the key relationships and points of alignment. A major benefit of roadmapping is the communication associated with the development and dissemination of roadmaps.

10.2 Where and why it is used

Although early applications of roadmapping were in large technology-intensive organizations in the electronics, aerospace and defence sectors, the approach is flexible and has been adapted for many different purposes such as planning and strategy in many different sectors. The major issues that roadmapping can address include:

- Identification.
- Exploitation.
- Learning.

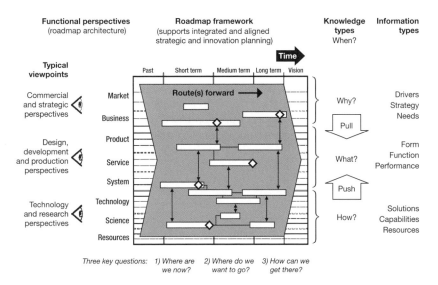

Figure 10.1   Schematic roadmap

The innovation process is often represented as a funnel, as shown in Figure 10.2, and a similar model can be applied to the strategy process. At the start (the 'fuzzy front end'), the process is divergent and exploratory, with the aim of identifying as many potential opportunities as possible and then assessing and filtering these down to those that show the most promise. The process is iterative, typically managed by a series of review points or stage-gates (see details in Chapter 12). The approach on the right-hand side of the funnel is very different – the focus is more on the implementation of innovations and strategic plans, where a tightly controlled, efficient process is appropriate.

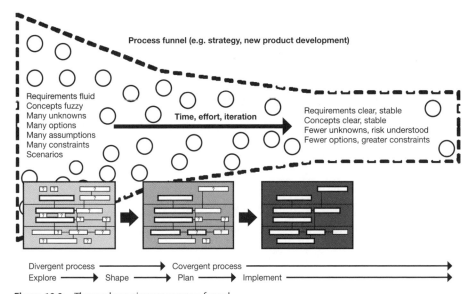

Figure 10.2   The roadmapping process as a funnel

Roadmapping can be applied throughout the funnel. At the front end, the method can be used to structure, capture and explore strategic issues, focusing and agreeing key actions to move forward. Later on, roadmapping has some similarities to project management such as Gantt charts, providing a high-level 'programme' view of a project, ensuring that the various activities are aligned.

The format of roadmaps, and the process for developing them, is different at the front and back ends of the process funnel. Workshop-based methods feature strongly at the start, while software often becomes necessary to manage the data associated with the roadmaps later on.

10.3 Process

Roadmapping as a process should not be divorced from the business processes (strategy, innovation, new product development and so on) that are supported by the development and deployment of roadmaps. The roadmapping process itself should be thought of as a simple systems-based organizing framework for enabling the capture, exploration, analysis, synthesis and reporting of strategic issues associated with the business process.

Garcia and Bray (1997) provide a description of the technology roadmapping process developed by Sandia National Laboratories in the USA, which is divided into three broad phases:

1 Preliminary activity.
2 Development of the technology roadmap.
3 Follow-up activity.

The preliminary activity consists of three separate steps:

1 Success factors should be considered at the start of the process, including the perceived need for roadmapping and collaborative development, and the input and participation of all relevant groups, for example functions, customers, suppliers, partners, government agencies and universities.
2 Committed leadership/sponsorship is needed from key decision makers and those involved in implementing the roadmap because of the effort required to develop a roadmap.
3 The context of the roadmap needs to be understood, including a definition of the vision for the organization, the aims of the roadmapping initiative, scope and boundaries, level of required detail and time frames.

The development of the technology roadmap phase has seven tasks/steps:

1 The product needs and focus should be agreed if buy-in is to be achieved and sustained. Garcia and Bray (1997) recommend the use of scenario planning if there is major uncertainty about the project needs.
2 Critical system requirements need to be defined, including time-based targets. These requirements relate to the functions and performance required from the product or system.

3 The major technology areas that can contribute to the critical product or system requirements need to be specified.

4 The product or system requirements and targets need to be translated into technology drivers and targets for the major technology areas. These are criteria that can be used to evaluate the benefits of the technology as a basis for differentiating the various options for selection purposes.

5 Technology alternatives need to be identified, which have the potential to respond to the technology drivers and achieve the targets.

6 The most attractive technologies need to be selected, which have the potential to achieve the desired targets. Various tools and techniques may be helpful during this step to support analysis and decision making, although expert judgement is often a key factor, benefiting from a collaborative process. The output from this step is the graphical representation that is the focal point of the roadmap document or report.

7 The information generated from the first six steps needs to be pulled together into an integrated report, including the graphical roadmap, description of each technology and its current status, critical risks and barriers, gaps and technical and implementation recommendations.

The follow-up activities include three steps:

1 The validation of the roadmap is needed. Development of the first (draft) version of the roadmap usually involves a relatively small group of key participants. Broader consultation is beneficial for validation purposes, to address key gaps identified and to build broader buy-in from those involved in or who influence its implementation.

2 The development of an implementation plan requires activities and projects to be planned, resourced, coordinated and managed.

3 The review and update step keeps the roadmap up to date in order to reflect changing circumstances and learning (Chapter 5). Typically, this will be linked to business processes such as strategy and new product development or as future events require.

Companies are different, in terms of sector, size, markets, products, technology, organizational structure, business, processes, culture, history and characteristics of individual people. Although there are similarities at a high level, including some well-established and widespread practices, there is great variety in terms of the specific way that business processes are deployed and the particular circumstances that companies find themselves in at any given point in time.

There are many textbooks and journal papers that provide guidance on innovation and strategic management. These sources can provide useful guidance and support when implementing roadmapping, which generally needs to be customized to fit the particular organizational context.

One example is shown in Figure 10.3, which shows a fairly generic strategic innovation process (EIRMA, 1997), combining both market pull and technology push aspects. In this example, the roadmapping creation is a single stage in the overall process. However, as highlighted in Figure 10.2, roadmapping can be used throughout the process, but applied in a different way at the 'front end' compared to the later stages.

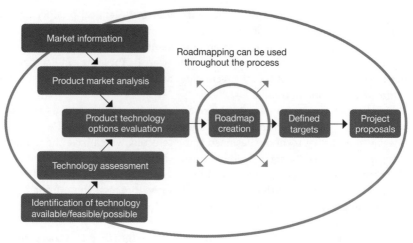

Figure 10.3 A sample strategic innovation process
Source: Based on EIRMA (1997).

Roadmapping is an inherently flexible technique, in terms of:

- The wide range of aims to which it can contribute.
- The time frame covered by the roadmap – past and future.
- The structure of the roadmap – layers and sublayers, which can be adapted to fit the particular application.
- The process that is followed to develop and maintain the roadmap(s).
- The graphical format that is selected to present information and communicate the roadmap.

However, this flexibility is subject to certain constraints, including the level of resources available and the need to integrate roadmapping with other systems, processes and management tools within the firm, for example the use of portfolio methods, balanced scorecard and stage-gates in the new product development process.

The key areas to consider when planning a roadmapping activity are:

- *Context*: the nature of the issue that triggered the interest in roadmapping needs to be explored, together with any constraints that will affect the approach adopted. Careful consideration should be given to establishing a clear business need and ownership, defining aims and scope, and identifying key people across the organization who should be involved.
- *Architecture*: the layout of the roadmap needs to be designed (see Figure 10.1), considering both time frame and structure, comprising layers and sublayers. The roadmap can be considered a 'dynamic systems framework', providing a structure within which the evolution of the system of interest can be mapped. Generally, this system relates to innovation, at the firm or sector level, where there is a need to align markets (know-why) with applications and processes (know-what) and technology and resources (know-how), over time (know-when). The roadmap framework provides a 'common language',

which supports communication between different communities, such as functions, technical disciplines or organizations.

- *Process*: this comprises the staged set of activities needed to build the roadmap content, make decisions, identify and agree actions and maintain the roadmap that is developed. Typically, the process will involve one or more workshops, for which the agenda needs to be designed to incorporate a logical set of facilitated activities, which can be combined in a flexible way to address the issues of interest.

Workshops are often a key element of a roadmapping process, particularly at the front end, bringing the various stakeholders together to share their knowledge and experience. Some typical workshop activities are shown in Figure 10.4, which emphasize how the use of simple structures and activities can enable strategic dialogue. The roadmap structure provides a framework to capture and organize knowledge, typically following a logic such as that expressed in Figure 10.3, drawing on experience from workshop participants, other key stakeholders and other available information sources. The process can start at various points on the roadmap (often trends and drivers, business strategy or vision), and then progressively populating the rest of the roadmap.

Roadmapping can be challenging because of the broad scope and complexity of the issues being addressed, uncertainties associated with the future and gaps in available knowledge. There are also a number of organizational challenges to address when implementing roadmapping activities, which are often high-profile initiatives. Key hurdles to consider as the process is implemented include:

- Initiating the process (taking the first step) – developing 'roadmap version 1.0', which is 'fit for purpose', for example clarifying the business context, pointing the way forward and enabling key decisions to be made.
- Ongoing maintenance of the first roadmap; if required, roadmapping can be used as a one-off problem-solving/decision-making tool.
- Rolling out the roadmapping process within an organization, either in an 'organic' fashion (community of practice) or, more formally, linked to key business process review points, such as budgeting or product development stage-gates.

Figure 10.4   Typical roadmapping workshop activities

The following success factors should be considered when embarking on a roadmapping initiative:

- Establish a clear business need.
- Ensure commitment from senior management.

- Plan carefully and customize the approach to suit your circumstances.
- Phase the process to ensure that benefits are delivered early.
- Ensure that the right people and functions are involved.
- Link the roadmapping activity to other business processes and tools.
- Provide adequate support and resources.
- Keep it simple.
- Iterate and learn from experience.

10.4 Roadmapping emerging technologies

The early stage of a technology development project is difficult to handle because of ingenious problems of exploring the value proposition and improving the design of the technology development project while reducing the risk. The approach called value roadmapping seems to offer a framework for supporting technology evaluation and valuation for emerging technologies (Dissel et al., 2009). In principle, the approach can also be used to support the business case for technology investment decisions, qualitatively and quantitatively (in financial terms), when the technology reaches a higher maturity level (assessed in terms of technology readiness level). Thus, the value roadmapping concept provides a consistent framework that can be used to link technological and commercial perspectives throughout the technology lifecycle.

The process is typically conducted as a workshop or a set of workshops with both technical and commercial people involved. The approach is based on eight process stages:

Define strategic framework, vision and scenario

In the first step, it is important to define the strategic framework/vision/scenario that governs the technology exploitation, including any overall assumptions, boundaries and constraints that apply. Step 1 is typically done in the preparation phase, before the value roadmap workshop takes place.

Map technology development and investment milestones

Participants at the workshop are asked to map the technology development project milestones and investment (current and future/potential), in terms of the technical capabilities that will be achieved at key milestones, together with any knowledge of competing and complementary technologies. The results are captured in the technology research and technology programs layer of the value roadmapping architecture.

Define value streams

The technology developments and opportunities identified in step 2 are used to put into the context (strategic framework, market pull and technology push) so that the potential value that may result from the technology investment can be explored (and potentially calculated). The goal is to identify specific sources of potential future revenue and value, articulated as clearly as possible. Participants are encouraged to forecast or estimate revenue/value for each opportunity. For estimating value, traditional methods (such as NPV) or some rough estimates might be used.

If opportunities are prioritized and value is estimated, the decision tree/options methods can be used to aggregate the various value contributions, including dependencies and estimates of likelihoods, to give a single financial measure of value. The goal is to identify as many value-generating opportunities as possible, after which it is necessary to cluster.

Map market and business trends and drivers

The participants are requested to map the market, the business trends and drivers that influence the prioritized value opportunities. These are typically social, economic, environmental, technological and political drivers, knowledge about potential customer needs and competitors as well as the milestones and goals of the technology. The results are mapped in the appropriate layer of the value roadmapping architecture.

Map barriers and enablers

This step maps the technical and non-technical barriers and enablers associated with developing and exploiting the technology. The map also includes the associated and complementary assets and actions that must be in place to achieve the aim of the roadmap.

Review project plan and value roadmapping

The technology development project plan is reviewed against the results of the roadmapping. The review typically focuses on the key strategic business drivers (e.g., using ROI or SWOT Strengths-Weaknesses-Opportunities-Threats analysis) of the respective firm. It is important to have these drivers defined by the decision makers. In some cases this is a technology council who makes the final investment decision. In other cases this can be the business unit director or board. By doing so, the key linkages between the elements of the value roadmapping are further enhanced and a common picture is created. The review can either be carried out as a part of the workshop or afterwards by the process owner and the responsible technology project managers supported by the facilitator. The outcome can, for example, be a (revised) business case or an 'elevator pitch'.

Present visualization

Complex projects' value roadmaps might be dense and fragmented, with gaps and data of varying quality. For those types of project, additional effort will be required to tidy up the roadmap. This detailed roadmap can be considered as a database, containing relevant information at a fairly high level of granularity and is unlikely to be very helpful in communicating key messages about the project and its value. Thus, communication roadmaps that might be in a presentable format need to be developed. For example, elevator pitch roadmaps or templates were found to be useful in condensing the road-map information. The value roadmapping can also provide a useful resource for 'what if' and sensitivity analyses and to assess the impact of events and new information on the plan as a whole.

Maintain value roadmapping as a process

The resulting roadmap and associated documentation should be maintained on an ongoing basis as part of a core business process (e.g. project management, new product development, research management and strategic planning/budgeting).

 Case studies

Roadmapping is a generic technique to be used for any TM activity. The case of Lucent Technologies, a large telecommunications firm, shows the use of roadmapping for new products at Lucent and how links are established with the company-level strategy and building selection capabilities (Chapter 7).

Lucent Technologies

Lucent has a complicated new product development process that is managed by roadmapping.

Figure 10.5 shows the overall roadmapping process, where a series of structured tem-plates guide the team through the process, ensuring that the key required information

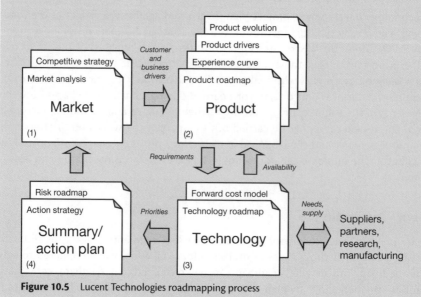

Figure 10.5   Lucent Technologies roadmapping process

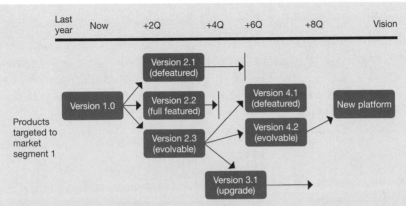

Figure 10.6 Lucent Technologies product roadmap

Source: Albright, R. E. and Kappel, T. A. (2003) 'Roadmapping in the Corporation', *Research-Technology Management*, **42**(2), 31–40.

is captured and summarized. The process starts with the market, considering both customers and competitors. This information, combined with inputs from the business strategy, drives the next step, which focuses on the product, including customer needs (requirements) and forecasts of product performance, leading to a product roadmap that sets out the key development phases (see Figure 10.6). Technology development must be considered in parallel, since product functionality and performance are closely linked to technological capability. Technology strategy is summarized in a technology roadmap (Figure 10.7), together with the associated costs, actions and risks.

The experience of Lucent Technologies highlights five key benefits from the process, focusing the team's thinking on the most important priorities at each step:

1 Linking strategy to product or technology plans, which are typically developed by different functional groups within the business.
2 Enabling corporate-level technology plans through the aggregation of product-level roadmaps.
3 Focusing on longer term planning by extending the planning horizon beyond strategy time frames.
4 Improving communication and ownership of plans through the joint development of integrated and aligned roadmaps.
5 Focusing planning on the highest priority topics by the use of structured visual representations of the various components of strategic planning.

Key Questions

1 What is roadmapping?
2 What are the advantages and disadvantages of roadmapping?
3 What is the process of roadmapping?

1. Bicycle company: Biko

Figure 10.7 below shows a roadmap developed by Biko, a traditional, but well-regarded, bicycle manufacturer with a strong brand and global manufacturing and distribution networks. Biko has just been acquired and its new owner has requested this technology roadmap to communicate Biko's business vision and strategic plan, as a basis for investment decisions.

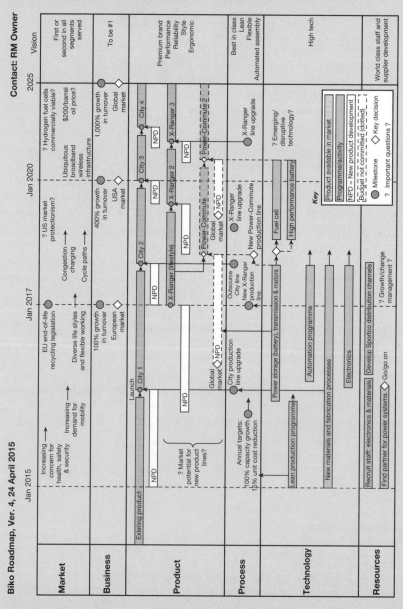

Figure 10.7 Biko's roadmap

Two key opportunities for product innovation have been identified: power-assisted bikes, typically for commuting; and high-performance 'lifestyle' bikes, such as mountain bikes. Roadmaps were produced for each of these options to explore how the existing product could be upgraded (in two years' time); the form a radical new product could take (in five years' time); and what a next generation product might look like (in ten years' time) – a product vision.

These product-level roadmaps were combined to create a business-level 'portfolio' roadmap (see Figure 10.7), showing how the existing product can provide a platform from which three distinct new product variants can be developed to serve different market segments: the robust 'City' bicycle range for general urban use, based directly on the current product; the 'X-Ranger' high-performance leisure bicycle, aimed at the affluent young professional; and the 'Power-Commute' power-assisted bicycle aimed at the growing professional urban commuting market.

With reference to the above roadmap, discuss:

a The meaning of each layer (market, business, etc.) of the roadmap.
b The critical links between layers, giving examples.
c Where the key strategic decision points are in the roadmap.
d What further information will be needed before investment decisions can be made with confidence.
e Discuss the relationship between roadmapping and innovation and business strategy processes in the firm and how roadmapping can support these.

Source: Center for Technology Management, University of Cambridge.

2. The Intelligent Transportation (ITS) Roadmap

Based on the information given below, try to build a technology roadmap for the Canadian government to build its ITS and discuss a strategy to follow.

The Vision: Canada becomes a key player in wireless backhaul systems for ITS by 2026. A 5% share of the world market is a reasonable goal. ITS should not be limited to highway systems – for example, Canada has a huge pipeline transportation system. The Strategy: Development of an integrated human resources response to exploit the product, technology and market drivers.

Product drivers

Passive Sensors – 2016–2019.
Risk Capital – 2019–2022.
Flexible Networks – 2019–2022.
Intelligent Sensors – 2018–2024.
Human Implant Sensors – 2018–2026.
Smart Cards – 2016–2019.

Market drivers

Personal Safety – 2016–2019.
Security of Information – 2016–2023.
Need for Real-Time Information – 2017–2024.
Aging Population – 2018–2026.
IP Compatibility – 2016–2019.

(Continued)

Technology drivers

Sensor Data Fusion – 2016–2024.
5G – 2019–2026.
Standards Know-How – 2018–2022.
Improved Battery Life – 2018–2023.
Nanotechnology (nano generators) – 2019–2025.
Encryption – 2018–2020.
Spectrum Limitations – 2021–2026.
Software Expertise – 2016–2023.

Response to drivers

- Encourage the formation of Canadian multinational enterprises in response to globalization. This will require improvements in our financing infrastructure, particularly in the availability of pools of Canadian buyout capital.
- Encourage collaboration between industry groups.
- Address software engineering. This is a global issue but Canadian policy makers should be aware of it.

Human resources issues

- Government monitors skills requirements and alerts industry and academia about impending shortages.
- A greater emphasis on soft skills development is recommended to deal with complex management systems which are in turn related to globalization.
- A greater emphasis on co-op programmes to accommodate the shift in corporate infrastructures brought about by globalization (for example large companies are not the training grounds they used to be).
- The processes involved in career selection should be better understood. Guidance counsellors play a critical role.

Key external factors

- Transfer of R&D and Manufacturing offshore.
- Globalization complicates the management of software development.

Source: http://www.ic.gc.ca/eic/site/trm-crt.nsf/eng/rm00259.html#return72 (Dates are fictitious)

 **Further reading**

Dissel, M., Phaal, R., Farrukh, C. J. and Probert, D. R. (2009) 'Value Roadmapping', *Research-Technology Management*, **52**(6), 45–55.
Phaal, R., Farrukh, C. J. and Probert, D. R. (2004) 'Customizing Roadmapping', *Research-Technology Management*, **47**(2), 26–37.

11

S-CURVE

11.1 Introduction

S-curves, also known as growth curves, have emerged from an analogy with biological life. S-curves illustrate the life cycle of a phenomenon that starts off slowly, grows rapidly, tapers or levels off and finally declines, as shown in Figure 11.1. The curve is used to describe many phenomena, including biological growth, demand for a new product and technology adoption rate (Rogers, 1995). The S-curve can be used as a strategic tool to understand the product, industry or technology life cycle. In the management literature, S-curves help to describe the invention, innovation, diffusion, growth and maturity phases of products/industries/technologies. The phases in the S-curve are labelled differently in the literature, although generally they refer to similar processes (Laroia and Krishnan, 2005). For example, in Figure 11.1, the S-curve phases are named as embryonic, growth, maturity and ageing. Each phase influences companies differently with respect to the capabilities and resources required to develop the innovation due to the differences in market conditions.

The specific application of S-curves in TM relies on the fact that the ultimate performances of all technical approaches are limited by physical laws. S-curves are defined at the industry level such that their y-axes represent increasing product performance and their x-axes represent the passage of time or the expenditure of engineering effort (Christensen, 1992). Thus, for a given technology, the S-curve defines the relative productivity of exploration or exploitation efforts.

When knowledge about the technology accumulates and the technology reaches a wide adoption phase, the growth rate in performance increases exponentially. This lasts until the maturity phase, where physical barriers make further development costly or sometimes even impossible. Then, a disruptive technology emerges with a new S-curve, replacing the old one (Christensen, 1997). In any industry facing a transition from one technology S-curve to another, or facing a rapid and continual series of technological changes, successfully managing transitions from one technology to another is crucial. Therefore, technology S-curves are fundamental in forming technology strategies.

Plotting S-curves for technologies at hand or for those seen as prospective areas for the company can help with the 'go' or 'no-go' decisions, help to adjust R&D budgets and timing and improve understanding of the competition at component and architectural level. However, it should also be noted that S-curves are usually a descriptive rather than a prescriptive tool (Christensen, 1992).

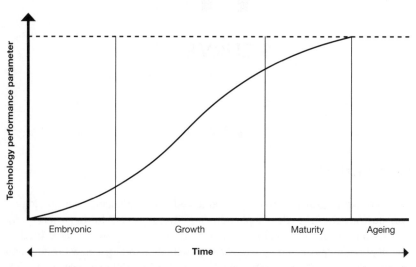

Figure 11.1 Typical S-curve

11.2 Where and why it is used

S-curves are used in a variety of ways, ranging from finding the growth of tumours in medicine to population growth in ecology (Rogers, 1995). In terms of TM, using S-curves offers the following key benefits:

- Acquisition.
- Exploitation.
- Identification.

In terms of acquisition, the analysis of S-curves shows managers where their technologies stand in the curve and how they should invest in technologies over time. If the technology in hand is mature and in decline, managers can decide to terminate all R&D in this area. Alternatively, an emerging technology can be identified and technology investments can be made in that field with a lower risk of failure. S-curves show the importance of technologies in a life cycle concept – the entire life cycle of a product/technology from its conception, through design and manufacture, to service and disposal (Bevilacqua et al., 2007). Thus, the use of S-curves might form the base of acquisition decisions along the product/technology lifetime, as discussed in Chapter 2.

The S-curve is helpful for exploitation capabilities (Chapter 3) since it maps growth of revenue or productivity against time. In the early stage of a particular innovation, growth is relatively slow as the new product establishes itself. At some point, customers begin to demand the product and product growth increases more rapidly. New incremental innovations or changes to the product allow growth to continue. Towards the end of its life cycle, growth slows and may even begin to decline. In the later stages, no amount of new investment in that product will yield a normal rate of return, so new approaches need to be tested such as focusing on user innovations (Gofman and Moskowitz, 2009). This is why the S-curve is used to analyse the status of the company's products and services within its market so the firm can react more quickly to growing or new markets. By observing changes in the life cycle of products, firms can easily plan component technology changes and utilize their products to gain high profits. In addition, S-curves help firms to analyse the adoption rate of new technologies, so they can organize launching and marketing activities of their products.

S-curves can highlight the threats in exploitation as well. In the growth stage, if strong patents do not exist to protect the innovating company's first mover advantage, new entrants may come into the market with architectural innovations and can profit significantly from a rapidly growing technology. This is called the 'innovator's dilemma' (Christensen, 1997). Managers should invest in protection and build enough complementary assets to survive in such competitive environments.

Another threat in exploitation might be the diluted concept of technology where new technology firms try to reduce their risks by increasing technology applications. But due to their limited resources, they cannot develop and launch a product that satisfies a wide variety of customers. This results in a 'chasm', where firms cannot reach a wide customer base with high revenues in order to continue their existence. In fact, the great majority of innovations never move off the bottom of the curve and never produce normal returns, widely known as the problem of 'crossing the chasm' (Moore, 1991).

The S-curve is further used to identify and forecast technologies, the core activity for identification mentioned in Chapter 4 (Martino, 1983). The S-curve is also used to identify the future trends of its existing technologies as well as new technologies that might become critical for the company. These S-curves can be used to gain insight into the relative payoff of investment in competing new technologies, as well as providing some insight into when and why some technologies overtake others in the race for dominance. For example, S-curve analysis is used for renewable energies and the findings indicate that wind energy and geothermal energy are poised to become more economical than fossil fuels within a relatively short time frame; R&D for wind and geothermal technologies has been underfunded by national governments relative to funding for solar technologies; and government funding of fossil fuel technologies might be excessive, given the diminishing performance of those technologies (Schilling and Esmundo, 2009). Sometimes life cycles move more quickly and sometimes they evolve more slowly. In faster cases, the reasons might be a competitor introducing a new technology to the market or a change in the technology in the market. By identifying technologies and their development times, managers can take the necessary actions.

According to Fichman and Kemerer (1995), the major advantages of using S-curves are:

- Evaluating the different stages of a technology.
- Pointing out the importance of being ready for technological discontinuities highlighting the importance of strategic positioning in case of a decline in gains.
- Giving the company the opportunity to be the first mover within a market.

The semiconductor industry is one of the best examples for showing how the S-curve was used for acquisition and identification purposes. From its inception in 1960, this industry has been driven by economics, speed and reliability to create chips with increasingly high functionality (Bowden, 2004). Building more functionality in a limited area involved improving the fabrication process, as well as keeping costs down and maintaining quality. The improved fabrication process allowed smaller transistors on the chip, increasing the overall speed and taking the cost of each transistor down. Since the production of transistors began, the number of transistors on a chip has doubled on average every 18 months. In

1965, this phenomenon was predicted by Gordon Moore and became known as 'Moore's law'. This law is believed to create a self-fulfilling prophecy for companies to double their transistor count in 18–24 months.

However, it is necessary to be cautious in using S-curves, since, according to Christensen (1992):

- The S-curve does not provide suggestions on how strategists should react to discontinuities in their technology.
- The advantage to be gained from new technologies cannot be quantified by the model.
- It is hard to conclude when to invest in new, and dispose of current, R&D.
- The S-curve does not reveal how the new technology could be foreseen by others or by whom it will be introduced.
- S-curves might not reflect the dynamic product or market changes.

The biggest shortcoming of the S-curve is its masking effect. A certain product or technology is often composed of many sub-technologies, going back to the simplest physical and chemical rules (Christensen, 1992; Bowden, 2004). Although the slope of performance-increase rate can be observed as declining in a certain technology, it does not mean this technology will eventually move into the mature phase. If one of the underlying technologies is improved or replaced, the overall product or technology may again move into a growth phase. It is important to analyse the S-curve thoroughly before deciding whether to invest in component technologies or evolve the current design through architectural change (Bowden, 2004; Debo et al., 2006).

11.3 Process

Drawing and using S-curves requires three main steps:

1 Longitudinal data collection on the basis of a performance metric.
2 Observing the evolution and plotting the curve.
3 Using the resulting curve for decision making.

After deciding on a performance metric, longitudinal data need to be collected for that particular performance dimension. The performance metric might change over time but it is necessary to choose the most appropriate and measurable criterion. For example, the speed of passenger aeroplanes was a widely used metric in S-curves, but it was replaced by fuel economy after all aeroplanes reached a certain speed. Furthermore, other metrics, like number of patents, level of overall research or profitability, can also be used in S-curve analysis, but none of these can give as accurate results as standard, easily observable performance metrics.

For mature technologies, it is easy to fit data into a curve. However, for those emerging technologies, it is necessary to make some assumptions and use forecasting techniques to draw a potential S-curve as a proxy and update that curve whenever data become available.

Once a curve is drawn, the evolution of technology can be predicted by making assumptions based on the stage of the technology in hand. For this analysis, different approaches can be used, depending on what decision is to be taken, such as buying a technology or identifying when to dispose of a technology.

To illustrate how S-curve analysis might be used for decision making, the model developed by Abernathy and Utterback (1978) will be briefly introduced. According to their model, the stages of the S-curve are named as fluid, transient and specific. In addition, product innovation, process innovation, competitive environment and organizational structure are closely linked together. All decisions are made on the basis of these links.

In the fluid phase, corresponding to the embryonic period, a high degree of experimentation takes place. Technological and market uncertainties exist. The manufacturing process relies on high-skilled labour and general purpose equipment. The major threats come from the old technology itself and the entrance of new firms. A company might follow different strategies. For example, it might attempt to compete with its competitors by making agreements with distributors and marketing investments to influence customers' perceptions.

In the transition period, growth starts. Producers start to learn more about the technology application and customers' needs. Thus, some standardization emerges. Acceptance of the innovation starts to increase and the market starts growing. The convergence pattern will lead to the appearance of a product design whose main components and underlying core characteristics do not vary from one model to another, called 'dominant design'. Firms in this phase will use strategies to consolidate their product positioning and start increasing production capacity and process innovation.

Although being the first firm in the market is expected to be profitable, in some cases the followers gain profits. One such example is the Betamax case, in which Sony was outclassed by JVC, who entered the market later, but JVC identified a customer need for longer play/record time and made a small change to the product (Cusumano et al., 1992). If the company does not have sufficient resources to mass produce or market the technology, the beginning of this transition phase is the most efficient time to sell the technology.

In the specific phase, the combination of growth and maturity stages, competition shifts from differentiation to product performance and costs. Companies now have a clear picture of market segments and might therefore concentrate on serving specific customers. Manufacturing uses highly specialized equipment and the bargaining power of suppliers and customers will increase. As a consequence, firms are able to secure their position through supplier relations, distribution channels and other complementary assets that will create barriers to firms planning to enter the market.

11.4 Managing IP through life cycle

Technology life cycle might be used in a number of ways ranging from strategy to protection. A study offers management of IP according to the phases of technology life cycle: emerging, growth, maturity and decline (Cao and Zhao, 2011). This is because each phase has its own characteristics in terms of cost, market risks, technology understanding/knowledge, market stability and standardization. Depending on these features, managers might make decisions about how to protect their technologies that are discussed in Chapter 6.

In the emerging period, the number of patent filings is relatively low and slowly increasing. The main task of a manager is to prevent the diffusion of information and materials related to the company's core technology from being revealed to the public or competitors. In the case of open innovation, a team involving researchers and patent attorneys should decide on IP strategy for all partners at the outset of the project. Meanwhile, the company should underwrite a confidential agreement with the employee who can get the core technology information and materials. Once the technology under development becomes successful, managers protect these achievements by aggressively patenting.

In the growth stage, innovations are made and the dominant technology emerges. If the company's technology has not won, the company might either withdraw from the industry or shift over to the dominant design. For the winning technology, proper IP management methods are acquired at this specific critical stage before project findings are made public. At the same time, employees who developed the technology should be rewarded. If the patent or technology does not relate to the company's core business model, or if the company lacks the ability to launch the products to the market, the company which owns the dominant technology might choose to license or sell the patent and/or technology to other companies. No matter which company commercializes the dominant technology, the technology tends to mature and standards are formed during this stage.

In the maturity phase, it is difficult for dominant companies to gain a long-term lead in technology R&D. Technology begins to diffuse on a large scale during this period. Managers might develop standards, license or cross-license, and technology transfer. At the final stage, it is in the decline period where the technology cannot produce much more profit from the original market. The legal protection of some patents may expire. New technology may outperform the old, rendering the old partially or possibly totally obsolete. The company might quit the current market by transferring the technology to other companies who think that this technology is still serviceable in the market of their districts or countries.

Case study

The latecomer firms in developing countries follow different paths to advance their technological and economic growth. These firms not only move from the back end to the front end of the value chain, but they also move from peripheral parts to core technologies and core components. An evolutionary model developed by Ouyang (2010) investigates the technological development with the S-curve analysis. The model is composed of five phases: trading and/or assembling, manufacturing under licensing/contracts, independent manufacturing, independent design and development and innovation. In each phase, different capabilities are targeted and built. When a latecomer country moves from one phase to another, firms in that country expand and upgrade their capabilities.

The existence of the dynamic S-curve does not mean that the move to the next phase is automatic and inevitable. Actually, there are several important chasms/gaps in the evolution that an imitator has to cross in order to become an innovator on technological frontiers, as shown in Figure 11.2:

- Chasm I – the chasm of licensed manufacturing.
- Chasm II – the chasm of independent manufacturing.
- Chasm III – the chasm of independent development.
- Chasm IV – the chasm of innovation.

These chasms may vary in width and challenges, and crossing these chasms may require different facilitators.

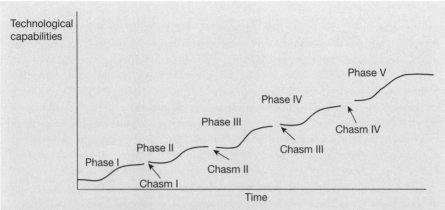

Figure 11.2 Dynamic imitator-to-innovator S-curve chasms

There are three types of factor that affect whether a latecomer firm can cross these chasms and move to the next phase: firm-level, industry-level and national-level. Firm-level factors include absorptive capacity, leader's ambition, commitment to R&D and tolerance of risk and change, available resources and cross-function cooperation and coordination. Their role changes as the latecomer firms move up the S-curve. Crossing the first two chasms depends on how well firms can identify, interpret and assimilate both the explicit and tacit knowledge (i.e. their absorptive capacity). During these early chasms, latecomer firms have little industry and technology knowledge and they rely on clients and licensing for technologies and industry knowledge. In addition, the technology and market risks and uncertainties are lower, thus the importance of financial resources and development capacity is relatively low. However, the chasms become wider and uncertainties become greater when the firm moves up the technological capability curve.

The following example shows how a firm might cross chasms. In the 1980s, Hyundai Motor Company made cars with outdated engine technologies. Hyundai wanted to get licences for the latest technologies from Mitsubishi and other leading carmakers, but they did not sell their technologies. Thus, in 1984 Hyundai established the Advanced Engineering and Research Institute in order to develop the modern engines on its own. Then, in 1986, it opened the Hyundai Technical Center in the US and in Germany to monitor the technological development in the auto industry in the advanced countries. Hyundai also increased its R&D staff significantly, reaching close to 10% of its workforce. After hundreds of engine design changes and breakdowns of engine prototypes, Hyundai management developed the alpha engine in 1992, which outperformed comparable Japanese models.

At the industry level, there are at least two factors affecting the latecomer firms' efforts in crossing the chasms: the competition level and the existence of highly segmented markets. For example, two years after Huawei started importing and selling telephone switches, more than 2,000 firms entered the market. The price competition and increasingly thin margin forced Huawei to exit and move into a new industry: manufacturing of telephones. High competition may be an important driver to push firms across the first chasm, however in the following three phases, too fierce competition and the consequent low margin may not generate an opportunity. This is because firms will need a significant amount of resources to cross the following chasms and this could be hard to generate in low-margin businesses. When there are a large number of customers who want to pay reasonable prices, latecomer firms might accumulate resources for R&D and help them cross the final two chasms.

At the national level, government plays a key role for latecomer firms. In the first two phases, latecomer firms are either assemblers or contract manufacturers. Their clients and market are stable and their technologies are simple and ready to use. Moreover, they are under the guidance of multinational firms, so the government's role is not essential. When it comes to operating in the final two phases and crossing the final two chasms, the latecomer firms face enormous challenges in resources, technologies and market competition. Government assistance becomes important to help them accumulate resources and improve their development capability. This may facilitate their crossing the final two chasms, becoming independent designers, developers and innovators.

Overall, the imitator-to-innovator transition demonstrates some features of the development of capabilities. The transition is cumulative and evolutionary. As capabilities in the later phases are built upon those gained in previous phases, it may take some latecomer firms less time to build some higher-order capabilities. For example, Samsung Electronics spent almost nine years learning how to fabricate 64K DRAM with the help of Micron, whereas it took Samsung Electronics only two years to develop and fabricate 1M DRAM independently.

As a final note, the move to the next phase is not automatic and linear. Although a small number of East Asian firms were successful in making the transition from imitator to innovator, many others failed and retreated to OEM. Thus, if latecomer firms want to become successful, they need to cross the four chasms and transform themselves from imitation to innovation.

Source: Ouyang, H. S. (2010) 'Imitator-to-Innovator S Curve and Chasms', *Thunderbird International Business Review*, **52**(1), 31–45.

 Key Questions

1 What is an S-curve?
2 What are the advantages and disadvantages of the S-curve?
3 What is the process of the S-curve?

Exercise

1. Trends company

As the marketing manager of Trends, a developer of website development software and designer of custom web pages, you have been charged with the responsibility of forecasting the growth of the Web and the consequent market potential for your products. You have obtained information regarding the growth of the Web over the past several years as shown in Table 11.1. This information has been happily received within Trends since, as the president put it, 'the upside potential for growth appears unlimited'. You, however, are more skeptical. Consequently, you decide to try to get a handle on the limits to growth of the Web.

Part A. First, forecast the growth of the Web assuming that its growth is linear. Assume that this constant (linear) growth continues into the future. How many websites do you forecast for January 2020? January 2025? Do you believe that this forecast is credible?

Part B. The Web appears to be growing exponentially. Forecast the future growth of the Web if its exponential growth continues. How many websites do you forecast for January 2020? January 2025? Do you believe that this forecast is credible? When will the number of websites equal the population of the earth (say ten billion)?

Part C. You are confident that the upside potential of the Web is not in fact unlimited, and that the number of sites will level off at some point. You consequently determine to model the growth of websites as a logistic function. How many websites do you forecast for January 2020? January 2025? Do you believe that this forecast is credible? What maximum number of web hosts do you forecast? In what year will the total number of websites equal 99% of this maximum?

Table 11.1 The number of websites

Year	Websites* launched
2013	672,985,183
2012	697,089,489
2011	346,004,403
2010	206,956,723
2009	238,027,855
2008	172,338,726
2007	121,892,559
2006	85,507,314
2005	64,780,617
2004	51,611,646
2003	40,912,332
2002	38,760,373
2001	29,254,370
2000	17,087,182
1999	3,177,453
1998	2,410,067
1997	1,117,255
1996	257,601
1995	23,500
1994	2,738
1993	130
1992	10
1991	1

Source: NetCraft and Internet Live Stats.

Based on http://www.internetlivestats.com/total-number-of-websites/ and http://web.archive.org/web/20010307224515/http://bus.colorado.edu/faculty/lawrence/TOOLS/SCurve/scurve.htm

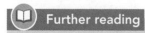
Further reading

Cao, Y. and Zhao, L. (2011) 'Intellectual Property Management Model in Enterprises: A Technology Life Cycle Perspective', *International Journal of Innovation and Technology Management*, **8**(2), 253–272.

Chen, C.-J., Huang, Y.-F. and Lin, B.-W. (2012) 'How Firms Innovate through R&D Internationalization? An S-curve Hypothesis', *Research Policy*, **41**(9), 1544–1554.

Foster, R. (1986) *Innovation: The Attacker's Advantage* (New York: Summit Books).

Hacklin, F., Raurich, V. and Marxt, C. (2005) 'Implications of Technological Convergence on Innovation Trajectories: The Case of ICT Industry', *International Journal of Innovation and Technology Management*, **2**(3), 313–330.

Ouyang, H. S. (2010) 'Imitator-to-Innovator S Curve and Chasms', *Thunderbird International Business Review*, **52**(1), 31–45.

Taylor, M. and Taylor, A. (2012) 'The Technology Life Cycle: Conceptualization and Managerial Implications', *International Journal of Production Economics*, **140**(1), 541–553.

12

STAGE-GATE

12.1 Introduction

Intense competition has forced companies to launch more new products in a shorter period of time but achieving a successful product/service is not an easy goal. According to a study by Cooper and Edgett (2006), 25% of commercialized projects succeed, while 33% of all launched new products fail. Thus, the need for improved product/service development initiated a search for appropriate development techniques. Since market conditions are changing rapidly as well as the technology used, traditional management systems fail in managing these projects. The Stage-Gate® system,[1] which was proposed by Cooper in the late 1980s, is a project management tool for new product development (Cooper, 1988, 1990). After the introduction of the method and wide usage in new product development by companies such as P&G, it has been extended and used in process technology development by companies such as Exxon and Eastman Chemicals (Cooper, 2008).

In this system, a new product idea goes through stages and gates before the decision to launch is made. Stages consist of the activities to gather knowledge and obtain information about the new product idea. Each stage is cross-functional, necessitating more than one department working on the project idea at each stage. After each stage, the idea passes through a gate, where the critical decision of whether to abandon or continue the project is made utilizing the information created at the previous stage. There are three common elements for each gate; inputs, criteria and outputs:

- *Inputs* are the information and analysis made at the previous stage.
- *Criteria* for qualitative and quantitative attributes depend on the gate number, although financial criteria become more crucial as the project moves towards completion.
- *Outputs* at gates are decisions made about the project idea, which can be 'go', 'kill', 'recycle' or 'hold'.

Additionally, operational and marketing plans and prioritization levels are the other outputs at the gates.

The stage-gate method maps the necessary actions of each stage as well as the essential goals of the stage. At each stage, decisions will be made regarding the criteria in production, marketing, finance and technology (Buggie, 2002; Rocque and Viali, 2004). Besides 'go' and 'no go', a third option is postponing the gate decision until the required actions are taken. The essential part is that collaborative work is required throughout the whole method since the decision-making process requires the participation of different stakeholders, while the tasks of each stage should be performed by cross-functional teams.

12.2 Where and why it is used

Although the stage-gate process was initially proposed for new product development and has been claimed to be the most important discovery in this area, it can be used in any kind of investment and research project as a structured decision-making tool, which takes into account different perspectives and stakeholders (Buggie, 2002). The method has been implemented by 80% of North American companies to manage the new product/service/process development process (Cooper, 2008).

The main goal of the framework is to reduce the costs and time while increasing the effectiveness of projects (Cooper and Edgett, 2006). Since most of the new product/service/process development projects fail, a no-go decision before the launch saves a lot of money and effort, while enabling employees to focus on a better project instead of the killed one.

Further, case studies prove that the stage-gate method offers many benefits (Cooper 1990, 2008):

- Reduces time to market.
- Reduces project risks and losses by the evaluations made after each stage.
- Sustains structured project management.
- Enables structured decision making about diversified criteria.
- Leverages the participation of different stakeholders and cross-functional teams.
- Includes different perspectives by means of the criteria that should be considered after each milestone.
- Monitors and evaluates IP throughout the stages.
- Improves resource allocation.
- Guides project funding by use of the gates.

The major criticism is its inflexibility.

All these benefits indicate why the stage-gate method is useful for project management tasks embedded in all TM activities, but it is particularly critical for:

- Identification.
- Protection.
- Selection.

12.3 Process

The stage-gate process defines all the activities that should be completed in order to succeed. According to Cooper (1988), there are 13 critical product innovation activities that should be managed, directed and controlled so as to be able to develop a new product successfully. These activities are:

- Initial screening.
- Preliminary market assessment.
- Preliminary technical assessment.
- Detailed market study/marketing research.
- Business/financial analysis.

- Product development.
- In-house product testing.
- Customer tests of products.
- Test market/trial sell.
- Trial production.
- Pre-commercialization business analysis.
- Production start-up.
- Market launch.

Most of the time, new product/service development efforts lack one or some of these critical activities, leading to inefficient product innovation trials. Therefore, Cooper (2008) developed the Stage-Gate system®, a methodology that could be utilized to ensure that all critical activities are applied in the new product development process. He also emphasizes that this system is applicable to services and thus he uses the term 'product' as an umbrella term.

In a typical stage-gate system, there are five gates and five stages:

1 Idea screening (gate) – scoping (stage).
2 Second screen (gate) – building business cases (stage).
3 Go to development (gate) – development (stage).
4 Go to testing (gate) – test/validation (stage).
5 Go to launch (gate) – launch (stage).

Idea generation is the first step of the process and consists of the new project idea proposed by the employees. Generally, anybody in the organization may propose a new project and should be encouraged to do so. In some cases, the idea proposals may be reviewed by an 'early committee' before passing the proposals to the first gate committee.

Gate 1   *Idea screening*: this includes criteria focused on the customers/market size, technological and economical feasibility, dependent on cost analysis.

Stage 1   *Scoping* is performed for the projects that pass through the idea screening gate. Initial marketing surveys are performed and the problem statement is prepared as well as the technical and business requirements and their respective budgets.

Gate 2   *Second screen*: includes criteria from three perspectives – strategic fit, market attractiveness and technological edge. Not all the criteria are 'must-conform' criteria, but at least one of them should be.

Stage 2   *Build business case* is where the project is assigned to a project manager. The problem statement and the requirements are developed to include more detail, the initial design is determined as well as the approach. As an input for the third gate, a cost–benefit analysis is performed depending on the cost estimates.

Gate 3   *Go to development*: here the project is approved for the development of detailed plans. Again, three key perspectives are used in evaluation. The competitive edge of the project, required business commitments and the clarification of the goals and tasks are evaluated in order to advance.

Stage 3   *Development* includes the activities performed to prepare detailed planning, investigation and finding an early customer.

Gate 4   *Go to testing*: here the project is evaluated considering the availability of an early customer and the quality of the system.

Stage 4   *Testing and validation* consists of all the internal tests for the pilot system/ product and the trials performed by the early customers. Any problems should be solved in order to pass the last gate. Thus, a cyclic procedure is performed here until the problems are resolved.

Gate 5   *Go to launch*: this is the last gate, where the launch of the new project/product is decided on. Two main concerns are whether the projects are profitable and the problems have been resolved.

Stage 5   *Launch* is the final stage where full-scale production is performed and the product/project is commercialized.

A post-launch review is performed to decide whether to continue expanding the opportunities to increase profitability, market share and competitiveness.

Although the stage-gate process is defined as a five-stage process for large-scale projects, the case studies revealed that, for smaller projects, this number of stages and gates results in inefficiency. Therefore, the stages can be merged depending on the scale of the project. For example, the development stage can be merged with the testing and validation stage for a product improvement if the scope is not very broad (Cooper, 2008). Further, it is important to note that for a stage-gate application, each firm is required to generate its own version of the system according to firm and industry needs. In fact, there are many firms that have been applying modified versions of the Stage-Gate® system proposed by Cooper et al. (2002). For example, Bombardier Aerospace Group has implemented a stage-gate model of seven phases, while Rolls-Royce has implemented the same system with only four phases (Philips et al., 1999).

12.4 Next generation stage-gate models

As the creator of the Stage-Gate® process, Cooper (2014) offers a new expanded version of his idea-to-launch system. He revises his traditional model to include three distinct features: adaptive, agile and accelerated. He argues these new features allow the process to be applicable to any context of projects and companies.

The open innovation practices and heightened customer involvement force the next-generation idea-to-launch system to be more adaptive. This can be done through a series of build-test-revise iterations. The product may be less than 50% defined when it enters development, but it evolves, adapting to new information as it moves through development and testing. The system is also flexible in so far as the actions for each stage and the deliverables to each gate are unique to each development project, based on the context of the market and the needs of the development process. This is the opposite of the standard approach to product development, which prescribes standardized actions and deliverables. There are also fast-track versions of the process for lower-risk projects. Additionally, a risk-based contingency model dictates that appropriate activities and deliverables be determined based on an assessment of project assumptions and risks. Finally, go/kill criteria become flexible with no standard sets or universal criteria for each gate. In this new model, gates are integrated with portfolio management.

The next-generation system incorporates elements of agility. For example, the deliverable is something that can be demonstrated to the stakeholders rather than it being documented only. Equally, these new systems emphasize moving quickly from milestone to milestone and rely on a much leaner system with all waste removed thanks to no bureaucracy. As a final feature, the new stage-gate system is capable of acceleration. Projects in the system are properly resourced, especially major projects, and fully staffed by a dedicated cross-functional team for maximum speed to market. Activities within stages overlap, and even stages themselves overlap. There is more emphasis on the fuzzy front end in order to identify key unknowns, risks and uncertainties as early as possible. Finally, IT support is provided to reduce work, provide better communication and accelerate the process.

In addition to Cooper's suggestions, one study (Hutchins and Muller, 2012) offers a way of accommodating innovative projects into the stage-gate model. One critique on the stage-gate process is associated with unintended consequences that inhibit innovation. It is observed that in some firms, the stage-gate process confers too much certainty on initial investment presumptions. Most critical information about the nature of the opportunity is presumed to be known or can easily be learned. This approach to innovation fails to promote the advantageous surprises and sometimes disruptive discoveries that produce genuine breakthrough opportunities.

To overcome this critique and to revitalize the new stage-gate, Hutchins and Muller (2012) offer five suggestions to revitalize the stage-gate process: (1) Make all assumptions explicit and then test and adjust; (2) Allow for divergence in order to explore new possibilities; (3) Build the project plan around the opportunity, not vice versa; (4) Evaluate projects according to metrics and learning objectives; and (5) Broaden the decision set used after the assessment of projects while they cross the gates. Regarding the criteria, there are four new decisions to make at gates. The first one is to decide on 'recycle' where a venture is re-directed towards a new opportunity, if learning suggests the original concept is not viable. The second decision could be to 'spin in' so that the venture is folded into an existing business if the target market is not sufficiently different or large to warrant a stand-alone business. The third one is deciding on 'salvaging', meaning that a venture is broken up and key elements, such as patents, processes, technology or relationships are harvested for use elsewhere in the company. The final decision might be 'direct spinning off' or 'licensing'. Ventures that differ radically from the core business may be sold to other companies.

 Case study

In stage-gate applications, most of the implementation problems occur at the front end of the methodology, where the analysis and gate criteria are more qualitative than quantitative. The cases of AlliedSignal and Alcoa provide good examples, showing that front-end innovation phases are seen as fuzzy and inefficiently managed. Smith, Herbein and Morris, authors of the following case, have work experience in AlliedSignal and Alcoa, so they summarized what they learned from the model which they developed and used in these two companies in order to manage front-end innovation.

(Continued)

AlliedSignal and Alcoa

According to Smith et al. (1999), at the front-end innovation stages of ideation and concept development, it is critical to employ a 'fast failure' mechanism. They developed the 'front-end innovation process' (FEIP), which has its roots in some principles of lean manufacturing and Six Sigma approaches and uses statistical measurements.

At AlliedSignal (which was an aerospace, automotive and engineering company that acquired and merged with Honeywell for $15 billion in 1999, after which the new group adopted the Honeywell name) and Alcoa (the world's third largest producer of aluminium, behind Rio Tinto Alcan and Rusal), the idea generation step was not well defined and structured. Smith et al. highlight that benchmarking across US firms of the front-end innovation process has confirmed that out of 30,000 ideas, only 125 had been formally reported and only one idea (on average) succeeded. The FEIP model (Figure 12.1) was applied first at AlliedSignal and then at Alcoa.

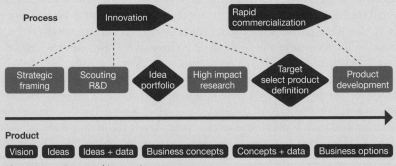

Figure 12.1 Front-end innovation process

The goal of the idea generation process is to create an idea portfolio considering the strategic frame and based on statistical data, eliminating those ideas that are more likely to fail.

The strategic frame is formed regarding the technological properties of the company and the environmental factors of technology. The most important elements in strategic framing are:

- Identification of technological trends in the markets.
- Knowledge of developments in science related to the core activities of the company.
- Observation of competitors with respect to their patents and long-term strategies.
- Technological SWOT analysis of the company.

The next step after strategic framing is defining the options. In order to detect flawed ideas in a shorter period of time and continue with the remaining options, several criteria and activities are defined, which are summarized in Table 12.1.

Table 12.1   Stage criteria for idea generation

Stage criteria	Process
Innovative technical vision	Allocation of approximately $2–5m initially
Potential for proprietary position	Fund projects based on competitive peer review or use small oversight technical board
Responsiveness to market trends	Immediate, responsive process with proposal submission and funding at any time, not constrained by budget cycles
Team composition and qualifications	Feedback to proposer within two weeks and start-up shortly thereafter
Literature and/or market research	Aim to rapidly support idea evaluation rather than criticize/defer
Risk/reward assessment – potential for $100m annual sales	Use metrics to drive speed, quality and success rate
Anticipated speed of execution	Specifically reward fast failures to emphasize process orientation

To execute FEIP as a fast failure mechanism, all new ideas are forbidden for the technical people, to make them focus only on the front-end activities and work at a rapid pace. The success of the FEIP model is the principle of quick idea evaluation – being aware that the vast majority of ideas would be unsuccessful.

The critical phases of the front-end process are stated as idea portfolio and target selection gates, as they are the key decision points. The scouting R&D/define-options stage becomes the focus of attention and control. Typical metrics utilized at this stage are shown in Figure 12.2.

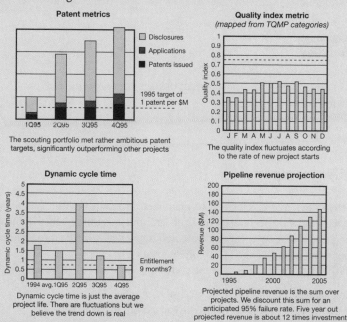

Figure 12.2   Typical metrics used for the 'define-options' stage of FEIP at AlliedSignal

(Continued)

The remaining steps of the stage-gate process are applied, as defined in the generic model. Integration of the FEIP to the remaining process is illustrated in Figure 12.3.

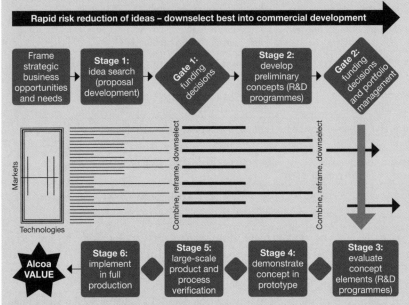

Figure 12.3 The stage-gate process at Alcoa

Source: Smith et al. (1999) 'Front-end Innovation at AlliedSignal and Alcoa', *Research-Technology Management*, **42**(6), 15–24.

Key Questions

1 What are stage-gates?
2 What are the advantages and disadvantages of stage-gate processes?
3 What is the stage-gate process?

Exercises

1. Wish coffee company

A coffee company called "Wish" is looking to manufacture a coffee maker that allows for one-cup processing with no filters; cup-sized grounds are utilized that come in individual serving sizes and a water carafe connected to the coffee maker must be kept full so the coffee maker is ready to go at a moment's notice.

Please sketch the stage-gate analysis for the coffee maker:

● How many stage-gates should Wish have? Please name them.
● What will be the tasks/activities needed to be carried out in each stage?
● What should be the decision criteria at each gate?

Consider that Wish plans to produce a new coffee maker product.

● Should the company change its stage-gate process? Why or why not? Discuss your reasoning for your answer.

Source: Adapted from http://www.brighthubpm.com/methods-strategies/92377-examples-of-the-stage-gate-process/

2. Local company

The Kellogg Company has three versions of its K-Way innovation process: the regular five-stage process to handle new products, a lighter three-stage process for smaller projects and a three-stage process to handle technology developments such as new science or invention projects. Based on this, consider possibilities of stage-gate processes in a small local company you know and discuss the applicability of different versions according to the company context. Please draw a hypothetical process and describe the tasks to be carried out at each stage based on your assumptions.

Note

1 Stage-Gate® is a registered trademark of the Product Development Institute Inc.

  Further reading

Cooper, R. G. (2001) *Winning at New Products: Accelerating the Process from Idea to Launch*, 3rd edn (Cambridge, MA: Perseus Books).

Cooper, R. G. (2014) 'What's Next? After Stage-Gate', *Research-Technology Management*, **57**(1), 20–31.

Jespersen, K. R. (2012) 'Stage-to-Stage Information Dependency in the NPD Process: Effective Learning or a Potential Entrapment of NPD Gates?', *Journal of Product Innovation Management*, **29**(2), 257–274.

Grönlund, J., Sjödin, D. R. and Frishammar, J. (2010) 'Open Innovation and the Stage-Gate Process: A Revised Model for New Product Development', *California Management Review*, **52**(3), 106–131.

Hutchins, N. and Muller, A. (2012) 'Beyond Stage-gate: Restoring Learning and Adaptability to Commercialization', *Strategy & Leadership*, **40**(3), 30–35.

13

VALUE ANALYSIS AND INNOVATION

13.1 Introduction

Value analysis/value engineering is an interdisciplinary problem-solving activity to improve the value of the functions required to accomplish the goal or objective of any product, process, service or organization (McGrath, 2004). The economic value of something is how much a desired object or condition is worth relative to other objects or conditions. In marketing, the value of a product is the relationship between the consumer's expectations of product quality and the actual amount paid for it. It is often expressed as the equation (Melnyk and Denzler, 1996):

value = benefits/price, or value = quality received/expectations

In a way, value is the perceived gain composed of individuals' emotional, mental and physical conditions plus various social, economic, cultural and environmental factors (Normann and Ramirez, 1993).

By identifying the functions of the product or service, it is possible to establish the worth of each one of these functions for customers, and provide only the necessary functions to meet the required performance at the lowest overall cost (Gage, 1967; Miles, 1972). Value analysis focuses on accomplishing the required functions at the lowest overall cost by eliminating or minimizing wasted material, time and product cost, which improves value to the customer. This establishes the link between value analysis and a variety of activities such as business process re-engineering, lean production and Six Sigma.

Value engineering is also referred as 'function analysis', 'value analysis' and 'value management'. It was further integrated into design activities in the 1990s, as in the well-known Toyota cost management process (Monden, 1992). This is why quality function deployment is an important value analysis technique, which extends the minimum essential product function and develops design functions into value engineering (Shillito, 1994).

Although value analysis was more or less developed as an engineering tool, it became a strategy tool after the contributions of strategy professors such as Normann and Ramirez (1993) and Kim and Mauborgne (1997, 2005). The original term 'value analysis' describes improving pre-existing products, processes or services (including the management of a company), but we prefer to use the term in line with the understanding of 'value innovation' to reflect the fact that innovations cannot be limited to improvements. The value innovation concept was first used by Kim and Mauborgne (1997). It is not about making trade-offs but about simultaneously pursuing exceptional value and lower costs. This is why value innovation is very much an outside-in, customer-oriented approach to innovation (Kim and Mauborgne, 2005). It can be formulated as:

value innovation = unprecedented benefits/lowered costs

Dillon et al. (2005) express value innovation as creating exceptional value for the customer. The goal is continuing success to drive a sustained increase in enterprise value.

Value and innovation should be considered as inseparable, since value without innovation can mean value creation that simply improves buyers' existing benefits, while innovation without value can be too technology driven (Kim and Mauborgne, 2005). In value innovation, instead of the conventional idea of staying ahead of the competition by matching or beating their rivals, firms are expected to focus on the demands of their customers and position themselves accordingly. Thus the value innovation concept provides a relevant support for questioning product or market strategies as well as underlying assumptions in five dimensions:

- Industry assumptions.
- Strategic focus.
- Customers.
- Assets and capabilities.
- Product and service offerings (Kim and Mauborgne, 1997).

13.2 Where and why it is used

Value analysis is generally useful in the process of improving innovation management in an enterprise, since it can be applied to any area of a firm where it is important to increase either the cost/quality ratio or other trade-offs in value. Value analysis methods have been applied to most company areas, for example manufacturing, product design and development, machinery design and TQM (Socitec, 1999). The application is not limited to just one phase of the company but affects the entire set of processes involved and which relate to each other. This is why value analysis might help to generate innovation at all stages of firms.

The Canadian Society of Value Analysis (2008) describes the major benefits of value analysis as:

- Improving a firm's ability to manage projects, solve problems, innovate and communicate.
- Providing a firm's staff with a definitive tool to improve value in any product, project or process.
- Cost savings, risk reduction, schedule improvements and even improved job satisfaction.
- High payback from the investment in value analysis, for example the payback may exceed a 10:1 ratio.
- Increasing responsiveness to client priorities.

From the TM perspective, the benefits of value analysis fall into three major areas:

- Acquisition.
- Identification.
- Selection.

By focusing on the real requirements of a company's customers rather than focusing on the industry situation or competitors' characteristics, value innovation leads to improved acquisition conditions (Chapter 2). Value innovation is based on large amounts of market and customer analysis, with many approaches and mental frameworks, which is why it supports the identification capability (Chapter 4). Regarding the selection capability (Chapter 7), value innovation supplies a strong base for creating a new market space and making the existing competition irrelevant.

No matter how differentiated the company is, the success and increased market share appeals to competitors sooner or later and hence they try to imitate the value curve of the company, so companies need to continuously introduce innovations at the product platform (such as physical product), the service platform (such as maintenance, customer service, warranties) and the delivery platform (logistics and the channel used to deliver the product to customers) (Kim and Mauborgne, 2005; Wingfield and Guth, 2006). This integrated approach crosses the functions in companies and hence brings production, marketing and R&D together.

13.3 Process

The methodology of value analysis can be applied to any area of activity in a company or organization, as well as to each of the development phases of products or services. For this reason, there are numerous variations in its application, depending on how, where and when it is applied. However, it is possible to define a basic structure common to value analysis methods and identify six stages which, although described in a consecutive fashion, are often undertaken concurrently or interactively (Socitec, 1999):

1 Preparation and orientation.
2 Information.
3 Functions.
4 Solutions.
5 Value.
6 Implementation.

In the preparation and orientation stage, the objectives and methods for the product/service are determined and work teams, responsibilities and time periods are defined. Then data about customer needs are compiled, organized and structured to form the information base. To clarify the functions of products and services, the different factors of the product or process are investigated, arranged, organized and structured. The goal is not only to eliminate or reduce the cost of components adding little value but also to enhance the value added by components that contribute significantly to functions important to customers. Then solutions are searched for. The products/services/processes are rethought in order to define alternative solutions by using creativity tools such as brainstorming. In order to attach values to each solution, the different proposed solutions are assessed with respect to the ratio of cost to functions. Finally, in the implementation phase, resources for the project are allocated and changes in product/service/process are implemented.

The stages described above are rather limited thinking on innovation, so value analysis could be transformed into value innovation analysis (Kim and Mauborgne, 2005). In such an analysis, a typical process consists of three main elements:

1 Creating the value curve.
2 Building new value curves.
3 Testing.

The value curve is important in showing how a customer sees the offerings of a company compared to that of its competitors. The possible aspects of customer value titled 'value elements' are shown on the horizontal axis and the relative level of the offering for each competitor is plotted on the vertical axis. For example, McDonald's, the US fast-food company, has decided to eliminate three value elements in the restaurant business: waiters, table settings and menu selection (Kim and Mauborgne, 2005). However, it increased radically its performance on four value elements: ubiquity, speed, quality and kid-friendliness. Thus, it placed its price in between the one-star and two-star restaurant evaluation system. By using such a strategy, McDonald's managed to change the value curve in the restaurant business by introducing the fast-food model.

The value curve helps to identify and articulate a company's existing strategic logic. Firms need to rethink the industry's assumptions, the company's strategic focus, the bundle of product and service offerings, as well as their approaches to customers, assets and capabilities and product and service offerings. To do this, managers are expected to ask four questions in order to drive a new value curve (Kim and Mauborgne, 2005):

- Which of the industrial factors taken for granted should be eliminated?
- Which factors should be reduced well below the industry's standard?
- Which factors should be raised well above the industry's standard?
- Which factors should be created that the industry has never offered?

In order to generate profitable growth, it is necessary to ask all four questions rather than just one or two. Value innovation aims to achieve superior value for buyers as well as lower cost for companies.

The case of Whirlpool is illustrative (Dillon et al., 2005). In 1999, Whirlpool reassigned 75 people and tasked them with answering the question: What other rooms in the home can Whirlpool bring value to? This customer-centric focus led to the introduction of 25 new products over three years – the family studio, a complete fabric-care and family activity centre for today's home and the personal valet clothes vitalizing system are examples. During the value modelling and analysis, Whirlpool utilized the following valuation techniques: options analysis, market-based valuations, discounted cash flow, NPV, future value assessment, probability assessment and value tracking. It also used value curves, value management systems, tornado diagrams, Monte Carlo analysis and influence diagrams.

In building new value curves, firms can follow one of the following tactics (Kim and Mauborgne, 2005):

- Looking across industries in order to compete with substitutes for the company's product rather than with direct competitors.
- Looking across strategic groups so that firms might avoid direct competition by positioning themselves between these groups.
- Looking across the chain of buyers to be effective to sell further downstream in the chain of buyers, creating 'pull' for the products.
- Looking across complementary offerings by looking at the whole system or process within which the customer uses a product or service. This is done by investigating customers' problems and seeking ways to provide a complete system or solution.
- Looking across functional or emotional appeal rather than positioning a product or service on its price or functionality.
- Looking across time (trends), as powerful trends can be the source of new value curves.

After generating the value path, the testing stage aims to observe the real impact. The planned portfolio of value offerings is implemented so that the company tests innovations. Based on feedback from customers, a company can progress and implement its new business model.

13.4 Expanding the value analysis

The concept of value is challenged with technological developments capable of closely integrating product, service and information. As well as the positive impact of technologies, the negative developments regarding increased environmental problems and concerns on economic crises are transforming the very idea of value itself. There is a call for a more human-centred future that will change people's lifestyles.

As discussed in Chapter 14, technologies such as sensors and information technologies result in new mixes of products, services and solutions. The blurred boundaries between products and services are based on high level integration of information, services, experiences and solutions, in and through specific contexts (e.g. the home, the car, the hospital, the hotel). Customers want to be able to customize their consumption in a way that is personal and fitting to them, as an individual or as a group. In a way, the idea of value attached to a standalone material object has started to shift to a value embedded in a system's intelligence and information. For example, technologies enable a home-centred health system in which users are connected to different circles of care, from family/friends to support professionals, expert patients, doctors and the hospital (Green, 2007). This more decentralized and user-centred system enables people to intuitively monitor and be aware of their health and wellbeing.

Besides technologies, mounting social and environmental problems are calling for a paradigm shift for businesses. This more human focus allows us to put people at the centre of the future, to explore more meaningful and wellbeing solutions and experiences and to re-introduce a normative approach to the future, meaning to think about preferable futures that make sense both to society and people. This development has two clear implications, on the one hand established firms are trying to find their ways in getting involved with the paradigm shift, while on the other hand new socially-led companies are arising. The new breed of company are social innovators dealing with social problems and introducing new social solutions. Most of these companies fall into the category of social entrepreneurs that run businesses based upon a double (financial and social or environmental) or triple (financial, social and environmental) bottom line. In other words, rather than relying on philanthropy or charity or public handouts, social entrepreneurs embed their social mission in business and reach self-sufficiency through earned income.

With respect to established firms, Nike might be an example. Nike was chosen to be the 7th innovative firm in 2014 according to the Fast Company because of its application called Making that helps companies measure the environmental impact of using different materials. Hannah Jones, Nike's VP of sustainable business and innovation, says that Nike created this enormous database of materials for the entire industry. Nike plans to eliminate the use of hazardous chemicals in the creation of its products by 2020. The company also expanded its ambitious Launch programme, which it created with NASA and the State Department. Hundreds of key players in the materials ecosystem come together to discover, incubate and accelerate companies developing innovative materials to be used on a wide scale. 'Sustainability can't be just a single product line; it has to be across everything we do.'

The example of social entrepreneur firms might be Aravind Eye Hospital established in India in 1976. The founder, Dr Venkataswamy, introduced a new business model where each paying customer paid for their cataract operations as well as two non-paying customers. All operations are customized to conduct large scale operations to reduce costs and offer high quality service. It has managed to cure more than four million customers since its establishment, and it keeps renovating itself in the field of ophthalmology.

In the road to a human-centred future, as Green (2007) clearly put forward: 'This transformation of a worldview, of social models and of more human ways of creating value, is also about a transformation of approaches and practices including new tools, new research and innovation, new leaders, new networks and new partnerships: cross-disciplinary, cross-industry, cross-border and public/private collaborations that will create the industries and markets of the future.'

Likely, there are available tools to help new leaders in helping them build the human-centred future. One such tool is design-driven innovation which stretches the view of value further. In general, the technology push ended in radical changes in product performance enabled by breakthrough technologies, whereas improved product solutions are enabled by better analysis of users' needs that are driven with market pull. As a third alternative, design-driven innovation changes the meaning of products and services. What designers do is basically define the meaning of products in people's lives. One of the best examples is Apple's iPod. It was a latecomer to the MP3-player market but its design features, the uniqueness of the look and feel, coupled with the integration of hardware, software services resulted in a change of meaning of a music player (Verganti, 2009) (Table 13.1).

Table 13.1   Type of innovations

Type of innovation	Type of need
Demand-pull innovation	Developed in response to an identified need
Technology-push innovation	Developed without consideration of whether it satisfies any need at all
Design-driven innovation	Finds value in something consumers never thought they'd need

Design offers a link between people, technology and the future. This is because design is able to give intangible ideas and creativity a form that eventually increases the level of debate and interaction and facilitates dialogue, contribution and involvement from users as well as from stakeholders. When companies innovate, they consider creating a future product or service. While they do forecast, in a way they need to envisage the future, in other words to make it tangible. This is quintessentially a design task.

Design helps firms to focus on the interplay between the functional and semantic dimensions of a product. The case study of Kartell illustrates the principal interpretations of the role of technology in radical design-driven innovation: technology as an enabler of new product meanings for the customer and the importance of supply networks that allow manufacturers to change product technologies quickly and experiment with new technologies. Kartell, an Italian furniture company, was founded in 1949. The founder Castelli's technological competence and innate creativity allowed Kartell to give furniture products a new sense of modernity through the use of plastic materials. Dell'Era et al. (2010) argue that Kartell's global market leadership in plastic household production is not only due to its ability to manage its image, its distribution skills and the way it markets and sells but it is also due to its traditional ability to work in plastic. New product development is managed in collaboration with mould manufacturers and chemical companies that help to define the materials and mould that will be used in production. As in many other design-driven companies, Kartell's R&D department aimed to provide a technological solution able to convey meanings conceptualized by the designer and ensure the innovativeness of the initial idea. To some extent, the designer is the owner of product meanings, while the R&D department provides product languages and technologies that embed values conceptualized by the designer.

Therefore, Dell'Era et al. (2010) argue that 'it is not sufficient to be sensitive only to socio-cultural messages, it is also necessary to transfer distinct inputs and stimuli into real projects in order to exploit accumulated knowledge about socio-cultural phenomena and transform it into new product meanings and languages.' Even if designers can support company exposure to emerging trends in society, this 'listening' activity has to be integrated with research on technologies that allow products to embed appropriate languages and consequently to convey coherent meanings.

This listening activity is also suggested by Verganti (2009) as a practice that a successful design-driven company should do. That is why Verganti calls for companies to work not only with customers as end-users but also to actively search and find 'interpreters' such as scientists, customers, suppliers, intermediaries, designers and artists who could deeply understand and shape the markets they work in. Green (2007) further suggests working with cultural innovators and creative communities as well as collaborating with social entrepreneurs.

Design-thinking approaches are also helpful in thinking of value in a network of companies and organizations acting as a community in order to generate new ways of living and changing the perception of value. An example to this is the Slow Food movement in Italy (Green, 2007). It is a network of restaurants that source their inputs produced locally. Over time, it has become a bigger European movement based on the generation or re-generation of local economies. This decentralized approach to value, rather than global production and consumption, promises to be more sustainable for the future as it offers transparency, a lower ecological footprint, increased diversity and the enhancement of local contexts, communities and livelihoods. It also has the power to help us re-think our relationship to time and to experience. Rather than focusing on speed and a superficial experience, it allows us to tap into and experience greater depth based on local environmental and social qualities. Understanding where things come from and how they are produced gives them greater meaning.

Company managers should consider the management of innovation processes together with their supply-chain relations as well as communities so that they can tackle the integration of learning mechanisms. By doing so, firms might develop an ability to systematically create value innovation initiatives (Berghman et al., 2012). In other firms, integration brings three potential benefits: the creation of new and substantially superior customer value, a redefinition of the business model and the altering of roles and relationships among industry players and stakeholders.

Porter and Kramer (2011) even call this value network an opportunity for shared value creation in order to re-invent capitalism and unleash a new wave of innovation and growth. Rather than focusing on customers per se, a shared view demands social value creation as an essential dimension of businesses. In summary, companies are expected to create shared value opportunities in three ways: (1) Re-conceiving products and markets so that companies can meet social needs while better serving existing markets, accessing new ones or lowering costs through innovation; (2) Redefining productivity in the value chain in order to improve the quality, quantity, cost and reliability of inputs and distribution while they simultaneously act as a steward for essential natural resources and drive economic and social development; and (3) Enabling local cluster development for reliable local suppliers, a functioning infrastructure of roads and telecommunications, access to talent and an effective and predictable legal system.

Overall, a human-centred future invites managers, leaders, engineers and academicians to come up with new thinking and tools that will help creative problem solving and the development of innovative and impactful solutions. Numerous methods for creativity have been developed over the years. A study determined the most popular and the most effective methods for creating game-changing ideas (Cooper, 2011). The most effective ideation methods include the following tools:

- Ethnography: camping out with customers or observation of customers for extended periods, watching and probing as they use or misuse the product or go about their tasks or life. This is the most effective of all methods, but not so popular since it is expensive and difficult to do.
- Customer visit teams: cross-functional company teams meet with customers or users; they conduct in-depth interviews to uncover problems, needs and desire for new products. This is also a very effective method, but much more popular due to cost and ease.
- Focus groups: running focus groups with customers or users specifically to identify needs, wants, problems, points of pain and suggestions for new products.
- Lead user analysis: working with particularly innovative customers or users, usually meeting in a group or holding a workshop, to identify problems and potential solutions.
- Customer designs: inviting customers or users to help you design your next new product.

The tools developed in management literature coincide with the industrial designers' tools. In practice, it is known that industrial designers (a) perform ethnography; (b) undertake concept prototyping and refinement with users; (c) factor in available materials, suppliers and manufacturing constraints; and (d) balance form and function to achieve a distinctive design and branding. On top of that, engineers pursue a number of specific activities in cost designing, which include (a) defining product line architecture, (b) specification of components and materials used for subsystems within the architecture, (c) costing these components and materials and (d) working on conversion/manufacturing costs to create finished products. When industrial designers and engineers get together and combine their tools, there are plenty of tools to conduct value analysis and become innovative.

Case studies

In recent years, value innovation has evolved into a sophisticated, reliable approach. Thus, the capability in using the approach is seen by some as a key tool in their strategic planning process. More organizations are seeking to better understand the value innovation approach, linking it to key differentiating consumer insights and so identifying market-breaking concepts. Some insights can be gained from real-life experiences, as described in the Samsung and Aplicare case studies below.

Samsung Electronics

In 1993, Samsung, a global electronics company, created a corporate culture of 'innovation is everything'. Korea's Samsung has driven itself upmarket, making a world-leading shift from innovation follower to innovation leader. With annual revenues of $60 billion, recent profits of $10 billion, a market value of over $100 billion and world leadership in key technologies such as LCD displays and dynamic random access memory (DRAM), Samsung is now consistently seen as the innovation leader in the consumer electronics sector.

In achieving its ambition to become the world's best company, Samsung decided to innovate continuously on six parallel tracks:

- *Product innovation*: to deliver a continual stream of stylish, innovative products that deliver unexpected delight.
- *Technology innovation*: to quickly develop and retain key technologies and core R&D investments that separate the company from its competitors.
- *Marketing innovation*: to create fresh approaches at every level of customer contact, continue to build the brand and drive sales.
- *Cost innovation*: to control costs in ways that complement and encourage innovation and increase market impact worldwide.
- *Organizational culture innovation*: to create work environments where everyone shares the freedom to learn from mistakes and succeed.
- *Global management innovation*: to develop highly localized product strategies, which link strong local insight and key market presence with an ability to accelerate the decision-making process and rapidly seize major opportunities worldwide.

To help to identify the core opportunities to outcompete its peers, in the late 1990s, Samsung opened a dedicated Value Innovation Program Center in Suwong. This is an integrated five-floor facility where value innovation is taught as a process and applied across many product lines. The first floor is devoted to value innovation training, the second, third and fourth floors are available for project teams to work on value innovation projects, ranging from strategy development to new business models to new products and the fifth floor is a mini-hotel where teams often stay until the project is finished.

By identifying and exploiting value innovation opportunities across all six innovation tracks, this facility has fast become a key source of new concepts that have helped grow market share and margins.

Key products from Samsung's Value Innovation Program have included:

- The SGH T-100 wireless phone, which sold over ten million units.
- A five-foot plasma display, currently in development.
- The world's first 40-inch LCD TV, which represented breakthroughs in size and wide-angle viewing.
- The SPH-E3200 digital camera phone, which has no antenna.

All these products have changed the value curve for the most important customers in their respective markets and are making a significant contribution to Samsung's increasing revenues, margins and market share.

Aplicare Inc.

Aplicare is a market leader in the formulation, production and packaging of topical antiseptic and personal care products for use in the US professional healthcare setting. It is a privately held company with annual sales of just under $100 million whose customers include doctors' offices, home healthcare agencies, hospitals, healthcare distributors, procedural kit and tray manufacturers and surgical centres.

In 2004, in order to drive organic growth and improve gross margins, Aplicare made a strategic decision to forward integrate into kit manufacturing in a unique and defensible way. To achieve this, Aplicare focused the value innovation methodology on a commodity dressing change kit, produced by at least six manufacturers. The president of Aplicare wanted a breakthrough product that was unique and defensible.

In response, the product development team first recognized that the most important customer was not the purchasing agent but the nurse, and so set about identifying the problems nurses experience using existing products. It developed a new value curve, identifying new elements of performance, such as procedural compliance, antiseptic effectiveness, means to package soiled/used materials and ease of opening and use, which would address the problems identified by nurses:

- Not compliant with procedure to leave the patient unattended after nurses have removed the old wound dressing to wash their hands – an unsecured catheter can move if the patient moves, potentially infecting the site.
- Confusion over the order the nurse uses the alcohol and povidone-iodine to clean the site.

Interestingly, the price dropped from most important (scored 1) for the purchasing agent to low importance (scored 8) for the nurse. This led to a dramatic new design for dressing change kits, which the company introduced at a nursing convention in May 2006. The response from end users and distributors was described as 'phenomenal'. Priced at a premium to current kits, the new value-driven design demonstrates that it is possible to transform a commodity into a breakthrough.

The Samsung and Aplicare examples highlight that, when market opportunity, corporate capability and core customer insights are aligned, companies not naturally culturally predisposed to innovating through the value chain can nevertheless use a

(Continued)

disciplined approach to identify and deliver value-innovating concepts. Some common characteristics of successful examples show that:

- CEOs champion innovation and their personality and style influence what companies do and how they do it.
- Company growth strategy and business models are clear to all employees.
- Decisions are made quickly with little dithering.
- Cycle times from concept to finished business model, product or service are being reduced to weeks from months and years.
- The organizational culture and working environment support risk taking, with innovation permeating the company.
- Ideas are sought after and welcomed from anywhere – within and outside the firm.
- Value innovation can occur anywhere, at any level, at any time.

Source: Jones T. and Lee, D. (2006) 'Samsung, Others Adopting Value Innovation', *Research-Technology Management*, **49**(5), 5–7.

Key Questions

1 What are value analysis and value innovation?
2 What are the advantages and disadvantages of value analysis?
3 What is the process of value analysis?

Exercises

1. Sun Software Company

Jasmine is a software development manager for a software house. She and her team handle short software enhancements for many clients. As part of a team development day, she and her team think about how they can deliver excellent service to their clients.

During the Activity Analysis part of the session, they identify the following activities that create value for clients:

- Order taking.
- Enhancement specification.
- Scheduling.
- Software development.
- Programmer testing.
- Secondary testing.
- Delivery.
- Support.

Jasmine also identifies the following non-client-facing activities as being important:

- Recruitment: choosing people who will work well with the team.
- Training: helping new team members become effective as quickly as possible, and helping team members learn about new software, techniques and technologies as they are developed.

Jasmine marks these out on her whiteboard.

Next, she and her team focus on the Order Taking process, and identify the factors that will give the greatest value to customers as part of this process. They identify the following Value Factors:

- Giving a quick answer to incoming phone calls.
- Having a good knowledge of the customer's business, situation and system, so that they do not waste the customer's time with unnecessary explanation.
- Asking all the right questions and getting a full and accurate understanding of the customer's needs.
- Explaining the development process to the customer and managing his or her expectations as to the likely timetable for delivery.

They then look at what they need to do to deliver the maximum value to the customer. These things are shown in a list under the title of "Changes Needed".

They then do the same for all other processes.

Once all brainstorming is complete, Jasmine and her team may be able to agree their priorities for implementation.

Source: Adapted from http://www.mindtools.com/pages/article/newTMC_10.htm

2. A New Start-up: Yellow

Yellow is a group of entrepreneurs who want to start a new company to produce pens. The team of engineers and marketing people come together and try to brainstorm on the features of the pen and potential ideas to make changes in their product.

The tasks to be completed for the team are as follows:

Functions:

- Identify the item to be analysed and the customers for whom it is produced.
- List the basic functions (the things for which the customer is paying). Note that there are usually very few basic functions.
- Identify the secondary functions by asking 'How is this achieved?' or 'What other functions support the basic functions?'
- Determine the relative importance of each function, preferably by asking a representative sample of customers (who will always surprise you with what they prefer).

Analyse contributing functions:

- Find the components of the item being analysed that are used to provide the key functions.
- Measure the cost of each component as accurately as possible, including all material and production costs.

Seek improvements:

- Eliminate or reduce the cost of components that add little value, especially high-cost components.
- Enhance the value added by components that contribute significantly to functions that are particularly important to customers.

Just to give an idea how to calculate and analyse based on costs and values, use the following example given in Figure 13.1. Accordingly, costs of components are: barrel (42 cents), top (18 cents), nib (114 cents), clip (120 cents). The value perceptions of customers for general functions are given out of 100-scale as follows: mark paper (80), protect nib (60), prevent leaks (40), looks attractive (80).

As a team member, based on your list of functions, try to develop a similar analysis. Please make some assumptions on value scale as you wish and try to change your assumptions and develop an alternative. Compare your results for different product ideas.

Eventually, discuss what should be your team's product suggestion to the owner of the company.

Source: Partially driven from the example of http://creatingminds.org/tools/value_engineering.htm

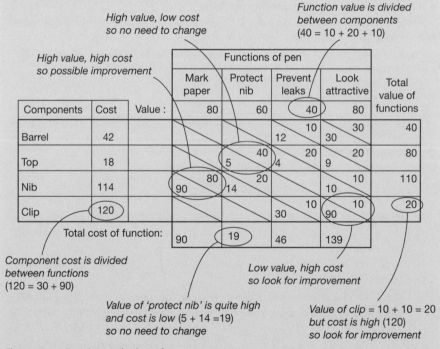

Figure 13.1 Functions and values of a pen

📖 **Further reading**

Berghman, L., Matthyssens, P. and Vandenbempt, K. (2012) 'Value Innovation, Deliberate Learning Mechanisms and Information from Supply Chain Partners', *Industrial Marketing Management*, **41**(1), 27–39.

Cooper, R. G. (2011) 'Perspective: The Innovation Dilemma: How to Innovate When the Market is Mature', *Journal of Product Innovation Management*, **28**(S1), 2–27.

Dell'Era, C., Marchesi, A. and Verganti, R. (2010) 'Mastering Technologies in Design-driven Innovation', *Research-Technology Management*, **53**(2), 12–23.

Kim, W. C. and Mauborgne, R. (2005) *Blue Ocean Strategy: How to Create Uncontested Market Space and Make the Competition Irrelevant* (Boston, MA: Harvard Business School Press).

Porter, M. E. and Kramer, M. R. (2011) 'Creating Shared Value', *Harvard Business Review*, **89**(1/2), 62–77.

Stabell, C. B. and Fjeldstad, Ø. (1998) 'Configuring Value for Competitive Advantage: On Chains, Shops, and Networks', *Strategic Management Journal*, **19**(5), 413–437.

Tebo, P. V. (2005) 'Building Business Value through Sustainable Growth', *Research-Technology Management*, **48**(5), 28–32.

Verganti, R. (2009) *Design Driven Innovation* (Cambridge, MA: Harvard Business School Press).

14

CONCLUSION: MANAGING TECHNOLOGY AND THE CHALLENGES AHEAD

14.1 TM for competitive advantage

Global competition is dominantly technology-driven. Technological innovation cannot be achieved without corporate management devoting considerable energy and investment to developing effective linkages between science, engineering and management. Efficient and effective management of these linkages can ultimately produce and provide products, processes and services that represent a distinctive corporate technological competence. This competence, then, becomes a primary tool for achieving competitive advantage.

Technology's role in competition is explicitly shown in a study measuring competitiveness at a firm level (Cetindamar and Kilitcioglu, 2013) and it is based on three pillars for competition as shown in Figure 14.1. The first pillar is called the 'outcome' since a company needs to show performance in all aspects of what it does to compete. The second pillar is named 'resources', an umbrella term to describe competencies of a firm. The third pillar is entitled 'managerial processes and capabilities' to include the role of management in the transfer of inputs to outputs. This transfer mechanism is not only a static result of processes and structures but also conscious involvement of management where managerial skills affect the whole process.

Competitiveness can be sustainable if and only if the resources resulting in competitiveness are kept alive and the company can establish a set of managerial processes where these resources are developed and utilized. As shown in Figure 14.1, the key resources for competitiveness are not only human and financial but also 'technology, innovation and design based resources'. Technology includes all technical knowledge and assets, while innovation covers all new or modified/improved developments and finally design capacity either complements technological innovations or integrates them in new forms through design features.

Technology's role as one of the key elements of competition is particularly important in industries with dynamic environments where ambidextrous organizations have a high probability of survival. An **ambidextrous organization** maintains a high degree of balance between exploitation (learning via local search, experiential refinement and reuse of existing knowledge) and exploration (learning gained through processes of concerted variation, planned experimentation and play) (Simsek, 2009). The assumption made by research on ambidexterity is that enterprises operating ambidextrously perform better as a result. An extensive study (Derbyshire, 2014) has backed this assumption based on information from the Community Innovation Survey covering 15 countries and 45,113 enterprises. The paper shows a strong, positive effect on growth in sales turnover from ambidexterity in the manufacturing and the scientific and technical services sectors.

Organizations competing in dynamic environments must be strategically flexible and efficient because customer needs and competitor activities demand immediate action.

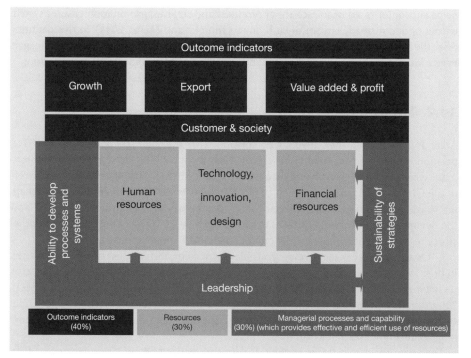

Figure 14.1   The model for competitiveness of firms
Source: Cetindamar, D. and Kilitcioglu, H. (2013).

Agility calls for active experimentation (Thomke and Manzi, 2014). Learning from a business experiment is not necessarily as easy as isolating an independent variable, manipulating it and observing changes in the dependent variable. Environments are constantly changing, the potential causes of business outcomes are often uncertain or unknown and so links between them are frequently complex and poorly understood. Thus, companies typically have to make trade-offs between reliability, cost, time and other practical considerations. Three methods can help to reduce the trade-offs and increase the reliability of the results: (1) randomized field trials, (2) blind tests and (3) **big data** (Thomke and Manzi, 2014). In particular, big data is becoming a significant managerial skill, because extremely large data sets may be analysed computationally to reveal patterns, trends and associations, especially relating to human behaviour and interactions.

McKinsey Global report (2010) shows that nearly 12 terabytes are created each day in tweets alone and there are many more data from social media streams, digital images, banking and transaction records, sensors, GPS signals and countless other sources. And the flow is accelerating; 90% of the data in the world today was created in the last two years and there will be 44 times more of it by the year 2020 (Chui et al., 2010). This is big data, and it will be pivotal for decision making. However, big data can provide clues only about the past behaviour of customers and might not necessarily help understand how customers will react to radical changes. Thus, when it comes to innovation, most managers must operate in a world where they still lack sufficient data to inform their decisions. This is the reason why managers need to build ambidextrous organizations: while exploration helps encounter rapid obsolescence of products and services, exploitation ensures system efficiency and a steady stream of cash flows (Thomke and Manzi, 2014). In this daunting task, the critical resource seems to be dynamic capabilities. Thus, technology managers have a lot to offer in managing big data and contributing to ambidextrous organizations.

14.2 TM as a profession

Adler and Ferdows in their 1990 article conclude that the chief technology officer (CTO) position is not a management fad and that it has a critical integrating role in an environment where technological changes are dynamic. Since then, a lack of attention to the role of the CTO in management research inspired Tschirky et al. (2003) to entitle a book chapter 'Wake-up call for general management: It's technology time' in order to highlight how the rare resource of technology needs to be managed by a CTO in a similar fashion to other scarce resources that companies rely on, such as human and financial capital.

CTOs are corporate executives responsible and accountable for their firm's TM practices. In practice, there are many names given to CTO-type positions, such as technical director, technology director, chief scientist, vice president of R&D and innovation director (Tobias, 2000; van der Hoven et al., 2012). In some cases the chief information officer (CIO) provides technical input at a senior level, but limited IT specific practices, rather than the broader range of technologies that a firm may rely on.

The seven main roles/tasks of the CTO are summarized below (Cetindamar and Pala, 2011):

1 CTOs establish coordination of technological efforts among business units and corporate research to ensure synergy and economies of scale. This task is mainly aimed at avoiding duplication of technological efforts between business units and facilitating the transfer of technology from one to the other.

2 CTOs represent technology within the top management by providing expert opinion on technological questions, recommending a long-term view of technology and fostering infant technology development projects.

3 CTOs should monitor the technological advances in order to capture the developments in technology fields that might impact on company operations.

4 CTOs supervise R&D labs and other technology development units. Therefore one task of the CTO is managing teams that participate in projects.

5 CTOs assess technological aspects of major strategic initiatives. This includes the assessment of the technological implications of proposed acquisitions, joint ventures, strategic alliances and lines of business. Technology assessment also includes the assessment of long-term trends in pertinent technologies.

6 CTOs usually manage the relationship of the company with technological actors in the external technology environment such as universities and regulatory agencies (Smith, 2003; Herstatt et al., 2007). The main tasks related to research organizations are to provide guidelines for the research that the corporation sponsors and to gather intelligence on important technical developments. The tasks related to regulatory agencies are to make sure that the innovations of the corporation comply with regulations, identifying trends in regulatory constraints and managing the efforts of the corporation to influence the regulatory process.

7 Smith (2003) states that sometimes CTOs should be included in marketing and media relations. He states that the attention of the media to the products of the company is crucial for the success of those products. Although media relations are usually pursued by the marketing department, when the focal product is a technological one, CTOs can communicate with the media to build the image of these products as (s)he is probably the one who knows most about the capabilities and technical features of the product.

Having a CTO makes a difference to firm performance as well. Based on a survey of 49 electronic and machinery firms in Turkey, a study found that even though the CTO position does not prevail, CTO roles are performed in varying degrees (Cetindamar and Pala, 2011). The findings confirm that performing decisional CTO roles (disturbance handler, entrepreneur, negotiator and resource allocator) increases profitability of firms and the educational background of a manager carrying out CTO roles strengthens this positive impact. The informational roles of a CTO (monitor, disseminator and spokesperson) result in a positive impact on profitability when the CTO has frequent communication with the CEO. In other words, the higher the extent of networking, the higher profits achieved from the realization of informational roles.

Regardless of being a CTO or not, there is demand for technology managers and the expected duties of them are in increasing demand. The wide recognition is that TM is mainly a profession for companies developing technologies or manufacturing companies that are utilizing technologies. But the impact of technology is pervasive across all sectors and it is blurring all the borders among them. Given the dynamic nature of how technology evolves, Badawy (2009) describes in detail the pervasiveness of the diffusion of technologies across many services such as technology diffusion in health care, telecommunications (such as voice over the Internet), wireless broadband, mobile banking, online media, online publishing, digital marketing and genetic engineering.

In addition, technology managers are not only needed by companies but by a wide range of organizations. The increase in the rate of public and private investment in technology has manifested itself in numerous 'technology-based economic development' and technology transfer initiatives at the regional, state and national levels. This development results in the rise of collaborative research and commercialization that demands more technology managers. In addition, the formation and growth of new technology-based firms, as well as the development and implementation of new technologies in large companies (and 'corporate entrepreneurship'), contribute to increased demand for professionals who can understand and function as technology managers. Many professions might also need to expand their skills to understand TM so that they can practise their own professions such as university technology transfer/licensing officers, scientists and engineers, corporate executives and independent entrepreneurs.

14.3 Challenges for technology managers

The need for professionals dealing with TM is increasing, but in a dynamic world these roles are repeatedly evolving due to challenges to the field. Six major challenges for technology managers are listed below: digitization, innovation process, innovation actors, services, sustainability and paradigm shift.

Digitalization

Innovations are an integral part of everyday life. They change the way we live but also influence the way we respond. This two-way interaction is a process of dynamic evolution. The recent radical change is based on digital technologies; they drive '**digitalization**': an emerging business model that includes the extension and support of electronic channels, content and transactions.

Digital technology is transformational due to its three key features (Iansiti and Lakhani, 2014): being transmitted without error, replicated indefinitely and communicated to the incremental consumer at zero marginal cost. Due to these features, digital technologies are revolutionizing products. Some researchers call the changes the third wave of IT (Porter and Heppelmann, 2014) while others emphasize the radical transformation as the second machine age (Brynjolfsson and McAffee, 2014). While the former highlights the period after 2000 as the new wave of IT where IT has become an integral part of the product itself, the later view considers a new era starting somewhere around 2006 where the exponential growth of digital technologies (with hardware, software and networks at their core) reinvents lives and economies in the world.

In their book The Second Machine Age, Brynjolfsson and McAffee (2014) draw an analogy to the industrial revolution which implicitly suggests that the digital revolution will be comparable in its effects on long-run economic growth. According to the authors, Moore's law, the doubling of integrated circuit computing power roughly every 18 months, has counterparts in other elements of computational technology. A closely related aspect of contemporary technological change is the proliferation of low-cost sensors and the resulting growth of machine-to-machine communication, allowing devices to interact with each other and respond to new conditions without human intervention. And with the digitization of 'just about everything' come streams of data making possible a ubiquitous 'Internet of things' and providing the necessary information for continuing improvement and new discoveries about complex processes (Chui et al., 2010; Iansiti and Lakhani, 2014). This has a profound impact in all sectors including services as discussed below.

Digitalization is not pure technologies but the use of technologies and a number of new collaborative ways of doing business with a wide variety of partners. A good example is the story of Nest, a company producing the digital thermostat and smoke detector that was acquired by Google in 2014 for $3.2 billion. (Iansiti and Lakhani, 2014). The Nest thermostat creates value by digitizing the entire home-temperature-control process from fuel purchase to temperature setting to powering the heating, ventilation and air-conditioning system. This company is based on a new business model since the revenue is not based only on its direct service: temperature measurement and smoke detection. Nest can make money from electric utilities on the basis of outcomes: Google can aggregate data on energy consumption patterns and offer the utilities a service in return for a percentage of their savings; in addition it can pass some of those savings back to consumers. Another partner of Nest is Jawbone, a company that produces wearable technology. Its products detect when someone has awakened and then dynamically adjust the home temperature by communicating with Nest. There are all sorts of possibilities to connect digital data collected by Nest and its potential partners. The example of Nest is quite illustrative of what smart products might offer in the coming future and the challenges they pose for managers.

Innovation process

In 2013, as part of its 75th anniversary celebration, the Industrial Research Institute (IRI) commissioned a project to consider the shape of R&D in IRI's 100th year. IRI 2038 explored how trends emerging today might affect the art and science of research and TM into the future.

The IRI conducted a project to explore how the trends of today might affect research and TM in 2038 (Farrington and Crews, 2013). The study described detailed sets of scenarios, one of which is summarized here to provide an insight about what the future might look like in 2038 from a technology manager's perspective.

The scenario is titled 'Three roads to innovation' and it discusses three new paths towards innovation: Hollywood R&D, communities of brains and innovation tribes. Taking these in turn, many corporations will work like Hollywood movie studios, in which a small production company assembles freelance talent on a project-by-project basis, while another path emerges as individuals directly connect their brains to cloud-based communities. These communities will attempt to solve social problems and develop transformational science, providing R&D via the network. Others will form insular communities (tribes) that work in secrecy to prevent outsiders from obtaining their intellectual property.

Based on this scenario, the study lists four implications for research and TM (Farrington and Crews, 2013):

R&D Value Proposition: R&D will not only identify future customer needs but also pick the best research model to solve these needs. Companies will value speed-to-market and strong evidence of demand; the use of fast prototyping and user feedback will mean projects get market exposure and feedback before being handed over to formal marketing and sales systems.

Talent Management: there will be an increasing reliance on freelance talent, so managers need to spend a lot of time building a community of talent. They will form teams quickly by using their community. Simulation will help increase speed and accuracy in assembling the right team. As software moves into talent and project management, researchers will need to develop an ability to manage or be managed by artificial intelligence or expert systems. This will include the need to maximize human creativity in a world of automation.

Portfolio Management: the ability to articulate exactly what the company is looking for is critical in managing the portfolio. Managers will handle many different types of projects, from highly open crowd-sourced models to tightly controlled internal programmes. Managing the flow of information for each project to maximize creativity and protect trade secrets will be a key source of advantage.

Project Management: stage-gate systems do not disappear, but are automated and the number of gates is reduced by using simulations and mapping a project's progress. Managers concentrate on being more collaborative and integrated with the rest of the organization or community rather than on daily project management. This complex task will be possible thanks to the use of intelligent software. Assembling and managing team capabilities will become a critical management skill.

Based on various scenarios, the IRI study highlights four major implications that are common across all scenarios, and which technology managers should pay particular attention to in the near term:

- Artificial intelligence and talent management will become key responsibilities for managers.
- Open innovation practices will increase and the management of intellectual property will become difficult. Managers will need to balance the benefits of connectivity and information sharing against the advantages of trade secrets.

- Needs identification and speed to market will require developing skills in customer research, ethnography, technology scouting and rapid prototyping.
- Projects serving customer needs will compete with the increasingly urgent needs of the planet itself. Urbanization and the rise of the megacity will also greatly influence R&D's role in these larger, more transformational projects for sustainability.

Although future scenarios might be very different, managers should begin to build relevant organizational competencies as the global market for R&D and TM changes. Careful attention to the evolving future will allow managers and their organizations to develop the relevant capacities and create competitive advantage.

Developing countries as innovation players

Product and service innovations aimed at resource-constrained customers in emerging markets highlight the reality that innovation and TM need to apply across cultures and geographies. Innovations originating in or directed to emerging markets typically result in products that may seem inferior compared with advanced technologies, in that they may not offer a wide range of features, or they may be smaller or made of less expensive materials (Hang et al., 2010). However, these products are characterized by other features, such as low cost, small size or simplicity of use, that make them accessible and attractive for a lower-end market or niche market, and so may out-perform advanced technologies in these market contexts. Companies looking to develop these innovations need to be sensitive to consumers' context.

A recent study (Zeschky et al., 2014) goes further and distinguishes types of resource-constrained innovations on the basis of novelty of solution and typical traits. At one extreme is cost innovation: the novelty of solution is low; it offers cost-engineered emerging market solutions with traits such as cost-effective raw material, local sourcing and smaller package sizes. An example for cost innovation is the cell phones and infrastructure produced by the Chinese firm Huawei, which is able to sell advanced smart phones at about 20% of the cost of Western competitors. At the other end is reverse innovation: the novelty of solution ranges from low to medium; it is a cost/value/application-engineered global solution with traits such as cost-effective raw materials, local sourcing and new applications (i.e. portability) (see Chapter 3 for details). An example of reverse innovation is the Logiq book produced by GE, a portable ultrasound device that was initially produced for emerging markets but later diffused into advanced countries.

Innovativeness in developing countries is not limited to manufacturing. A study has shown the important role played by developing economies in the origin and types of innovations in financial services that are offered via mobile phones (van der Boor et al., 2014). The findings indicate that 85% of the innovations in this field have originated in developing countries and at least 50% of all mobile financial services were pioneered by users, approximately 45% by producers and the remaining were jointly developed by users and producers. They also highlight that the main factors contributing to these innovations occurring in developing countries are the high levels of need and the existence of flexible platforms, in combination with increased access to information and communication technology. Additionally, services developed by users diffused at more than double the rate of producer-innovations. Finally, the study observed that three-quarters of the innovations that originated in non-OECD countries have already diffused to OECD countries and that the (user) innovations are therefore globally meaningful. The findings call for a re-examination of the new sources of innovation and warn technology managers to be ready to collaborate across countries.

Services

The service sector has become a key application domain for engineering and TM since it represents 60–70% of GDP in developed economies. As Tidd and Bessant (2013) describe at length, many examples of technological innovation can be found in services. Clearly, information technologies have transformed many service industries including banking, insurance, health care and education.

Services vary widely in type, and the way in which they integrate with technologies differs correspondingly. For example, Hulshoff et al. (1998) show the value of categorizing services based on where the knowledge resides. They suggest that knowledge is based either in the provider of the service, the user of the service or the infrastructure or system that provides the service. In summary: (1) knowledge-based services knowledge resides with the service provider, (2) knowledge-embedded services knowledge resides in the system and (3) knowledge-extracted services knowledge resides entirely in the user of the service. In a knowledge-based economy, all types of services become a source of technology exploitation and utilization. That is why it is no surprise that the world's first business computer was used in a service company, namely to support bakery planning and logistics for the UK catering services company J. Lyons and Company (Tidd and Bessant, 2013).

Besides service industries, manufacturing companies are challenged with a transformation from being a product supplier into becoming a product-service provider. Increasingly, manufacturers sell the benefits from the use of a product rather than just the product itself as explained by the case of the passenger train manufacturer Alstom Transport (Euchner, 2014). The main rail line between London and Glasgow utilizes high-speed electric trains manufactured by Alstom. These are operated by Virgin and owned by a financial organization called Angel Trains, but maintained by Alstom. These three organizations: Virgin, Alstom and Angel Trains come together to deliver the train system. In addition to its role as manufacturer, Alstom maintains the performance, availability and reliability of the trains so that Virgin can focus on serving passengers. Virgin measures the performance of Alstom on metrics that relate to its own business process, such as any disruption experienced by passengers. Alstom then arranges its operations to perform against such metrics. For example, responsiveness is critically important, so Alstom has insourced activities which are necessary to delivering this. In addition it has also developed information communication technologies which help monitor the condition of the trains and how they are being driven. Also, it has processes in place to react if a train fails in service and has staffed its organization with people who have skills that enable them to work very closely with Virgin.

The integration of products and services is further strengthened with two developments: the wide application of sensors and the rise of design-driven innovations. The former indicates the possibility of gathering and using extensive information on products and services. A *McKinsey Quarterly* article on the topic describes how the proliferation of sensors is making possible a new level of automation in data collection, transmission and analysis (Chui et al., 2010). When products are embedded with sensors, companies can track the movements of these products and even monitor interactions with them. Business models can be fine-tuned to take advantage of this behavioural data. As discussed above under the title of digitalization, there are many opportunities arising for companies that can utilize digital technologies in their products. Porter and Heppelmann (2014) call the rise of new forms of business model 'Product as a service'. They highlight the transformation of smart and connected products into a system of systems where many products and service systems interact with each other under new business models. For example, when sensors and network connections are embedded in a rental car, it can be leased for short time spans to registered members of a car service, rental centres become unnecessary and each car's use can be optimized for higher revenues. Zipcar has pioneered this model and more established car rental companies are starting to follow. The role of sensors is not only in new technology-based products, sensors are moving into every product. *Wired's* November 2012 issue included an article on a pair of entrepreneurs who are helping viticulturists refine their irrigation and harvesting practices by embedding water sensors in the vineyards (O'Briens, 2012). In the future, as sensors become ever more pervasive, the amount of data generated by things may outstrip that produced by humans, leading to new business models.

Similar to the profound impact of sensor technologies, design-driven innovation as a new managerial approach offers many advantages. Technologies coupled with design further help both service and manufacturing firms to change the meaning of their offerings in the eyes of their customers. As Verganti (2009) proposes, people do not buy products but they buy meanings; since people use things for profound emotional, psychological and socio-cultural reasons as well as utilitarian ones (see details in Chapter 13). Design-driven innovation becomes a new dimension for companies to compete. For example, the Nintendo Wii transformed consoles from a passive immersion in a virtual world approachable only by niche experts into an active physical entertainment for everyone through socialization. Nintendo had a new sensing technology as well as design features giving a unique look and feel. In short, companies might bring various innovations together and have a radical impact in markets, like the Wii case where the overlap of design- and technology-driven innovation changed the meaning of computer gaming from a largely solitary activity to an interactive family one.

The impact of design-driven innovation is profound, particularly for services. For example, restaurants move from emphasis on food towards experience innovation around restaurants as systems of consumption involving the product, its delivery, the physical and cultural context and so on (Tidd and Bessant, 2013). Service providers such as airlines, hotels or entertainment businesses are differentiating themselves along such experience innovations.

Whatever form the transformation associated with the integration of products and services takes, it is clear that technology managers will need to understand the dynamics of manufacturing and service industries, and they need to be ready to create new business models, improve business processes and reduce costs and risks through the extensive data they will gather on products and services. Thus, a different set of capabilities is needed to succeed in the integration of product-services, including business-model design, partner-network management, integrated-development process, reaching out to developing countries and service-delivery-network management (Chang et al., 2014). Companies seeking to offer high-value industrial product-service systems must find ways to develop these key capabilities in their own organizations, otherwise manufacturing companies neglecting to invest resources in managing the transition towards a product-service orientation may risk their long-term market competitiveness.

Sustainability

The World Wide Fund for Nature suggests that lifestyles in the developed world at present require the resources of around two planets and this will rise to 2.5 by 2050 (WWF, 2010). According to the Natural Edge Project, the next waves of innovation will be driven by simultaneously improving productivity and protecting the environment. As shown in Figure 14.2, technological innovations and design know-how have the potential to tackle many environmental problems cost effectively and profitably. For example, green buildings, hybrid cars, wind power, resource processing, transport systems and a wide array of recycling and other enabling technologies will have a major impact on the future sustainability of business and society. In addition, sustainable global economic growth is not possible without a portfolio of sustainable energy sources such as renewable technologies. Hopefully, many other new and impactful technologies are in the research pipeline.

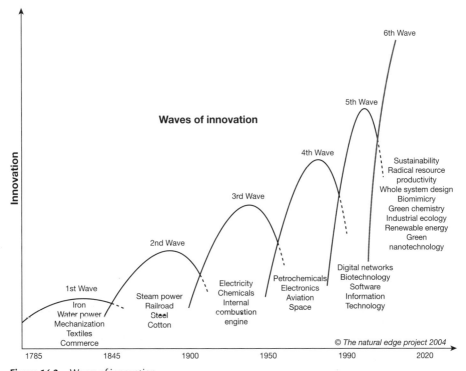

Figure 14.2   Waves of innovation
Source: http://creativecommons.org/licenses/by/3.0/

Sustainability is not only about technologies. It also requires sustainable products, processes and systems, particularly sustainable supply chains. The entire supply chain should be designed and managed from a total life-cycle perspective considering coordination between product, process and supply chain design. Only then will it become possible to efficiently reduce environmental and societal impacts of supply chains while maintaining profitability. Coordinating product and supply chain design decisions will play a critical role in improving the performance across the supply chain. Product design determines future costs, which in turn depend on the supply chain configuration such as the number and location of suppliers, their capabilities and capacities. There are many tools available for life-cycle cost assessments as discussed in Chapter 2. Therefore, coordinating sustainable product and supply chain design decisions requires consideration of all product life-cycle stages and incorporating a closed-loop flow within the supply chain.

Sustainability-driven innovation at Philips

In 2003, a structured sustainable supply chain programme was introduced and the Philips Environmental Report (first published in 1999) was extended into a Sustainability Report. In 2009, the Philips Annual Report covered all aspects of sustainability in Philips' business practices that focus on reducing the Environmental or Ecological Footprint of all Philips products.

Since 2004, Philips defines 'green' products as those offering significant environmental improvements in one or more key focal areas: energy efficiency, packaging, hazardous substances, packaging, weight, recycling and disposal and lifetime reliability. The lifecycle approach is used to determine a product's overall environmental improvement over its total life cycle. Most green products directly contribute to EcoVision5's second and third targets: energy efficiency and closing the material loop. For example, the Consumer Lifestyle division has launched its first 'Cradle to Cradle' inspired products, such as the Performer EnergyCare vacuum cleaner, made from 50% post-industrial and 25% bio-based plastics. It is extremely energy efficient, but it earns its designation as a Green Product primarily because it scores so highly in the focal area of recycling.

With the launch of EcoVision4, Philips introduced a target for Green Innovation. Within five years until 2012, a total of €1bn would be invested in Green Innovation contributing to the green key focal areas and leading to green products. This target was already reached in mid-2010. Therefore in 2010, the EcoVision5 programme was launched for the first time setting sustainability targets aiming at both the social and environmental dimensions of sustainability.

- Green Product sales increased to 51% of total sales (€ 11.8 billion) in 2013, two years ahead of schedule.
- €509 million was invested in Green Innovation, dedicated to addressing global challenges related to health care, materials and energy efficiency.
- A Circular Economy approach was launched to further enhance Green value creation.
- The lives of 1.8 billion people were improved in 2013.
- 14,000 tonnes of recycled content was included in its products by focusing on the material streams for plastics, aluminium, refurbished products and spare parts harvesting.
- Philips was recognized as an industry leader in the 2013 Carbon Disclosure Project. (CDP), scoring an 'A' for performance.

Source: Seebode, D., Jeanrenaud, S. and Bessant, J. (2012) 'Managing Innovation for Sustainability', *R&D Management*, **42**(3), 195–206.
and

http://www.philips.com/about/company/missionandvisionvaluesandstrategy/vision2015.page

Paradigm shift

A paradigm shift is taking place in innovation, which is being democratized with active user roles and open innovation processes, and where the scope is widening from product and service innovation to business model and societal innovation. Different stakeholders are involved from the public sector, the business world (local and international companies), academia, NGOs, citizens and users. Information and communication technology is a key enabler for mobilizing and aggregating 'collective intelligence and creativity' (Green, 2007). An example and expression of this shift in innovation can be seen in the launch of the European Network of Living Labs in 2006. The labs bring together users and experts to foster collaborative innovation and are a step towards a European Innovation System based on open co-creative labs for jobs, growth and global competitiveness.

The paradigm shift invites innovation to take place in managerial thinking. Existing literature brings forward two theories to help managers: dynamic capabilities and design thinking. Chapter 1 describes dynamic capabilities as a multidisciplinary framework to explain long-term enterprise performance. Teece (2014) has clearly highlighted that organizational ambidexterity and other related frameworks are tailored versions of dynamic capabilities. Thus, TM can be conceived as a set of dynamic capabilities for dealing with the complexities of the world. Since this book already utilizes the dynamic-capability approach, a second helpful tool for technology managers is discussed here: design thinking.

In its simplest form, design shapes ideas to become practical and attractive propositions for users or customers. Design is not only a problem-solving activity but also a knowledge-generation and integration activity, covering a wide range of fields, activities and tasks, including product performance, process efficiency, cost, ease of manufacturing, aesthetics, user friendliness, durability and ergonomics. Hobday et al. (2011) argue that economic growth and the expansion of wealth rely in part on the design and creation of new spaces for technological possibility. These spaces, in turn, require the human ability to design and create stories, forms and concepts that underpin business and wider economic innovation. In other words, design thinking is a model that allows firms to integrate design into their core activities as a spur to innovation, and it becomes a critical consideration for technology managers.

According to one of the leading thinkers of the subject, Martin (2009) introduces design thinking as a challenge to managers in order to think outside the box. Design thinking is based on three key concepts: the knowledge funnel, the distinction between reliability and validity and abductive reasoning (Martin, 2009; Leavy, 2009). The knowledge funnel is a pathway with three main stages – mystery (and hunch), heuristic (turning a hunch into an initial heuristic or rule-of-thumb) and algorithm (converting the heuristic into a repeatable formula or algorithm). The goal of reliability is to 'produce consistent, predictable outcomes,' while the goal of validity is to 'produce outcomes that meet a desired objective.' Abductive reasoning refers to the logic of what might be. This thought process is a kind of informed conjecture that can only be verified through the generation of new data (usually through prototyping and testing in most business applications). So it is neither associated with analytical thinking (relevant to exploitation) nor intuitive thinking (like in exploration). In fact, this is exactly what the November 2014 issue in Harvard Business Review (Thomke et al., 2014) invites managers to experiment with.

Why might such thinking help managers dealing with technologies? As described above, managers are faced with the challenges of developing and managing ambidextrous organizations. Design thinking appears to be a tool to balance two key conflicts: (1)

exploration-exploitation and (2) reliability-validity. Exploration includes things captured by terms such as search, variation, risk taking, experimentation, play, flexibility, discovery and innovation. Exploitation includes such things as refinement, choice, production, efficiency, selection, implementation and execution. Adaptive systems that engage in exploration to the exclusion of exploitation are likely to find that they suffer the costs of experimentation without gaining many of its benefits. They exhibit too many undeveloped new ideas and too little distinctive competence, while systems that engage in exploitation to the exclusion of exploration are likely to find themselves trapped below optimal equilibrium. As a result, maintaining an appropriate balance between exploration and exploitation is a primary factor in system survival and prosperity. Design thinking helps to balance exploration and exploitation.

The second balance where design thinking might be helpful is the reliability-validity dimension. In practice, programs like Six Sigma typify the reliability-orientation, while R&D represents the kind of exploratory activity most associated with validity. Leavy (2009) defines a process as reliable if it produces a predictable result time and again, and a process is valid when it flows from 'designers' deep understanding of both user and context'. In order to compete, firms need to build their processes to balance reliability-validity expectations.

Finally, abductive reasoning encourages experimentation to find solutions. Various tools from design are offered as valuable instruments for generating solutions. From architecture, such tools include various forms of visualization, including drawings, sketches, computer graphics and prototypes; from new product design, companies like IDEO (a design consultancy) propose creative processes that include 'un-focus' groups and ethnographic techniques. So a design attitude assumes that the main challenge is to generate and develop alternative solutions from which to choose.

Further, design thinking could be instrumental in understanding multiple users across countries and markets. The IRI 2038 study identifies the importance of needs identification and speed-to-market in order to quickly identify opportunities for research and technology to serve new customer needs and understand each customer in his/her specific context. This means developing skills in culture, society, customer research, ethnography, technology scouting and rapid prototyping that are the key tools in design thinking. Additionally, these skills will need to be global, as new consumers and researchers from emerging markets around the globe demand more attention.

Besides the creation and diffusion of innovations for particular customer needs, culture is influential in commercialization and scaling processes. Both national and company culture could influence the result of innovation. Culture plays an important role that bridges invention and innovation; invention can be transferred to innovation with a culture which can support the invention, and invention can be inspired by an innovative culture. In summary, the balance of multiple perspectives of decision-making and the roles of diversity and government policy are all crucial for the success of an innovation in a global context.

14.4 Implications for technology managers and educators

The evidence on the need for a TM education is compelling. The five major forces that contribute to this (Badawy, 2009) are the necessity of understanding the complex problems of managing technology, the critical need for a broad vision of technology as an integral link in corporate strategy, managing technological innovation as a top-management responsibility, the context and core competence of technology-based organizations and the unique characteristics of technical professionals.

On top of that, the challenges outlined above, namely the intensification of innovation, the integration of services and manufacturing and increased concern on sustainability, TM is challenging current managerial practices and calls for fundamental change in TM education. Since sustainability and innovation go beyond organizational boundaries and require managers to act in networks across functional and national borders, technology managers need to be equipped with new expertise and new skills in organizing, collaborating and communicating both internally and externally. This trend will increase and strengthen open innovation practices such as the rise of 'open-source' innovation (e.g. Linux, a software operating system that has captured substantial market share) and new organizational forms (e.g. research joint ventures and technology alliances).

TM's overarching concern is to help management understand, assimilate, integrate and direct technology and technology-facilitated innovation for the benefit of the enterprise, customers and society. Given that need, technology managers and students with career plans in TM should find ways of preparing themselves for the future. Educators also have to find ways to respond to the new challenges.

TM naturally rests on knowledge developed over many years. As shown through the analysis of literature from 1987 to 2006, the existing body of TM is based on six topics (Duan, 2011): (1) core competence and competitive advantage; (2) information system planning and changes; (3) the management of innovation and organizations; (4) TM approaches; (5) technology strategy; and (6) organizational learning and KM. Any educational programme needs to address these topics as the basis of the knowledge to be transferred to students.

On top of that base, professionals and students need to be equipped with a broad set of skills, ranging from generic to specific (Wright et al., 2008). Within the context of TM education, a recent study considered generic skills such as those taught in courses on strategy, marketing, organizational behaviour, finance, project management and operations management. These courses are characterized by their emphasis upon theory, often abstracted from a single industry or technology. By contrast, according to the same study, specific skills are considered to be creative problem solving, new technology evaluation, business plan development and cross-disciplinary communication. This is because those skills are rooted within the industry or technology context where the technologists are based.

Effective management of technology calls for different managerial skills, techniques, styles and ways of thinking. Thus, the challenge facing management educators in determining what managers in the 21st century should know about technology is daunting. What is needed is a new breed of managers who are as adept in TM as they are in traditional business skills. Technology-based corporations increasingly need a capacity for rapid innovation in strategies, products, processes and services as distinct from traditional high-volume mass production or service companies of past decades. Managers of technology, therefore, need to acquire the knowledge and skills that will enable them to compete effectively in world markets. In particular, design thinking deserves to be a key part of education programmes.

As it stands, literature also offers some studies with suggestions for educators. Van Wyk and Gaynor (2014) propose a template for graduate level studies that covers the comprehensive body of knowledge for TM in four groups: (1) knowledge of technology, (2) knowledge of technology-linked management topics, (3) knowledge of general management topics and (4) knowledge of supporting disciplines. The knowledge to be transmitted in education might be broad enough but the challenges call educational institutions to enrich these categories to develop and adopt a different set of managerial concepts, competencies and skills for the effective management of technology. There is a need for broadening the knowledge set to include design thinking and sustainability.

A European wide study confirms the need for technology entrepreneurship and commercialization skills (Clarysse et al., 2009). Another study highlights greater attention to the management and commercialization of IP (Thursby et al., 2009). It is clear that there is a shift towards more entrepreneurially-based courses that require interdisciplinary skills and team learning (Phan et al., 2009).

On the issue of collaborations, another study (Austin et al., 2009) highlights that the technology manager needs to orchestrate the integration of different kinds of knowledge, from specialized/domain specific to general/domain spanning, requiring familiarity with both technological and managerial issues. The study considers the example of arriving at a recommendation of which technology to adopt. Such a decision requires access to deep technical knowledge as well as an ability to conceptually separate technical from management concerns and involve decision makers with the knowledge, skills, authority and incentives appropriate to each. Technology managers should be ready for these challenging tasks.

Considering the global nature of technologies and their diffusion, it is no surprise that there needs to be a set of skills to help managers face cultural and global concerns. A study on developing a global mindset (Javidan and Walker, 2013) shows that cultural issues might diffuse into knowledge and skill sets for managers to get ready for diversity in global markets. In particular, managers aiming to become global leaders should develop their intellectual, psychological and social capital, and some guidelines for this are suggested below:

1 Global intellectual capital refers to a set of knowledge relating to: global industry, global competitive business and marketing strategies, assessment of risks of doing business internationally, supplier options in other parts of the world, cultures in different parts of the world, geography, history, important persons of several countries, economic and political issues, concerns and hot topics of major regions of the world.

2 Global psychological capital constitutes passion for diversity, quest for adventure and self-assurance. Passion for diversity means the enjoyment of exploring, travelling and living in other parts of the world, as well as getting to know people there. Quest for adventure covers interest in dealing with challenging situations, the willingness to take risks and to test one's abilities as well as the enjoyment of dealing with unpredictable situations. Finally, self-assurance skills are needed such as being energetic, self-confident, comfortable in uncomfortable situations and witty in tough situations.

3 Global social capital covers three traits: intercultural empathy, interpersonal impact and diplomacy skills. Intercultural empathy is based on an ability to work well with people from other parts of the world, an ability to understand nonverbal expressions of people from other cultures, an ability to emotionally connect to people from other cultures and to engage people from other parts of the world to work together. Interpersonal impact is associated with experience in negotiating contracts/agreements in other cultures, strong networks with people from other cultures and with influential

people and reputation as a leader. Finally, diplomacy refers to skills such as ease of starting a conversation with a stranger, an ability to integrate diverse perspectives, an ability to listen to what others have to say and willingness to collaborate.

One last reminder about skills is from the book written by Brynjolfsson and McAffee (2014): technologies like big data and analytics, high-speed communications and rapid prototyping have augmented the contributions made by more abstract and data-driven reasoning, and in turn have increased the value of people with the right engineering, creative or design skills. Thus, digital technologies are offering many opportunities for those who are ready to capture them with the required skill set.

In sum, there is more to be done to figure out how to succeed in a future world that will be different from today. We end with a quotation from Kocaoglu (2009):

Technology cannot solve every problem in society; but there are very few problems that can be solved without proper utilization of technology. Proper utilization requires proper management. That is what our discipline does. Those who manage technology will be the winners in the coming generations, those who are managed by technology will be left in the footnotes of history. The challenge awaiting us is to make sure that our societies will be among the winners.

 Key Questions

1 How can technology contribute to the competitiveness of firms?
2 Does design-driven innovation contribute to the understanding of TM?
3 What is an ambidextrous organization? What are the main characteristics of these organizations?
4 What are the managerial roles of technology managers in a company?
5 Please explain the challenges technology managers face in the coming years.
6 What should educators take into consideration while renewing the curriculum of TM?

 Further reading

Adler, P. S. and Ferdows, K. (2009) 'The Chief Technology Officer', *California Management Review*, **32**(3), 55–62.

Austin, R., Nolan, R. L. and O'Donnell, S. (2009) 'The Technology Manager's Journey: An Extended Narrative Approach to Educating Technical Leaders', *Academy of Management Learning & Education*, **8**(3), 337–355.

Badawy, A. F. (2009) 'Technology Management Simply Defined: A Tweet Plus Two Characters', *Journal of Engineering and Technology Management*, **26**(4), 219–224.

Brynjolfsson, E. and McAffee, A. (2014) *The Second Machine Age* (New York: Norton).

Cetindamar, D. and Kilitcioglu, H. (2013) 'Measuring the Competitiveness of a Firm for an Award System', *Competitiveness Review*, **23**(1), 7–22.

Cetindamar, D. and Pala, O. (2011) 'Chief Technology Officer Roles and Performance', *Technology Analysis & Strategic Management*, **23**(10), 1031–1046.

(Continued)

Chang, S.-B., Lai, K.-K. and Chang, S.-M. (2009) 'Exploring Technology Diffusion and Classification of Business Methods: Using the Patent Citation Network', *Technological Forecasting & Social Change*, **76**(1), 107–117.

Chui, M., Löffler, M. and Roberts, R. (2010) 'The Internet of Things', McKinsey Quarterly, http://www.mckinsey.com/insights/high_tech_telecoms_internet/the_internet_of_things

Clarysse, B., Mosey, S. and Lambrecht, I. (2009) 'New Trends in Technology Management Education: A View from Europe', *Academy of Management Learning & Education*, **8**(3), 427–443.

Derbyshire, J. (2014) 'The Impact of Ambidexterity on Enterprise Performance: Evidence from 15 Countries and 14 Sectors', *Technovation*, **34**, 574–581.

Duan, C.-H. (2011) 'Mapping the Intellectual Structure of Modern Technology Management', *Technology Analysis & Strategic Management*, **23**(5), 583–600.

Farrington, T. and Crews, C. (2013) 'The IRI 2038 Scenarios', *Research-Technology Management*, **56**(6), 23–32.

Green, J. (2007) *Democratizing the Future: Towards a New Era of Creativity and Growth* (Eindhoven: Philips Electronics N. V.).

Hobday, M., Boddington, A. and Grantham, A. (2011) 'An Innovation Perspective on Design: Part 1', *Design Issues*, **27**(4), 5–15.

Hobday, M., Boddington, A. and Grantham, A. (2012) 'An Innovation Perspective on Design: Part 2', *Design Issues*, **28**(1), 18–29.

Iansiti, M. and Lakhani, K. (2014) 'Digital Ubiquity: How Connections, Sensors, and Data Are Revolutionizing Business', *Harvard Business Review*, **92**(11), 91–99.

Javidan, M. and Walker, J. L. (2013) *Developing Your Global Mindset* (Edina, MN: Beaver's Pond Press).

Kocaoglu, D. F. (2009) 'Engineering Management – Where it Was, Where it is Now, Where it is Going', *Engineering Management Journal*, **21**(3), 23–25.

Leavy, B. (2009) 'A Design-thinking – A new Mental Model for Value Innovation', *Strategy and Leadership*, **38**(3), 5–14.

Martin, R. (2009) *The Design of Business: Why Design Thinking is the Next Competitive Advantage* (Cambridge, MA: Harvard Business Review Press).

McKinsey (2011) Big Data: The Next Frontier for Innovation, Competition, and Productivity. http://www.mckinsey.com/insights/business_technology/big_data_the_next_frontier_for_innovation

O'Briens, J. M. (2012) 'The Vine Nerds', *Wired's*. http://www.wired.com/2012/10/mf-fruition-sciences-winemakers.

Parida, V., Sjödin, D. R. and Kohtamäki, M. (2014) 'Mastering the Transition to Product-service Provision', *Research-Technology Management*, **57**(3), 44–52.

Phan, P. P., Siegel, D. S. and Wright, M. (2009) 'New Developments in Technology Management Education: Background Issues, Program Initiatives, and a Research Agenda', *Academy of Management Learning & Education*, **8**(3), 324–336.

Porter, M. E. and Heppelmann, J. E. (2014) 'How Smart, Connected Products are Transforming Competition', *Harvard Business Review*, **92**(11), 64–88.

Seebode, D., Jeanrenaud, S. and Bessant, J. (2012) 'Managing Innovation for Sustainability', *R&D Management*, **42**(3), 195–206.

Simsek, Z. (2009) 'Organizational Ambidexterity: Towards a Multilevel Understanding', *Journal of Management Studies*, **46**(4), 597–624.

Teece, D. J. (2014) 'The Foundations of Enterprise Performance: Dynamic and Ordinary Capabilities in an (Economic) Theory of Firms', *Academy of Management Perspectives*, **28**(4), 328–352.

Tidd, J. and Bessant, J. (2013) *Managing Innovation: Integrating Technological, Market and Organizational Change*, 5th edn (Chichester: John Wiley).

Thomke, S. and Manzi, J. (2014) 'The Discipline of Business Experimentation', *Harvard Business Review*, **92**(12), 70–79.

Thursby, M. C., Fuller, A. W. and Thursby, J. (2009) 'An Integrated Approach to Educating Professionals for Careers in Innovation', *Academy of Management Learning & Education*, **8**(3), 389–405.

Tobias, Z. (2000) 'Chief Technology Officer', *Computerworld*, **34**, 76–77.

Tschirky, H., Jung, H.-H. and Savioz, P. (2003) *Technology and Innovation Management on the Move: From Managing Technology to Managing Innovation-driven Enterprises* (Zurich, Switzerland: Orell Fuessli Verlag).

Van der Hoven, C., Probert, D., Phaal, R. and Goffin, K. (2012) 'Dynamic Technology Leadership', *Research-Technology Management*, **55**(5), 24–33.

Van Wyk, R. J. and Gaynor, G. (2014) 'An Academic Template for Graduate Programs in Engineering and Technology Management', *IEEE Engineering Management Review*, **42**(4), 119–124.

WWF (2010) *Living Planet Report 2010. Biodiversity, Biocapacity and Development* (Gland, Switzerland: WWF International).

Zeschky, M. B., Winterhalter, S. and Gassman, O. (2014) 'From Cost to Frugal and Reverse Innovation: Mapping the Field and Implications for Global Competitiveness', *Research-Technology Management*, **57**(4), 20–27.

APPENDIX: LINKING TM ACTIVITIES WITH TM TOOLS

This book is based on the micro-level analysis of TM in order to understand how firms carry out their TM activities and what tools and techniques are needed. Technological changes are continuously creating new challenges and opportunities for application to new product, service and process development. However, these opportunities need to be captured and turned into value through effective TM where development and implementation of technological capabilities are needed.

TM is the ability to improve and develop products, processes and existing technology as well as to generate new knowledge and skills in response to the competitive business environment. Each TM activity is related to a certain technological capability, comprising one or more processes/routines/competencies. Technology capabilities are accumulated and embodied in skills, knowledge, experience and organizational systems. Since TM activities help to develop and implement generic technological capabilities, Part I introduced these generic capabilities and activities – acquisition, exploitation, identification, learning, protection and selection.

It is difficult to describe exactly where firms exercise these activities due to the complex nature of firms and industries. In the TM framework presented in Figure 1.1, TM activities are typically linked to or embedded within three core business processes: strategy, innovation and operations. This is why after identifying the actual business processes behind strategy, innovation and operations, managers are able to integrate TM processes into them. Depending on a number of contextual conditions such as size, firms gradually accumulate technological capabilities through the various processes, procedures, routines and structures embedded in practice. Managers need to identify the various common processes/routines forming the key technological capabilities that reflect what goes on within their individual companies. In other words, each organization will have their specific elements that show their own individual picture. If the organization is a large company with considerable R&D activity, the story/completed picture might include all elements in the TM activities model. However, if the organization has no R&D and the innovation is incremental, the corresponding activities will be different. For example, a small firm might develop only the exploitation and learning capabilities to survive in the market. Once managers identify their key technological capabilities, they can manage technology effectively.

It is true that effective TM is based on dynamically developing skills and knowledge. However, skills and knowledge are a necessary but not sufficient condition for managing technologies. Turning these skills and knowledge into practice is as important as developing them, making TM activities and tools the two sides of the same coin. In this book, tools include devices for supporting both action/practical application and frameworks for conceptual understanding. The word 'tool' indicates that the user controls how it is applied and how well it is used. Thus the tools can be adapted by a company to fit its own purposes and situation and can be used singly or in various combinations. Part II introduced six TM tools and techniques – patent analysis, portfolio management, road-mapping, S-curve, stage-gate and value analysis – which are useful for carrying out the TM activities mentioned in Part I.

In this Appendix, the goal is to link TM activities with the tools. However, few studies have been undertaken that link TM activities with the available set of tools in a comprehensive format. One notable exception is *Temaguide: A Guide to Technology Management and Innovation for Companies* (Cotec, 1998), which, as part of a study funded by the EU in 1998, considers how TM tools can be applied, as shown in Figure A.1. *Temaguide* proposes 18 types of TM tools that can be used in six major tasks:

- Gathering external information.
- Gathering internal information.
- Deciding on workload and resources for various technology projects.
- Facilitating ideas and supplying solutions to problems.
- Improving efficiency and flexibility.
- Managing groups/teams in a company.

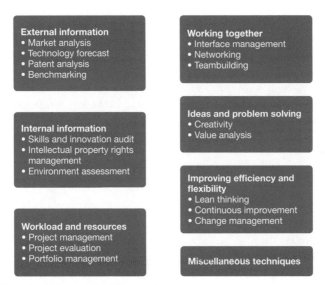

Figure A.1   TM tools and their application potential
Source: Cotec (1998).

For example, if a manager wants to gather external information, *Temaguide* proposes the use of four main techniques – market analysis, technology forecast, patent analysis and benchmarking.

Dhillon (2002) does not describe any particular TM activity but offers nine different sets of tools to be used for engineering and technology management in general:

- *Decision-making tools*: decision trees, optimization techniques, discounted cash flow analysis, learning curve analysis, depreciation analysis, fault tree analysis and forecasting methods.

- *Project management tools*: project selection methods and models, project management techniques and project managers' responsibilities, qualifications, selection and reporting.
- *Engineering design and product costing tools*: design types and approaches, engineering design manpower, design reviews and design review team, reasons for product costing, product life cycle costing and new product pricing.
- *Creativity and innovation.*
- *Concurrent engineering.*
- *Value engineering.*
- *Reverse engineering.*
- *TQM.*
- *Maintenance management.*

Some of the tools mentioned above, such as reverse engineering and decision making, are applicable to many managerial activities, so they are not specific to TM per se. Some others such as TQM directly help to manage quality rather than technology.

Another notable study reviewed major TM journals to identify TM tools that can be used for specific TM activities (Cetindamar et al., 2006). The following journals were searched with the keywords 'tools' and 'activities', for the period 1995–2005 using the ABI Proquest and Elsevier ScienceDirect databases: *Research Policy, Journal of Product Innovation Management, Journal of Business Venturing, IEEE Transactions on Engineering Management, R&D Management, International Journal of Technology Management, Technology Analysis and Strategic Management, Journal of Engineering & Technology Management, Research-Technology Management, Journal of High Technology Management Research* and *Technovation*. The results identified 122 relevant articles, but analysis showed that there is no integrated study available that groups TM tools on the basis of TM activities or vice versa.

In the above study (Cetindamar et al., 2006), TM activities are listed under 11 categories:

- Technology utilization.
- KM.
- Technology acquisition.
- R&D management.
- Technology integration.
- Technology protection.
- Technology transfer.
- Technology planning and forecasting.
- Technology strategy.
- Technology assessment.
- Technology commercialization and marketing.

These activities are rather confusing, since broad managerial tasks such as KM are at the same level of analysis as other individual tasks such as technology planning. As discussed in Chapter 1, KM crosses all activities in TM-specific activities. However, the study proposes an ad-hoc model of linking TM tools with TM activities.

Table A.1 shows how the tools can be used in different TM activities. Some of these tools are used in more than one activity. For example, patent analysis might be used for technology protection, technology transfer and KM. The combination of tools and the way they will be used in a company will vary depending on the company's structural characteristics as well as its specific need.

Table A.1 The relationship between TM techniques/methods and activities

TM tools and techniques	Related TM activities
Strategic thinking techniques SWOT analysis, Porter's five forces analysis	Technology strategy
Techniques for identification of technologies Value chain analysis	Technology acquisition, technology transfer
Market analysis Cost-benefit analysis, statistical decision-making models	Technology strategy, technology acquisition, technology planning
Benchmarking	Technology strategy, technology transfer, technology assessment
Technology forecast Mathematical programming techniques, monitoring, simulation, technology road mapping, decision trees, methodological forecasting techniques, trend extrapolation, technology life-cycle analysis, technology-product matrix analysis, modelling, expert opinion	Technology planning and forecasting, technology assessment
Intellectual property rights Licensing, patent analysis	Technology transfer, technology protection, licence/patent purchasing, technology commercialization and marketing, KM
Portfolio management Two to three dimensional matrices, value-success probability matrix, technological position – maturity matrix, technology efficiency analysis, check lists, technology analysis (technical and economical)	R&D development, technology utilization, technology integration
Project evaluation Risk-return analysis, capacity and bottleneck calculations, reverse engineering	Technology assessment, technology utilization
Continuous improvement Brainstorming	R&D development, technology utilization, KM
Creativity Promote creativity and change, scenario building, teamwork, education for professional development	R&D development, KM

Source: Cetindamar et al. (2006).

Studies in the literature focus mainly on a specific TM activity, for which tools are developed and applied. For example, Daim and Kocaoglu's (2008) study describes the tools for technology acquisition. De Piante Henriksen's (1997) study of technology assessment classified useful assessment tools into nine categories (Table A.2):

- Economic analysis.
- Information monitoring.
- Technical performance assessment.
- Decision analysis.
- Risk assessment.
- Systems engineering/systems analysis.
- Market analysis.
- Technological forecasting.
- Externalities/impact analysis.

Table A.2 Technology assessment toolkit for TM in the globally competitive enterprise

Economic analysis	Risk assessment
Cost/benefit analysis, cost-effectiveness analysis, life-cycle cost assessment (LCA), return on investment (ROI), net present value (NPV), internal rate of return (IRR), breakeven point analysis, residual income, total savings, increasing returns analysis	Simulation modelling and analysis, probabilistic risk assessment, environment, health and safety studies, risk-based decision trees, litigation risk assessment
Information monitoring	**Systems engineering/systems analysis**
Electronic databases, internet, technical/scientific literature reviews, patent searches, Bayesian confidence profile analysis	Technology system studies, system dynamics, simulation modelling and analysis, project management techniques, system optimization techniques, linear, integer and non-linear programming, technology portfolio analysis, externalities analysis
Technical performance assessment	**Market analysis**
Statistical analysis, surveys/questionnaires, trial use periods, beta testing, technology decomposition theory, S-curve analysis, human factors analysis, ergonomics studies, ease-of-use studies, outcomes research	Fusion method, market push/pull analysis, surveys/questionnaires, S-curve analysis
Decision analysis	**Technological forecasting**
Multi-criteria decision making, multi-attribute utility theory scoring, group decision support systems (GDSS), Delphi/group Delphi, analytic hierarchy process (AHP), Q-sort, decision trees, fuzzy logic	S-curve analysis, Delphi/AHP/Q-sort, R&D researcher hazard rate analysis, trend extrapolation, correlation and causal methods, probabilistic methods
Externalities/impact analysis	
Social impact analysis, political impact analysis, environmental impact analysis, ethical issues analysis, cultural impact analysis	

Source: De Piante Henriksen (1997).

Table A.2 indicates how complicated it could be just to look at the tool list given for a specific TM activity. It is possible that not all tools need to be applied, since some have dual or multiple purposes and can be used as a substitute for others. In addition, companies can change their assessment criteria according to the type of technology. For example, simulation modelling might give enough information to make an assessment of a technology, but in other cases, it might require the use of additional techniques.

The management discipline consists not only of knowledge but also a wide variety of skills, among which the ability to use managerial tools in practice is a critical one. The value of management tools is occasionally brought into question, since they are sometimes seen as some form of crutch that managers deploy instead of thinking creatively (Brady et al., 1997). There are a few studies investigating which managerial processes and tools are most often used by boards and senior management groups in practice. One such study was conducted by a consultant firm called Bain & Company, whose tools study goes back to 1993. In 2005, Bain surveyed 960 global executives to investigate the use of 25 major management tools. The most widely used tool to help run a business was strategic planning (79% of respondents), while mission and vision statements were reported as widely used (72%) and change management programmes were reported as used by 59% (Rigby and Bilodeau, 2005).

Even though the management discipline has been developing general tools for use across disciplines, such as finance and marketing, and specific tools devoted to sub-disciplines, the TM literature rarely offers a list of tools relevant to managing technology in companies, although it has been described as a necessity (Brady et al., 1997; Whitney, 2007). This is why it is important to conclude the book by offering a list that will satisfy the needs of TM activities. This is a wider list than the six key tools discussed in the book, in order to give a wider framework to understand how tools and activities could be matched.

On the basis of the dynamic-capability-based model of the TM framework developed in Chapter 1, the link between the major TM activities and tools is mapped (Table A.3). Table A.3 attempts to include as many tool groups as possible, but it is not an exhaustive list, since there are as many ways of doing the same tasks in management (TM is no exception) as there are in any social science. For example, to increase creativity, mind mapping or lateral thinking techniques could be used interchangeably. In the same way, forecasting could be done by scenario analysis or the Delphi method.

In order to find out which type of tools will be needed to carry out each TM activity, we studied the processes described in Part I for that particular activity and developed general tool categories. For example, Chapter 2 describes how internal and external acquisition processes work, including processes ranging from portfolio management, new product/service/process development, to specific external collaboration management such as finding partners. Given this set of acquisition processes, managers will want to tap into tools that will be useful for assessing, developing creativity, managing projects and strategy building. Depending on the particular need, managers can adapt one or more tools and form a portfolio of tools in dealing with the acquisition problem at hand. As shown in Table A.3, managers might use mind mapping, patent analysis and roadmapping, among others.

Table A.3 shows eight general tool categories useful for carrying out TM activities:

- Assessment.
- Creativity.
- Decision making.
- Forecasting.
- KM.
- Problem solving.
- Project management.
- Strategy.

The names given to these general tool categories might vary, but we believe they capture what managers need. For example, in acquiring technologies, managers need to assess technologies, be creative in developing new ideas, manage innovative projects and develop strategies for collaborations and projects. Given these needs, the corresponding names for these four general tool categories become assessment, creativity, project management and strategy.

Some examples are given for each tool category in Table A.3. In the case of assessment, exemplar tools are benchmarking, real options, quality function deployment and S-curves, while in the case of strategy tools, three examples are roadmapping, SWOT and value analysis.

Table A.3 TM tools and their applications

Activities	General tool categories	Examples
Acquisition	Assessment techniques Creativity tools Project management tools Strategy tools	Real options, S-curve* Mind mapping, lateral thinking Portfolio management*, stage-gate* Roadmapping*, value analysis*
Exploitation	Assessment techniques Problem solving Project management tools Strategy tools	Benchmarking, S-curve* Fishbone diagram, TRIZ Portfolio management*, stage-gate* Roadmapping*, value analysis*
Identification	Assessment techniques Forecasting techniques KM tools Strategy tools	Quality function deployment, S-curve* Delphi method, roadmapping* Knowledge mapping, patent analysis* SWOT, value analysis*
Learning	Creativity tools KM tools Project management tools Strategy tools	Six hats, cause and effect analysis Brainstorming, patent analysis* Portfolio management*, stage-gate* Roadmapping*, value analysis*
Protection	Assessment techniques KM tools Project management tools Strategy tools	Cost-benefit analysis, S-curve* Patent analysis*, value mapping Portfolio management*, stage-gate* Roadmapping*, value analysis*
Selection	Assessment techniques Decision-making tools Project management tools Strategy tools	S-curve*, STEEPA Balanced scorecard, decision trees Portfolio management*, stage-gate* Roadmapping*, value analysis*

Key: * these tools are presented in Part II.

Table A.3 aims to capture the links between TM activities and the tools that help to manage these activities. Identifying the major tools that facilitate the development and application of technological capabilities is particularly important for offering practical guidelines to apply and reinforce TM concepts within the business so that managers can incorporate TM into their daily routines.

Given that management is an art, there is no single best way to manage technology in a company and there is no mechanistic route to success. There are, however, lessons that can be learned from other companies and theoretical frameworks to guide thinking and decision making, and tools and techniques to assist analysis. This book is an attempt to simplify a complicated world by offering a starting point to deal with the management of technology. Table A.3 shows how different sets of tools might be used to carry out six key TM activities and how the six tools covered in this book form a small but critical set of tools, since they prevail across all activities. As discussed in Chapter 1, the selection criteria for the six key tools are:

- Simplicity and flexibility of use.
- Degree of availability.
- Standardization level.
- The prevailing ones across TM processes and capture internal and external dynamics.

The goal of this book is to be a practical, handy guide for engineers, managers and students who plan to become technology managers in the future. Thus, it recommends the key TM activities and a small number of tools and techniques that will be used to carry out these tasks: six technological capabilities and six tools. However, as clearly shown in Table A.3, real life is complicated and there are many tools that could be of benefit. Managers need to start somewhere and the six TM activities and six tools presented in this text provide a useful starting point.

Further reading

Dodgson, M. (2000) *The Management of Technological Innovation* (Oxford: Oxford University Press).

Dorf, R. C. (1999) *The Technology Management Handbook* (Florida: CRC Press/IEEE Press).

Gaynor, G. H. (ed.) (1996) *Handbook of Technology Management* (New York: McGraw-Hill).

Gregory, M. J. (1995) 'Technology Management: A Process Approach', *Proceedings of the Institution of Mechanical Engineers*, **209**, 347–356.

Hidalgo, A. and Albors, J. (2008) 'Innovation Management Techniques and Tools: A Review from Theory and Practice', *R&D Management*, **38**(2), 113–127.

Liao, S. (2005) 'Technology Management Methodologies and Applications: A Literature Review from 1995–2003', *Technovation*, **25**(4), 381–393.

Phaal, R., Farrukh, C. J. and Probert, D. R. (2006) 'Technology Management Tools: Concept, Development and Application', *Technovation*, **26**(3), 336–344.

Rush, H., Bessant, J. and Hobday, M. (2007) 'Assessing the Technological Capabilities of Firms: Developing a Policy Tool', *R&D Management*, **37**(3), 221–236.

Straker, D. (1997) *Toolbook for Quality Improvement and Problem Solving* (New York: Prentice Hall).

Tidd, J., Bessant, J. and Pavitt, K. (1998) *Managing Innovation: Integrating Technological, Market and Organizational Change*, 3rd edn (Chichester: John Wiley).

GLOSSARY

Absorptive capacity measures a firm's ability to value, assimilate and apply new knowledge on multiple levels – individual, group, firm and national level. Antecedents are prior-based knowledge, that is, knowledge stocks and knowledge flows, as well as communication. It involves a firm's innovation performance, aspiration level and organizational learning. Absorptive capacity is particularly important for companies to invest in R&D instead of simply buying the results such as patents.

Acquisition is how a company obtains the technologies valuable for its business, based on the buy-collaborate-make decision. Technologies might be developed internally, by some form of collaboration or acquired from external developers. The management of acquisition differs on the basis of the choice made.

Activity is used interchangeably with 'process' or 'routine', and is associated with the concept of capability. When the capability reaches some threshold level of practised or routine activity, the performance of an activity can be claimed to constitute a capability.

Alliances are collaborations among several organizations ranging from firms to intermediaries. Several types of alliance are possible, ranging from an ad-hoc partnership formed to solve a specific problem, through complex alliances and joint ventures to complete acquisition.

Ambidextrous organization refers to an organization's ability to be efficient in its management of today's business and also adaptable for coping with tomorrow's changing demand.

Auditing generally refers to the evaluation of a person, organization, system, process, project or product. Audits are performed to ascertain the validity and reliability of information, and also to provide an assessment of a system's internal control. For example, a technology audit provides details of the technologies available in-house and their status.

Assessment is the systematic identification, analysis and evaluation of the potential secondary consequences, whether beneficial or detrimental, of technology in terms of its impacts on social, cultural, political and environmental systems and processes.

Base/enabling technologies are essential to be in business and are widely exploited by competitors, so their competitive impact is low. **Critical/key technologies** are well embodied in products and processes and their competitive impacts are high. **Pacing technologies** might be under experimentation by some competitors and if the technology succeeds, its competitive impact is likely to be high. **Emerging technologies** are at an early research stage or emerging in other industries and their competitive impact is unknown, although they are expected to be tomorrow's pacing technologies.

Balanced scorecard is an accounting method used to ensure well-rounded performance, especially from managers, by designing an evaluation that takes into account the perspective of clients/ customers, managers, peers and subordinates on four dimensions: customer service, internal business processes, learning and growth and financials.

Benchmarking uses standards or measures from high-performing organizations as a basis for comparison. The results from benchmarking need to be used as part of an overall change process; just doing the benchmarking doesn't lead to change.

212

Big data is a broad term for large or complex data sets.

A **business model** is a framework for creating economic, social and/or other forms of value. The term 'business model' is thus used for a broad range of informal and formal descriptions to represent core aspects of a business, including purpose, offerings, strategies, infrastructure, organizational structures, trading practices and operational processes and policies.

Business process re-engineering (BPR) is a TQM tool used to increase performance by radically redesigning the organization's structures and processes, including starting from the ground up.

Capability is an ability to do something, consisting of strategies and operational activities. Capability is the ability to perform actions and since it applies to human capital, capability is the sum of expertise and capacity. Capacity is the ability to hold, receive or absorb knowledge.

Commercialization is the process of introducing a new product/service into the market. The actual launch of a new product/service is the final stage of new product/service development. Commercialization includes the activities of finalizing development and preparing the product/ service to customers as well as dealing with marketing, such as advertising and sales promotion and after-sales efforts.

Complementary assets are the assets, infrastructure or capabilities needed to support the successful commercialization and marketing of a technological innovation, other than those assets fundamentally associated with that innovation. These assets offer services almost always needed to commercialize an innovation, such as marketing, competitive manufacturing and after-sales support. Three main complementary assets are 'generic assets', which do not need to be tailored to a particular innovation; 'specialized assets', which have unilateral dependence with the innovation; and 'co-specialized assets', where a bilateral dependence exists between the innovation and the complementary asset.

Concurrent engineering is a process in which appropriate disciplines are committed to work interactively to conceive, approve, develop and implement products/service projects that meet predetermined objectives. Concurrent engineering is applied to the engineering design philosophy of cross-functional cooperation in order to create products that are better, cheaper and more quickly brought to market.

Continuous improvement improves performance and customer satisfaction through continuous and incremental improvements to processes, including removing unnecessary activities and variations – often represented as a quality initiative.

Contracting R&D is where a company uses the services of a contract research organization or some other party to develop a new process or product.

Core competencies are competencies that are applicable to a wide variety of products and business markets, are not imitable and make a significant contribution to the perceived customer benefits of the end product. Core competencies are particular strengths relative to other organizations in the industry, which provide the fundamental basis for the provision of added value. Core competencies are the collective learning in organizations, and involve how to coordinate diverse production skills and integrate multiple streams of technologies.

Corporate entrepreneurship can broadly be defined as entrepreneurship within an existing organization. Employees, perhaps engaged in a special project within a larger firm, are encouraged to behave as entrepreneurs, with the resources and capabilities of the firm to draw upon. Corporate entrepreneurship includes all of an organization's innovation, renewal and venturing efforts.

Design is a plan or drawing produced to show the look and function or workings of a building, garment or other products/services before they are made.

Design-driven innovation is the radical change of user experience and meaning for products and services.

Design thinking is a formal method for practical, creative resolution of problems or issues, with the intent of an improved future result. It's a methodology for actualizing concepts and ideas.

The **development funnel** (also known as an idea/project funnel) illustrates the new product development process where the idea generation, development and product launch/commercialization activities are conducted. It is widely used in innovation management processes.

Diffusion is the process whereby a new technology is spread. Diffusion is also an endogenous characteristic of the innovation process itself, as the learning, imitation and feedback effects that arise during adoption further develop the initial innovation.

Digitalization refers to the emerging business model that is based on electronic channels, content and transactions thanks to the wide availability of digital technologies.

Diversification is a marketing strategy used by a company aiming to increase profitability through greater sales volume obtained from new products and new markets. The strategies of diversification can include internal development of new products or markets, acquisition of a firm, alliance with a complementary company, licensing of new technologies and distributing or importing a product line manufactured by another firm.

Dominant design indicates a key technological design that is a de facto standard in its marketplace. When a new technology emerges, rival firms will introduce a number of alternative designs and, through time, they will launch updated designs that incorporate incremental improvements. Then, at some point, the design becomes accepted as the industry standard.

Dynamic capabilities are the ability to reconfigure, redirect, transform and appropriately shape and integrate existing core competencies with external resources and strategic and complementary assets to meet the challenges of rapidly changing competition and imitation.

Eco-innovation means the creation of novel and competitively priced goods, processes, systems, services and procedures that can satisfy human needs and bring quality of life to all people with a life-cycle-wide minimal use of natural resources per unit output, and a minimal release of toxic substances.

Exploitation entails commercialization, but first the expected benefits need to be realized through the effective implementation, absorption and operation of the technology within the firm. Technologies are assimilated through technology transfer either from R&D to manufacturing or from external company/partner to internal manufacturing department. Exploitation processes include incremental developments, process improvements and marketing.

Forecasting means predicting the future. It is the process of estimation in unknown situations by use of qualitative (such as scenario-based) data or quantitative (such as time series, cross-sectional and longitudinal) data. Forecasting is applicable to many managerial tasks such as demand forecasting. Technological forecasting is forecasting the future characteristics of useful technological machines, procedures or techniques, as well as future market trends for technology products.

Identification is necessary for all sorts of technologies – enabling, critical, pacing or emerging. This process includes market changes as well as technological developments. Identification includes search, auditing, data collection and intelligence processes for technologies and markets.

Innovation is doing something new such as a product, process or service, including newness in the firm. It may refer to incremental, radical and revolutionary changes in thinking, technologies, products, processes, markets or organizations. Innovation has been studied in a variety of contexts, including technology, commerce, social systems, economic development and policy construction. So there are a wide range of approaches to conceptualizing innovation in the literature.

Innovation management is the discipline of managing innovation processes, so that novel ideas within an organization can be successfully implemented. These ideas are not limited to technologies.

Intelligence describes a property of the mind that encompasses many related abilities, such as the capacities to reason, plan, solve problems, think abstractly, comprehend ideas, use language and learn. There are several ways to define intelligence. In some cases, intelligence may include traits such as creativity, personality, character, knowledge or wisdom.

Intellectual assets are non-monetary assets that cannot be seen, touched or physically measured, are created through time and/or effort and are identifiable as a separate asset. There are two primary forms of intangibles: legal intangibles, such as trade secrets, copyrights, patents, trademarks and goodwill, known as 'intellectual property'; and competitive intangibles, such as knowledge activities, collaboration activities, leverage activities and structural activities, which directly impact effectiveness, productivity and opportunity costs within an organization.

Intellectual property (IP) is an umbrella term for various legal entitlements that attach to certain names, written and recorded media and inventions.

Intellectual property rights (IPR) refer to the rules governing the IP, which are defensible in a court of law.

Knowledge constitutes not only cognition or recognition (know-what), but also the capacity to act (know-how) as well as understanding (know-why) that reside within the mind.

Knowledge management (KM) collects and manages critical knowledge in an organization to increase its capacity for achieving results, often involving extensive use of computer technology; its impact depends on how well the enhanced, critical knowledge is applied to the organization.

Learning is a critical part of technological competency; it involves reflections on technology projects and processes carried out within or outside the firm. There is a strong link between this process and the broader field of knowledge management.

A **learning organization** is skilled at creating, acquiring and transferring knowledge, as well as modifying its behaviour to reflect new knowledge and insights.

Licensing refers to the conventional situation where a company holds a licence for the use of a product design/process/marketing package, or some combination of the three, on a franchise basis.

Market research aims to supply information to what, where, when, how and why questions about a company's business.

A **marketing innovation** is the implementation of a new marketing method involving significant changes in product design or packaging, product placement, product promotion or pricing.

M&A (mergers and acquisitions) refers to the buying, selling and combining of different companies that aid, finance or help a growing company in a given industry to grow rapidly without having to create another business entity. If two companies are more or less the same size, the term 'merger' is used.

Open innovation systems refer to how, in a world of widely distributed knowledge, companies cannot afford to rely entirely on their own research, but can buy or license processes or inventions from other companies.

An **organizational innovation** is the implementation of a new organizational method in the firm's business practices, workplace organization or external relations. **Patents** are granted for new, useful, and non-obvious inventions, and give the patent holder a right to prevent others from practising the invention without a licence from the inventor for a certain period of time.

Patent analysis is a tool to convert statistical information related to patents into useful information for a specific need.

Patent pool aggregates IPR of a number of patents related for the purpose of joint licensing.

Patent trolls are companies or individuals that buy up patents in bulk and block these patents' application in new innovations.

A **PESTEL** analysis is a framework or tool used by marketers to analyse and monitor the macro-environmental (external marketing environment) factors that have an impact on an organization. PESTEL stands for political, economic, social, technological, environmental and legal.

A **portfolio** is the collection of products in development and products in the market that focuses on achieving the company's strategic goals.

Portfolio management is the centralized management of one or more portfolios, by identifying, prioritizing, authorizing, managing and controlling projects and programmes to achieve the firm's strategic goals.

Process involves the transformation of inputs into outputs in order to achieve a managerial objective. A business process or business method is a collection of related, structured activities or tasks that produce a specific service or product (serve a particular goal) for a particular customer(s). It often can be visualized with a flow chart as a sequence of activities.

A **process innovation** is the implementation of a new or significantly improved production or delivery method.

A **product family** consists of products having similar features and the same model platforms. It provides an architecture based on commonality and similarity.

A **product innovation** is the introduction of a good or service that is new or significantly improved with respect to its characteristics or intended uses.

Protection aims to protect the intellectual assets within a firm, where formal processes such as patenting and staff retention need to be in place.

Quality function deployment is a TQM tool used in designing products on the basis of customer feedback; it extends value engineering in that it is not restricted to minimum essential product functions.

R&D (research and development) is a process of creating a firm's technologies in-house or through collaborations. In general, R&D activities are conducted by specialized units or centres belonging to companies, universities and state agencies. In the context of commerce, R&D normally refers to future-oriented, longer term activities in science or technology, using similar techniques to scientific research without predetermined outcomes and with broad forecasts of commercial yield.

Reverse innovation refers to product and service innovations aimed at resource-constrained customers in emerging markets.

Reliability is centred on the frequency of breakdowns, **maintainability** is focused on the time of breakdown and **availability** is viewed as being the consequence of reliability and maintainability.

Roadmapping provides an integrating framework that summarizes at a high level (on one page) the various strategic elements that must be aligned to achieve the overall organizational goals.

A **routine** describes a 'repetitive pattern of activity', a course of normative, standardized actions or procedures that are followed regularly.

Scenario analysis is a process of analysing possible future events by considering alternative possible outcomes.

S-curves are used to illustrate the life cycle of a phenomenon that starts off slowly, grows rapidly, tapers or levels off and then finally declines.

Selection takes account of company-level strategic issues, which requires a good grasp of strategic objectives and priorities developed at the business-strategy level. Then, the selection process aligns technology-related decisions with the business strategy.

STEEPA (social, technological, environmental, economic, political and aesthetic) is an assessment technique used to analyse these dimensions of a technology project: social, such as population growth rate and age profile; technological, such as impact of emerging technologies; environment, such as environmental laws; economic, such as current and future economic growth; political, such as government type and stability; and aesthetic, such as design.

The **stage-gate** process is a project management tool for new product development. A stage-gate model is a technique in which a product/process/system development process is divided into stages separated by gates. At each gate, the continuation of the development process is decided by (typically) a manager or a steering committee.

Sustainability refers to forms of progress that meet the needs of the present without compromising the ability of future generations to meet their needs.

A **SWOT analysis** is a structured planning method used to evaluate the strengths, weaknesses, opportunities and threats involved in a project or in a business venture.

Technology innovations refer to technologically new products, services and processes, as well as significant technological improvements in products, services and processes.

Technology intelligence is believed to capture and deliver technological information as part of the process whereby an organization develops an awareness of technology threats and opportunities.

Technology management (TM) is the management of technological capabilities to shape and accomplish the strategic and operational objectives of an organization.

The TM framework considers technology as a resource and emphasizes the dynamic nature of the knowledge flows that must occur between the commercial and technological functions in a firm, linking to the strategy, innovation and operational processes. An appropriate balance must be struck between market 'pull' (requirements) and technology 'push' (capabilities).

Technology transfer is the process by which the technology, knowledge and information developed by a creator are applied and utilized by an applier.

Technological capabilities consist of dynamic and operational capabilities that are a collection of routines/activities to execute and coordinate the variety of tasks required to manage technology.

Tools include devices for supporting action/practical application and frameworks for conceptual understanding. Many terms can be used interchangeably with tools, including 'techniques', 'procedures', 'processes', 'models', 'maps' and 'frameworks'.

Total quality management (TQM) ensures that the organization consistently meets or exceeds customer requirements and continually improves by measuring processes and imposing controls.

Utilization aims to maintain or continuously improve the existing use of technologies.

Value analysis (value engineering) is an interdisciplinary problem-solving activity for improving the value of the functions required to accomplish the goal or objective of any product, process, service or organization.

Value chain refers to a chain of activities. Products pass through all activities in the chain in order, and at each activity the product gains some value. The chain of activities gives the products more added value than the sum of added values of all activities.

A **value curve** shows how a customer sees the offerings of a company compared to that of its competitors.

Value proposition is a marketing concept indicating what the customer gets for their money/time. A customer can evaluate a company's value proposition on two broad dimensions with multiple subsets: relative performance, what the customer gets from the vendor relative to a competitor's offering, and price, what the customer pays to acquire the product or service plus the access cost.

BIBLIOGRAPHY

Abernathy, W. J. and Utterback, J. M. (1978) 'Patterns of Innovation in Technology', *Technology Review*, **80**(7), 40–47.

Abraham, B. and Moitra, S. (2001) 'Innovation Assessment through Patent Analysis', *Technovation*, **21**(4), 245–252.

Adler, P. S. and Ferdows, K. (2009) 'The Chief Technology Officer', *California Management Review*, **32**(3), 55–62.

Albright, R. E. and Kappel, T. A. (2003) 'Roadmapping in the Corporation', *Research-Technology Management*, **42**(2), 31–40.

Archer, N. P. and Ghasemzadeh, F. (1999) 'An Integrated Framework for Project Portfolio Selection', *International Journal of Project Management*, **17**(4), 207–216.

Argyris, C. and Schön, D. (1978) *Organisational Learning: A Theory of Action Perspective* (Reading, MA: Addison-Wesley).

Armbrecht, F. M., Chapas, R. B. Jr and Chappelow, C. C. (2001) 'Knowledge Management in R&D', *Research-Technology Management*, **44**(4), 28–48.

Ashkenas, R., Ulrich, D., Jick, T. and Kerr, S. (1995) 'Strengthening the Value Chain', in R. Ashkenas, D. Ulrich, T. Jick and S. Kerr (eds) *The Boundaryless Organization: Breaking the Chains of Organizational Structure* (San Francisco: Jossey-Bass).

Austin, R., Nolan, R. L. and O'Donnell, S. (2009) 'The Technology Manager's Journey', *Academy of Management Learning & Education*, **8**(3), 337–355.

Badawy, A. F. (2009) 'Technology Management Simply Defined: A Tweet Plus Two Characters', *Journal of Engineering and Technology Management*, **26**(4), 219–224.

Baiyin, Y., Watkins, K. E. and Marsick, V. J. (2004) 'The Construct of the Learning Organisation: Dimensions, Measurement, and Validation', *Human Resource Development Quarterly*, **15**(1), 31–55.

Beard, J. W. (2002) 'Management of Technology', *Knowledge, Technology & Policy*, **15**(3), 45–58.

Bell, M. (2003) *Knowledge Resources, Innovation Capabilities and Sustained Competitiveness in Thailand*, final report to NSTDA (Brighton: SPRU).

Bennett, D. (2013) 'Tracking the Trends in Manufacturing Technology Management', *Journal of Manufacturing Technology Management*, **24**(1), 5–8.

Bergek, A., Tell, F., Berggren, C. and Watson, J. (2008) 'Technological Capabilities and Late Shakeouts: Industrial Dynamics in the Advanced Gas Turbine Industry, 1987–2002', *Industrial and Corporate Change*, **17**(2), 335–392.

Berghman, L., Matthyssens, P. and Vandenbempt, K. (2012) 'Value Innovation, Deliberate Learning Mechanisms and Information from Supply Chain Partners', *Industrial Marketing Management*, **41**(1), 27–39.

Beruvides, M. G. and Khalil, T. (1990) 'Intra-firm Technology Transfer', in T. Khalil and B. Bayraktar (eds) *Management of Technology II* (Atlanta/Norcross, GA: Industrial Engineering and Management Press).

Bessant, J. and Caffyn, S. (1996) 'Learning to Manage Innovation', *Technology Analysis and Strategic Management*, **8**(1), 59–70.

Best, M. H. (2001) *The New Competitive Advantage: The Renewal of American Industry* (Oxford: Oxford University Press).

Bevilacqua, M., Ciarapica, F. E. and Giacchetta, G. (2007) 'Development of a Sustainable Product Lifecycle in Manufacturing Firms: A Case Study', *International Journal of Production Research*, **45**(18/19), 4073–4098.

Blau, J. and Wolff, M. F. (2006) 'Microsoft to Sell Non-core Technology', *Research-Technology Management*, **49**(4), 4–5.

Boerner, C. S., Macher, J. T. and Teece, D. J. (2001) 'A Review and Assessment of Organizational Learning in Economic Theories', in M. Dierkes, A. Antal, B. J. Child and I. Nonaka (eds) *Handbook of Organizational Learning and Knowledge* (New York: Oxford University Press).

Bontis, N., Dragonetti, N., Jacobsen, K. and Roos, G. (1999) 'The Knowledge Toolbox: A Review of the Tools Available to Measure and Manage Intangible Resources', *European Management Journal*, **17**(4), 391–402.

Bowden, M. J. (2004) 'Moore's Law and the Technology S-curve', *Stevens Alliance for Technology Management*, **8**(1), 4–7 and 11. http://www.stevens.edu/business/sites/business/files/SATM-Winter04-4_0.pdf

Bowonder, B., Miyake, T. and Muralidharan, B. (1999) 'Prediction of the Future: Lessons from Evolutionary Theory', *Technological Forecasting and Social Change*, **62**(1), 51–62.

Brady, T., Rush, H. and Hobday, M. (1997) 'Tools for Technology Management: An Academic Perspective', *Technovation*, **17**(8), 417–426.

Braun, E. (2000) *Technology in Context: Technology Assessment for Managers* (New York: Walter de Gruyter).

Breitzman, A. and Mogee, M. (2002) 'The Many Applications of Patent Analysis', *Journal of Information Science*, **28**(3), 187–205.

Breitzman, A. and Thomas, P. (2002) 'Using Patent Citation Analysis to Target/Value M&A Candidates', *Research-Technology Management*, **45**(5), 28–37.

Brown, D. (1997) *Innovation Management Tools: A Review of Selected Methodologies*, European Commission. EUR 17018.

Brynjolfsson, E. and McAffee, A. (2014) *The Second Machine Age* (New York: Norton).

Buggie, F. D. (2002) 'Set the Fuzzy Front End in Concrete', *Research-Technology Management*, **45**(4), 11–14.

Burgelman, R. A., Maidique, M. A. and Wheelwright, S. C. (2004) *Strategic Management of Technology and Innovation*, 4th edn (Chicago: Irwin).

Canadian Society of Value Analysis. (2008) *Improvements through Value Analysis*, www.scav-csva.org/aboutva.php.

Canez, L. and Garfias, M. (2006) 'Portfolio Management in the Literature', *Research-Technology Management*, **49**(4), 52–54.

Cao, Y. and Zhao, L. (2011) 'Intellectual Property Management Model in Enterprises', *International Journal of Innovation and Technology Management*, **8**(?), 253–272.

Carayannis, E. G. and Alexander, J. (1999) 'The Wealth of Knowledge: Converting Intellectual Property to Intellectual Capital in Co-operative Research and Technology Management Settings', *International Journal of Technology Management*, **18**(3/4), 326–352.

Carroll, P. B. and Mui, C. (2008) *Billion-dollar Lessons: What You Can Learn from the Most Inexcusable Business Failures of the Last 25 Years* (New York: Penguin).

Ccesoft. (2009) *The Value Curve of McDonald's Compared to that of its Two Competitors*, www.ccesoft.com/e-zine/value%20innovation.htm

Cetindamar, D. and Kilitcioglu, H. (2013) 'Measuring the Competitiveness of a Firm for an Award System', *Competitiveness Review*, **23**(1), 7–22.

Cetindamar, D. and Pala, O. (2011) 'Chief Technology Officer Roles and Performance', *Technology Analysis & Strategic Management*, **23**(10), 1031–1046.

Cetindamar, D., Pala, O. and Can, O. (2006) 'Technology Management Activities and Tools: The Practice in Turkey', PICMET 2006 Conference, 8–13 July, Istanbul, Turkey.

Cetindamar, D., Phaal, R. and Probert, D. (2009) 'Understanding Technology Management as a Dynamic Capability: A Framework for Technology Management Activities', *Technovation*, **28**(1), 45–58.

Chang, S.-B, Lai, K.-K. and Chang, S.-M. (2009) 'Exploring Technology Diffusion and Classification of Business Methods: Using the Patent Citation Network', *Technological Forecasting & Social Change*, **76**(1), 107–117.

Chang, Y.-C., Miles, I., and Hung, S.-C. (2014) Introduction to special issue: Managing technology-service convergence in Service Economy 3.0., Technovation, **34**(9), 499–504.

Cetindamar, D. and Ulusoy, G. (2008) 'Innovation Performance and Partnerships in Manufacturing Firms in Turkey' *Journal of Manufacturing Technology Management*, **19**(3), 332–345.

Chen, C.-J., Huang, Y.-F. and Lin, B.-W. (2012) 'How Firms Innovate Through R&D Internationalization? An S-curve Hypothesis', *Research Policy*, **41**(9), 1544–1554.

Chen, T.-Y., Yu, O.-S., Hsu, G. J.-Y., Hsu, F.-M. and Sung, W.-N. (2009) 'Renewable Energy Technology Portfolio Planning with Scenario Analysis, *Energy Policy*, **37**(8), 2900–2906.

Chesbrough, H. W. (2003) *Open Innovation* (Boston, MA: Harvard Business School Press).

Chiesa, V., Coughlan, P. and Voss, C. A. (1996) 'Development of a Technical Innovation Audit', *Journal of Product Innovation Management*, **13**(2), 105–136.

Chiesa, V., Giglioli, E. and Manzini, R. (1999) 'R&D Corporate Planning: Selecting the Core Technological Competencies', *Technology Analysis & Strategic Management*, **11**(2), 255–279.

Chiesa, V. and Manzini, R. (1998) 'Organizing for Technological Collaborations: A Managerial Perspective', *R&D Management*, **28**(3), 199–212.

Christensen, C. M. (1992) 'Exploring the Limits of the Technology S-curve, Part 1: Component Technologies', *Production and Operations Management Journal*, **1**(4), 334–338.

Christensen, C. M. (1997) *The Innovator's Dilemma: When New Technologies Cause Great Firms to Fail* (Boston, MA: Harvard Business School Press).

Chui, M., Löffler, M. and Roberts, R. (2010) 'The Internet of Things', McKinsey Quarterly, http://www.mckinsey.com/insights/high_tech_telecoms_internet/the_internet_of_things

Clarysse, B., Mosey, S. and Lambrecht, I. (2009) 'New Trends in Technology Management Education: A View from Europe', *Academy of Management Learning & Education*, **8**(3), 427–443.

Cohen, W. M. and Levinthal, D. A. (1990) 'Absorptive Capacity: A New Perspective on Learning and Innovation', *Administrative Science Quarterly*, **35**(1), 128–153.

Cohen, W. M., Nelson, R. R. and Walsh, J. P. (2000) 'Protecting their Intellectual Assets: Appropriability Conditions and Why U.S. Manufacturing Firms Patent', *NBER Working Paper*, No. 7552.

Cohendet, P. and Simon, L. (2007) 'Playing across the Playground: Paradoxes of Knowledge Creation in the Videogame Firm', *Journal of Organizational Behavior*, **28**(5), 587–605.

Comstock, G. L. and Sjolseth, D. E. (1999) 'Aligning and Prioritizing Corporate R&D', *Research-Technology Management*, **42**(3), 19–25.

Coombs, J. E. and Bierly, P. E. (2006) 'Measuring Technological Capability and Performance', *R&D Management*, **36**(4), 421–438.

Cooper, R. G. (1988) 'The New Product Process: A Decision Guide For Management', *Journal of Marketing Management*, **3**(3), 238–255.

Cooper, R. G. (1990) 'Stage-Gate Systems: A New Tool for Managing New Products', *Business Horizons*, **33**(3), 44–54.

Cooper, R. G. (2008) 'Perspective: The Stage-Gate® Idea-to-Launch Process: Update, What's New, and NexGen Systems', *Journal of Product Innovation Management*, **25**(3), 213–232.

Cooper, R. G. (2011) 'Perspective: The Innovation Dilemma: How to Innovate When the Market is Mature', *Journal of Product Innovation Management*, **28**(S1), 2–27.

Cooper, R. G. (2014) 'What's Next? After Stage-Gate', *Research-Technology Management*, **57**(1), 20–31.

Cooper, R. G. and Edgett, S. J. (1997) 'Portfolio Management in New Product Development: Lessons from the Leaders, I', *Research-Technology Management*, **40**(5), 16–29.

Cooper, R. G. and Edgett, S. J. (2006) 'Ten Ways to Make Better Portfolio and Project Selection Decisions', *Visions Magazine*, **30**(3), 11–15.

Cooper, R. G., Edgett, S. J. and Kleinschmidt, E. J. (1997) 'Portfolio Management in New Product Development: Lessons from the Leaders, II', *Research-Technology Management*, **40**(6), 43–53.

Cooper, R. G., Edgett, S. J. and Kleinschmidt, E. J. (1999) 'New Product Portfolio Management: Practices and Performance', *The Journal of Product Innovation Management*, **16**(4), 333–351.

Cooper, R. G., Edgett, S. J. and Kleinschmidt, E. J. (2001) *Portfolio Management for New Products* (Cambridge, MA: Perseus).

Cooper, R. G., Edgett, S. J. and Kleinschmidt, E. J. (2002) 'Optimizing the Stage-gate Process: What Best-practice Companies Do, I', *Research-Technology Management*, **45**(5), 21–28.

Cooper, R. G. and Kleinschmidt, E. J. (1994) 'Uncovering the Keys to New Product Success', *IEEE Engineering Management Review*, **21**(4), 5–18.

Cooper, R. G. and Slagmulder, R. (1997) *Target Costing and Value Engineering* (Portland, OR: Productivity Press).

Cotec. (1998) *Temaguide: A Guide to Technology Management and Innovation for Companies* (Brussels: EC funded project).

Crossan, M. and Beldrow, I. (2003) 'Organizational Learning and Strategic Renewal', *Strategic Management Journal*, **24**(11), 1087–1105.

Cusumano, M., Mylonadis, Y. and Rosenbloom, R. (1992) 'Strategic Maneuvering and Mass Market Dynamics: The Triumph of VHS over Beta', *Business History Review*, **66**(1), 51–94.

Daim, T. U. and Kocaoglu, D. F. (2008) 'How Do Engineering Managers Evaluate Technologies for Acquisition? A Review of the Electronics Industry', *Engineering Management Journal*, **20**(3), 44–52.

David, P. (1990) 'The Dynamo and the Computer: An Historical Perspective on the Modern Productivity Paradox', *American Economic Review*, **80**(2), 355–361.

Debo, L. G., Toktay, L. B. and van Wassenhove, L. N. (2006) 'Joint Life-cycle Dynamics of New and Remanufactured Products', *Production & Operations Management*, **15**(4), 498–513.

Dell'Era, C., Marchesi, A. and Verganti, R. (2010) 'Mastering Technologies in Design-Driven Innovation', *Research-Technology Management*, **53**(2), 12–23.

Derbyshire, J. (2014) 'The Impact of Ambidexterity on Enterprise Performance: Evidence from 15 Countries and 14 Sectors', *Technovation*, **34**, 574–581.

Desouza, K. C. (2005) *New Frontiers of Knowledge Management* (Basingstoke: Palgrave Macmillan).

Dhillon, B. S. (2002) *Engineering and Technology Management Tools and Applications* (Norwood, MA: Artech House).

Dibb, S., Simkin, L., Pride, W. M. and Ferrell, O. C. (2001) *Marketing: Concepts and Strategies*, 4th European edn (Boston, MA: Houghton Mifflin).

Dillon, T. A., Lee, R. K. and Matheson, D. (2005) 'Value Innovation: Passport to Wealth Creation', *Research-Technology Management*, **48**(2), 22–36.

Dissel, M., Phaal, R., Farrukh, C. J. and Probert, D. R. (2009) 'Value Roadmapping', *Research-Technology Management*, **52**(6), 45–55.

Docherty, M. (2006) 'Primer on 'Open Innovation": Principles and Practice'. *PDMA (Product Development and Management Association) Vision* (April 2006): 13–17.

Dorf, R. C. (1999) *The Technology Management Handbook* (Florida: CRC Press/IEEE Press).

Downes, L. and Nunes, P. (2014) *Big Bang Disruption: Strategy in the Age of Devastating Innovation* (New York: Penguin-Portfolio).

Doz, Y. and Hamel, G. (1997) 'The Use of Alliances in Implementing Technology Strategies', in M. L. Tushman and P. Andersen (eds) *Managing Strategic Innovation and Change* (Oxford: Oxford University Press).

Drake, M. P., Sakkab, N. and Jonash, R. (2006) 'Maximising Return on Innovation Investment', *Research-Technology Management*, **49**(6), 32–41.

Drejer, A. (1996) 'The Discipline of Management of Technology, based on Considerations relating to Technology', *Technovation*, **17**(5), 253–265.

Duan, C.-H. (2011) 'Mapping the Intellectual Structure of Modern Technology Management', *Technology Analysis & Strategic Management*, **23**(5), 583–600.

Dussauge, P., Hart, S. and Ramanantsoa, B. (1992) *Strategic Technology Management: Integrating Technologies into Global Business Strategies* (Chichester: John Wiley & Sons).

Dyer, J. H. and Nobeoka, K. (2000) 'Creating and Managing a High-performance Knowledge-sharing Network: The Toyota Case', *Strategic Management Journal*, **21**(3), 345–368.

Easingwood, C. and Koustelos, A. (2000) 'Marketing High Technology: Preparation, Targeting, Positioning, Execution', *Business Horizons*, **43**(3), 27–34.

Easterby-Smith, M. and Lyles, M. A. (eds) (2003) *The Blackwell Handbook of Organisational Learning and Knowledge Management* (Oxford: Blackwell).

EC (European Commission) (2004) *Innovation Management and the Knowledge-driven Economy*, Brussels: EC, ftp://ftp.cordis.lu/pub/innovation-policy/studies/ studies_innovation_manage ment_final_report.pdf

EC (European Commission) (2006) *InnoSupport: Supporting Innovation in SMEs*, Brussels, www.inno support.net

Eggers, J. P. (2012) 'All Experience is not Created Equal: Learning, Adapting, and Focusing in Product Portfolio Management', *Strategic Management Journal*, **33**(3), 315–335.

Ehrnberg, E. and Jacobsson, S. (1996) 'Managing Technological Discontinuities – a Tentative Framework', *International Journal of Technology Management*, **11**(3/4), 452–70.

EIRMA (European Industrial Research Management Association) (1997) 'Technology Roadmapping: Delivering Business Vision', Working Group Report No. 52 (Paris: EIRMA).

Eisenhardt, K. M. and Martin, J. A. (2000) 'Dynamic Capabilities: What are They?', *Strategic Management Journal*, **21**(10/11), 1105–1112.

Enkel, E. and Gassmann, O. (2010) 'Creative Imitation: Exploring the Case of Cross-industry Innovation', *R&D Management*, **40**(3), 256–270.

Ernst, H. (2003) 'Patent Information for Strategic Technology Management', *World Patent Information*, **25**(3), 233–242.

Euchner, J. (2014) 'Services-Led Business Models for Manufacturers', *Research-Technology Management*, **57**(2), 11–14.

Farrington, T. and Crews, C. (2013) 'The IRI 2038 Scenarios', *Research-Technology Management*, **56**(6), 23–32.

Farrukh, C. J., Fraser, P. and Hadjidakis, D. (2004) 'Developing an Integrated Technology Management Process', *Research-Technology Management*, **47**(4), 39–46.

Farrukh, C. J., Phaal, R. and Probert, D. R. (1999) *Tools for Technology Management: Dimensions and Issues* (Portland, OR: Proceedings of the Portland International Conference on Management of Engineering and Technology – PICMET 1999, 25–29 June).

Fichman, R. G. and Kemerer, C. F. (1995) 'The Illusory Diffusion of Innovation: An Examination of Assimilation Gaps', Working Paper Series No. 746, Katz Graduate School of Business, University of Pittsburgh.

Fleischer, T. and Grunwald, A. (2008) 'Making Nanotechnology Developments Sustainable. A Role for Technology Assessment?', *Journal of Cleaner Production*, **16**(8/9), 889–898.

Floyd, C. F. (1998) *Managing Technology for Corporate Success* (Burlington: Gower Aldershot).

Foden, J. and Berends, H. (2010) 'Technology Management at Rolls-Royce', *Research-Technology Management*, **53**(2), 33–42.

Ford, D. and Saren, M. (1996) *Technology Strategy for Business* (New York: International Thomson Business Press).

Ford, S. J., Mortara, L. and Probert, D. R. (2012) 'Disentangling the Complexity of Early -Stage Technology Acquisitions', *Research-Technology Management*, **55**(3), 40–48.

Fröhling, W. (2007) *Intellectual Property* (Brussels: EIRMA).

Gage, W. L. (1967) *Value Analysis* (Maidenhead: McGraw-Hill).

Gagnon, R. J. and Haldar, S. (1995) 'Assessing Advanced Technologies: Survey Results', *Engineering Management Journal*, **7**(1), 15–23.

Gallagher, S. R. (2012) 'The Battle of the Blue Laser DVDs,' *Technovation*, **32**(2), 90–98.

Galvin, R. (1998) 'Science Roadmaps', *Science*, **280**(5365), 803.

Garcia, M. L. and Bray, O. H. (1997) *Fundamentals of Technology Roadmapping* (Albuquerque, NM: Sandia National Laboratories).

Garvin, D. A. (1993) 'Building a Learning Organization', *Harvard Business Review*, **71**(4), 78–91.

Garvin, D. A. (2003) *Learning in Action: A Guide to Putting the Learning Organization to Work* (Boston, MA: Harvard Business School Press).

Gaynor, G. H. (ed.) (1996) *Handbook of Technology Management* (New York: McGraw-Hill).

Genus, A. and Coles, A. M. (2005) 'On Constructive Technology Assessment and Limitations on Public Participation in Technology Assessment', *Technology Analysis & Strategic Management*, **17**(4), 433–443.

Giordan, J. C. and Kossovsky, N. (2004) 'It's Time to Think Differently about R&D Assets and the CTO's Role', *Research-Technology Management*, **47**(1), 9–12.

Goffin, K. and Mitchell, R. (2005) *Innovation Management: Strategy and Implementation Using the Pentathlon Framework* (Basingstoke: Palgrave Macmillan).

Gofman, A. and Moskowitz, H. (2009) 'Steps towards a Consumer-driven Innovation Machine for "Ordinary" Product Categories in their later Lifecycle Stages', *International Journal of Technology Management*, **46**(1/2), 349–363.

Goldheim, D., Slowinski, G. and Daniele J. (2005) 'Extracting Value from Intellectual Assets', *Research-Technology Management*, **48**(2), 41–48.

Gomory, R. E. (1989) 'From the "Ladder of Science" to the Product Development Cycle', *Harvard Business Review*, **67**(8), 99–105.

Govindarajan, V. and Euchner, J. (2012) 'Reverse Innovation', *Research-Technology Management*, **55**(6), 13–17.

Graettinger, C. P. (2002) *Using the Technology Readiness Levels Scale to Support Technology Management in the DOD's ATD/STO Environments: A Findings and Recommendations Report* (Army CECOM, Pennsylvania: Carnegie Mellon Software Engineering Institute).

Granstrand, O. and Holgersson, M. (2014) 'The Challenge of Closing Open Innovation.' *Research-Technology Management*, **57**(5), 19–25.

Gregory, M. J. (1995) 'Technology Management: A Process Approach', *Proceedings of the Institution of Mechanical Engineers*, **209**, 347–356.

Green, J. (2007) *Democratizing the Future: Towards a new era of Creativity and Growth* (Eindhoven: Philips Electronics N. V.).

Groenveld, P. (1997) 'Roadmapping Integrates Business and Technology', *Research-Technology Management*, **40**(5), 48–55.

Grönlund, J., Sjödin, D. R. and Frishammar, J. (2010) 'Open Innovation and the Stage-Gate Process', *California Management Review*, **52**(3), 106–131.

Guzman, J. G., Fernández, D. C. A., Colomo-Palacios, R. and Velasco de Diego, M. (2013) 'Living Labs for User-Driven Innovation', *Research-Technology Management*, **56**(3), 29–39.

Hang, C.-C., Jin, C. and Subramian, A. M. (2010) 'Developing Disruptive Products for Emerging Markets', *Research-Technology Management*, **53**(4), 21–26.

Hargadon, A. and Sutton, R. I. (2000) 'Building an Innovation Factory', *Harvard Business Review*, **78**(3), 157–167.

Hatch, N. W. and Dyer, J. H. (2004) 'Human Capital and Learning as a Source of Sustainable Competitive Advantage', *Strategic Management Journal*, **25**(12), 1155–1178.

Hayes, R. H., Wheelwright, S. C. and Clark, K. B. (1984) *Restoring Our Competitive Edge* (New York: John Wiley).

Hayes, R. H., Wheelwright, S. C. and Clark, K. B. (1988) *Dynamic Manufacturing* (New York: Free Press).

Helfat, C. E. and Peteraf, M. A. (2003) 'The Dynamic Resource-based View: Capability Lifecycles', *Strategic Management Journal*, **24**(10), 997–1010.

Henriksen, A. D. (1997) 'Technology Assessment Primer for Management of Technology', *International Journal of Technology Management*, **13**(5/6), 615–638.

Hidalgo, A. and Albors, J. (2008) 'Innovation Management Techniques and Tools: A Review from Theory and Practice', *R&D Management*, **38**(2), 113–127.

Hobday, M. (2005) 'Firm-level Innovation Models: Perspectives on Research in Developed and Developing Countries', *Technology Analysis & Strategic Management*, **17**(2), 121–146.

Hobday, M., Boddington, A. and Grantham, A. (2011) 'An Innovation Perspective on Design: Part 1', *Design Issues*, **27**(4), 5–15.

Hobday, M., Boddington, A. and Grantham, A. (2012) 'An Innovation Perspective on Design: Part 2', *Design Issues*, **28**(1), 18–29.

Holt, K. (1992) 'The M-T Matrix. A New Strategic Tool' in T. Khalil, B. Bayraktar and J. Edosomwan (Eds.) *Management of Technology II* (Norcross, GA: Industrial Engineering and Management Press).

Huarng, K.-H. (2010) 'Essential Research in Technology Management', *Journal of Business Research*, **63**(5), 451–453.

Hull, R., Coombs, R. and Peltu, M. (2000) 'Knowledge Management Practices for Innovation: An Audit Tool for Improvement', *International Journal of Technology Management*, **20**(5/8), 633–657.

Hulshoff, H. E., Kirchnoff, J. J., Kirchnoff, B. A., Walsh, S. T. and Westhof, F. M. J. (1998) *New Services Strategic Study and Exploratory Survey of a Dynamic Phenomenon (Zoetermeer, NL: EIM Press)*.

Hunt, D., Nguyen, L. and Rodgers, M. (2007) *Patent Searching Tools & Techniques* (New York: John Wiley & Sons).

Hutchins, N. and Muller, A. (2012) 'Beyond Stage-gate: Restoring Learning and Adaptability to Commercialization', *Strategy & Leadership*, **40**(3), 30–35.

Iansiti, M. and Lakhani, K., (2014) 'Digital Ubiquity: How Connections, Sensors, and Data are Revolutionizing Business', *Harvard Business Review*, **92**(11), 91–99.

ICS UNIDO (International Centre for Science and High Technology UN Industrial Development Organization) (2008) *Forum for Technology Transfer, Training Course on Technology Management*, www.ics.trieste.it/TP_TechnologyManagement/

Javidan, M. and Walker, J. L. (2013) *Developing Your Global Mindset* (Edina, MN: Beaver's Pond Press).

Jespersen, K. R. (2012) 'Stage-to-Stage Information Dependency in the NPD Process', *Journal of Product Innovation Management*, **29**(2), 257–274.

Jin, J. and Zedtwitz, M. (2008) 'Technological Capability Development in China's Mobile Phone Industry', *Technovation*, **2**(2), 327–334.

Jobber, D. (2001) *Principles & Practice of Marketing*, 3rd edn (London: McGraw-Hill).

Johnes, G. K., Lanctot, A. and Teegeni, H. J. (2001) 'Determinants and Performance Impacts of External Technology Acquisition', *Journal of Business Venturing*, **16**(3), 255–283.

Johnson, G. and Scholes, K. (1999) *Exploring Corporate Strategy* (London: Prentice Hall).

Johnson, G., Whittington, R., Scholes, K., Angwin, D. and Regnér, P. (2014) *Exploring Strategy Text & Cases*, 10th edn (Harlow: Pearson Education).

Jones, T. and Lee, D. (2006) 'Samsung, Others Adopting Value Innovation', *Research-Technology Management*, **49**(5), 5–7.

Kahn, K. B. (2004) *PDMA Handbook of New Product Development*, 2nd edn (New York: John Wiley).

Kaplan, R. S. and Norton, D. P. (1996) *The Balanced Scorecard: Translating Strategy into Action* (Boston, MA: Harvard Business School Press).

Kerr, C., Farrukh, C., Phaal, R. and Probert, D. (2013) 'Key Principles for Developing Industrially Relevant Strategic Technology Management Toolkits', *Technological Forecasting and Social Change*, **80**(6), 1050–1070.

Kerr, C. I., Mortara, L., Phaal, R. and Probert, D. R. (2006) 'A Conceptual Model for Technology Intelligence', *International Journal of Technology Intelligence and Planning*, **2**(1), 73–93.

Kerzner, H. (2003) *Project Management: A Systems Approach to Planning, Scheduling, and Controlling* (Hoboken, NJ: John Wiley & Sons).

Khalil, T. (2000) *Management of Technology: The Key to Competitiveness and Wealth Creation* (Boston, MA: McGraw-Hill).

Khanna, T. and Palepu, K. G. (2010) *Winning in Emerging Markets: A Roadmap for Strategy and Execution* (Cambridge, MA: Harvard Business Press).

Kim, J. and Wilemon, D. (2002) 'Sources and Assessment of Complexity in NPD Projects', *R&D Management*, **33**(1), 16–30.

Kim, W. C. and Mauborgne, R. (1997) 'Value Innovation: The Strategic Logic of High Growth', *Harvard Business Review*, **75**(1), 103–112.

Kim, W. C. and Mauborgne, R. (2005) *Blue Ocean Strategy: How to Create Uncontested Market Space and Make the Competition Irrelevant* (Boston, MA: Harvard Business School Press).

Kocaoglu, D. F. (1994) 'Technology Management: Educational Trends', *IEEE Transactions on Engineering Management,* **41**(4), 347–50.

Kocaoglu, D. F. (2009) 'Engineering Management – Where it Was, Where it is Now, Where it is Going', *Engineering Management Journal,* **21**(3), 23–25.

Kolb, D. and Fry, R. (1975) 'Towards a Theory of Applied Experiential Learning', in C. Cooper (ed.) *Theories of Group Processes* (Chichester: John Wiley).

Korhohen, S. and Niemela, J. S. (2005) 'A Conceptual Analysis of Capabilities: Identifying and Classifying Sources of Competitive Advantage in the Wood Industry', *Liiketaloudellinen Aikakauskrija,* **54**(1), 11–47.

Kossovsky, N., Brandegee, B. and Giordan, J. C. (2004) 'Using the Market to Determine IP's Fair Market Value', *Research-Technology Management,* **47**(3), 33–42.

Kotler, P. and Keller, K. L. (2006) *Marketing Management,* 12th edn (Englewood Cliffs, NJ: Prentice Hall).

Krogh, G., Takeuchi, H., Kase, C. and Canton, C. G. (2013) *Towards Organizational Knowledge* (Basingstoke: Palgrave Macmillan).

Kuznets, S. (1930) *Secular Movements in Production and Prices: The Nature and their Bearing upon Cyclical Fluctuations* (Boston, MA: Houghton Mifflin).

Laroia, G. and Krishnan, S. (2005) 'Managing Drug Discovery Alliances for Success', *Research-Technology Management,* **48**(5), 42–50.

Larson, C. F. (2007) '50 Years of Change in Industrial Research and Technology Management', *Research-Technology Management,* **50**(1), 26–31.

Leavy, B. (2009) 'A Design-thinking – A New Mental Model for Value Innovation', *Strategy and Leadership,* **38**(3), 5–14.

Lee, C., Park, H. and Park, Y. (2013) 'Keeping Abreast of Technology-driven Business Model Evolution', *Technology Analysis & Strategic Management,* **25**(5), 487–505.

Lehmann, R. D. and Winer, R. S. (2004) *Product Management,* 4th edn (New York: McGraw-Hill/Irwin).

Leonard-Barton, D., Bowen, H. K. and Clark, K. B. (1994) 'Prototypes: Tools for Learning and Integrating', *Harvard Business Review,* **72**(5), 124–125.

Levitt, B. and March, J. (1988) 'Organizational Learning', *Annual Review of Sociology,* **14**(1), 319–340.

Liao, S. (2005) 'Technology Management Methodologies and Applications: A Literature Review from 1995–2003', *Technovation,* **25**(4), 381–393.

Liew, A. (2007) 'Understanding Data, Information, Knowledge and their Interrelationships', *Journal of Knowledge Management Practice,* **8**(2).

Lichtenthaler, U. (2011) 'Implementation Steps for Successful Out-Licensing', *Research-Technology Management,* **54**(5), 47–53.

Lind, J. (2006) 'Boeing's Global Enterprise Technology Process', *Research-Technology Management,* **49**(5), 36–42.

Lindsay, J. (2000) *The Technology Management Audit: The Tools to Measure How Effectively you Exploit the Technological Strengths and Know-how in your Company* (London: Financial Times/Prentice Hall).

Linstone, H. A. and Grupp, H. (2000) 'National Technology Foresight Activities Around the Globe', *Technological Forecasting and Social Change,* **60**(1), 85–94.

Liu, S. and Shyu, J. (1997) 'Strategic Planning for Technology Development with Patent Analysis', *International Journal of Technology Management,* **13**(5/6), 661–680.

Loutfy, R. and Belkhir, L. (2001) 'Managing Innovation at Xerox', *Research-Technology Management,* **44**(4), 15–24.

Lu, L. (2007) 'Protecting Intellectual Property Rights', *Research-Technology Management,* **50**(2), 51–56.

Maier, A. M., Moultrie, J. and Clarkson, P. J. (2012) 'Assessing Organizational Capabilities', *IEEE Transactions on Engineering Management,* **59**(1), 138–159.

Makridakis, S., Wheelwright, S. C. and Hyndman, R. J. (1998) *Forecasting: Methods and Applications*, 3rd edn (New York: John Wiley).

Martin, R. (2009) *The Design of Business: Why Design Thinking is the Next Competitive Advantage* (Cambridge, MA: Harvard Business Review Press).

Martino, J. (1983) *Technological Forecasting for Decision Making*, 2nd edn (New York: North-Holland).

Mathews, S. (2011) 'Innovation Portfolio Architecture, Part – 2: Attribute Selection and Valuation', *Research-Technology Management*, **54**(5), 37–46.

McGrath, M. E. (2004) *Next Generation Product Development: How to Increase Productivity, Cut Costs, and Reduce Cycle Times* (New York: McGraw-Hill).

McGrath, R. G. (2013) *The End of Competitive Advantage: How to Keep Your Strategy Moving as Fast as Your Business* (Boston, MA: Harvard Business Review Press).

McKinsey. (2011) Big Data: The Next Frontier for Innovation, Competition, and Productivity, http://www.mckinsey.com/insights/business_technology/big_data_the_next_frontier_for_innovation

McMillan, A. (2003) 'Roadmapping: Agent of Change', *Research-Technology Management*, **42**(2), 40–47.

Melnyk, S. A. and Denzler, D. R. (1996) *Operations Management: A Value-driven Approach* (Chicago: Irwin).

Meyer, M. H., Anzani, M. and Walsh, G. (2005) 'Innovation and Enterprise Growth: How IBM Develops Next Generation Product Lines', *Research-Technology Management*, **48**(4), 34–44.

Meyer, M. H. and Poza, H. (2009) 'Venturing next to the Core: From Defense to Homeland Security', *Research-Technology Management*, **52**(3), 24–37.

Mikkola, J. H. (2001) 'Portfolio Management of R&D Projects: Implications for Innovation Management', *Technovation*, **21**(7), 423–435.

Miles, L. D. (1972) *Technique of Value Analysis and Engineering* (New York: McGraw-Hill).

Minzberg, H. (1994) *The Rise and Fall of Strategic Planning* (New York: Free Press).

Mintzberg, H., Ahlstrand, B. and Lampel, J. (1998) *Strategy Safari: A Guided Tour through the Wilds of Strategic Management* (New York: Free Press).

Mogee, M. and Kolar, R. (1994) 'International Patent Analysis as a Tool for Corporate Technology Analysis and Planning', *Technology Analysis & Strategic Management*, **6**(4), 485–504.

Moncada-Paterno-Castello, P., Rojo, J. and Bellido, F. (2000) *User's Manual and Tutorial: Technology Identification Methodology – IPTS-TIM Software V.1.1* (Seville: European Commission Institute for Prospective Technological Studies).

Monden, Y. (1992) *Toyota Production System: An Integrated Approach to Just-in-time* (Atlanta, GA: Industrial Engineering & Management Press).

Moore, G. (1991) *Crossing the Chasm* (New York: HarperBusiness).

Mortara, L. and Ford, S. (2012) *Technology Acquisitions: A Guided Approach to Technology Acquisition and Protection Decisions* (Cambridge: University of Cambridge).

Mortara, L., Kerr, C. I., Phaal, R. and Probert, D. R. (2007) *Technology Intelligence: Identifying Threats and Opportunities from New Technologies* (Cambridge: CTM, University of Cambridge).

Navens, T. M., Summa, G. L. and Uttal, B. (1990) 'Commercializing Technology: What the Best Companies Do', *Harvard Business Review*, **63**(4), 154–163.

Nissing, N. (2007) 'Would you Buy a Purple Orange?', *Research-Technology Management*, **50**(3), 35–39.

Nonaka, I. and Konno, N. (1998) 'The Concept of "Ba": Building a Foundation for Knowledge Creation', *California Management Review*, **40**(3), 40–55.

Nonaka, I. and Takeuchi, H. (1995) *Knowledge-creating Company* (New York: Oxford University Press).

Norburn, D. (2005) *Blackwell Encyclopaedic Dictionary of Strategic Management* (New York: Blackwell).

Norling, P. M., Herring, J. P., Rosenkrans, W. A., Stellpflug, M., and Kaufman, S. B. (2000) 'Putting Competitive Technology Intelligence to Work', *Research-Technology Management*, **43**(5), 23–29.

Normann, R. and Ramirez, R. (1993) 'From Value Chain to Value Constellation: Designing Interactive Strategy', *Harvard Business Review*, **71**(4), 65–77.

NRC (National Research Council) (1987) *Management of Technology: The Hidden Competitive Advantage* (Washington, DC: National Academy Press).

O'Briens, J. M. (2012) 'The Vine Nerds', *Wired's*, http://www.wired.com/2012/10/mf-fruition-sciences-winemakers

OECD (Organization for Economic Co-operation and Development) (1995) *The Oslo Manual* (Paris: OECD).

Ouyang, H. S. (2010) 'Imitator-to-Innovator S Curve and Chasms', *Thunderbird International Business Review*, **52**(1), 31–45.

Parida, V., Sjödin, D. R. and Kohtamäki, M. (2014) 'Mastering the Transition to Product-Service Provision', *Research-Technology Management*, **57**(3), 44–52.

PD-Trak Solutions. (2006) *A Practical Approach to Portfolio Management*, www.npd-solutions.com/portfolio.html

Pecas, P., Ribeiro, I., Folgado, R. and Henriques, E. (2009) 'A Life Cycle Engineering Model for Technology Selection,' *Journal of Cleaner Production*, **17**(9), 846–856.

Pelc, K. I. (1996) 'Knowledge Mapping: A Tool for MOT', in G. H. Gaynor (ed.) *Handbook of Technology Management* (New York: McGraw-Hill).

Petrick, I., Rayna, T. and Striukova, L. (2014) 'The Challenges of Intellectual Property', *Research-Technology Management*, **57**(5), 9–11.

Phaal, R., Farrukh, C. J. and Probert, D. R. (2004a) 'A Framework for Supporting the Management of Technological Knowledge', *International Journal of Technology Management*, **27**(1), 1–15.

Phaal, R., Farrukh, C. J. and Probert, D. R. (2004b) 'Customizing Roadmapping', *Research-Technology Management*, **47**(2), 26–37.

Phaal, R., Farrukh, C. J. and Probert, D. R. (2006) 'Technology Management Tools: Concept, Development and Application', *Technovation*, **26**(3), 336–344.

Phaal, R., O'Sullivan, E., Routley, M., Ford, S. and Probert, D. (2011) 'A Framework for Mapping Industrial Emergence,' *Technological Forecasting and Social Change*, **78**(2), 217–230.

Phaal, R. and Palmer, P. J. (2010) 'Technology Management – Structuring the Strategic Dialogue', *Engineering Management Journal*, **22**(1), 64–74.

Phan, P. P., Siegel, D. S. and Wright, M. (2009) 'New Developments in Technology Management Education', *Academy of Management Learning & Education*, **8**(3), 324–336.

Philips, R., Neailey, K. and Broughton, T. (1999) 'A Comparative Study of Six Stage-gate Approaches to Product Development', *Integrated Manufacturing Systems*, **10**(5), 289–297.

Porter, M. (1985) *Competitive Advantage* (New York: Free Press).

Porter, M. (1990) 'The Competitive Advantage of Nations', *Harvard Business Review*, **68**(2), 73–93.

Porter, A. L. and Cunningham, S. W. (2005) *Tech Mining: Exploiting Technologies for Competitive Advantage* (New York: Wiley).

Porter, A. L., Roper, A. T., Mason, T. W., Rossini, F. A., Banks, J. and Wiederholt, B. J. (1991) *Forecasting and Management of Technology* (New York: Wiley).

Porter, M. E. and Heppelmann, J. E. (2014) 'How Smart, Connected Products are Transforming Competition', *Harvard Business Review*, **92**(11), 64–88.

Porter, M. E. and Kramer, M. R. (2011) 'Creating Shared Value', *Harvard Business Review*, **89**(1/2), 62–77.

Powells, W. W. (1998) 'Learning from Collaboration', *California Management Review*, **40**(3), 228–240.

Prahalad, C. K. and Hamel, G. (1990) 'The Core Competence of the Corporation', *Harvard Business Review*, **68**(3), 79–91.

Probert, D., Dissel, M., Farrukh, C., Mortara, L., Thorn, V. and Phaal, R. (2013) 'The Process of Making the Business Case for Technology', *Technological Forecasting and Social Change*, **80**(6), 1129–1146.

Ramamurti, R. and Singh, J. V. (2009) *Emerging Multinationals in Emerging Markets* (Cambridge: Cambridge University Press).

Reger, G. (2001) 'Technology Foresight in Companies: From an Indicator to a Network and Process Perspective', *Technology Analysis and Strategic Management*, **13**(4), 533–553.

Rigby, D. and Bilodeau, B. (2005) 'The Bain 2005 Management Tool Survey', *Strategy & Leadership*, **33**(4), 4–12.

Ritala, P. and Hurmelinna-Laukkanen, P. (2013) 'Incremental and Radical Innovation in Coopetition – The Role of Absorptive Capacity and Appropriability', *Journal of Product Innovation Management*, **30**(1), 154–169.

Roberts, E. B. (2004) 'A Perspective on 50 Years of the Engineering Management Field', *IEEE Transactions on Engineering Management*, **51**(4), 398–403.

Rocque, L. B. and Viali, W. A. (2004) *At the Stage Gate: Critical Questions for IT Project Sponsors* (Anaheim, CA: PMI Global Congress Proceedings).

Rogers, E. M. (1995) *Diffusion of Innovations*, 3rd edn (New York: Free Press).

Rothaermel, F. T. (2013) *Strategic Management: Concepts* (Columbus, OH: McGraw-Hill/Irwin).

Rothwell, R. (1994) 'Towards the Fifth-generation Innovation Process', *International Marketing Review*, **11**(1), 7–31.

Routley, M., Phaal, R., Athanassopoulou, N. and Probert, D. (2013) 'Mapping Experience in Organisations', *Engineering Management Journal*, **25**(1), 35–47.

Rush, H., Bessant, J. and Hobday, M. (2007) 'Assessing the Technological Capabilities of Firms: Developing a Policy Tool', *R&D Management*, **37**(3), 221–236.

Rush, H., Bessant, J., Hobday, M., Hanrahan, E. and Medeiros, M. Z. (2014) 'The Evolution and Use of a Policy and Research Tool', *Technology Analysis & Strategic Management*, **26**(3), 353–365.

Sakkab, N. Y. (2002) 'Connect & Develop Complements Research & Develop at P&G', *Research-Technology Management*, **45**(2), 38–45.

Schiederig, T., Tietze, F. and Herstatt, C. (2012) 'Green Innovation in Technology and Innovation Management – An Exploratory Literature Review', *R&D Management*, **42**(2), 180–192.

Schilling, M. A. and Esmundo, M. (2009) 'Technology S-curves in Renewable Energy Alternatives: Analysis and Implications for Industry and Government', *Energy Policy*, **37**(5), 1767–1781.

Schnaars, S. P., Chia, S. L. and Maloles, C. M. III. (1993) 'Five Modern Lessons from a 55-year-old Technological Forecast', *Journal of Product Innovation Management*, **10**(1), 66–74.

Scott, G. (2000) 'Critical Technology Management Issues of New Product Development in High-tech Companies', *Journal of Product Innovation Management*, **17**(1), 57–77.

Seebode, D., Jeanrenaud, S. and Bessant, J. (2012) 'Managing Innovation for Sustainability', *R&D Management*, **42**(3), 195–206.

Senge, P. M. (1990) *The Fifth Discipline* (New York: Doubleday).

Shapiro, C. and Varian, H. (1999) 'The Art of Standards Wars', *California Management Review*, **41**(2), 8–32.

Shillito, M. L. (1994) *Advanced QFD: Linking Technology to Market and Company Needs* (New York: John Wiley & Sons).

Shillito, M. L. and De Marle, D. J. (1992) *Value, its Measurement, Design, and Management* (New York: John Wiley & Sons).

Shipton, H., Zhou, Q. and Mooi, E. (2013) 'Is there a Global Model of Learning Organizations? An Empirical, Cross-nation Study', *International Journal of Human Resource Management*, **24**(12), 2278–2298.

Simsek, Z. (2009) 'Organizational Ambidexterity: Towards a Multilevel Understanding', *Journal of Management Studies*, **46**(4), 597–624.

Slowinski, G., Hummel, E., Gupta, A. and Gilmont, E. R. (2009) 'Effective Practices for Sourcing Innovation', *Research-Technology Management*, **52**(1), 27–34.

Slowinski, G. and Zerby, K. W. (2008) 'Protecting IP in Collaborative Research', *Research-Technology Management*, **51**(6), 58–65.

Smith, R. D. (2003) 'The Chief Technology Officer: Strategic Responsibilities and Relationships', *Research-Technology Management*, **46**, 28–36.

Smith, R. G., Herbein, W. C. and Morris, R. C. (1999) 'Front-end Innovation at AlliedSignal and Alcoa', *Research-Technology Management*, **42**(6), 15–24.

Snyder, N. T. and Duarte, D. L. (2008) *Unleashing Innovation: How Whirlpool Transformed an Industry* (New York: Jossey-Bass).

Socitec. (1999) *Innovation Management: Building Competitive Skills in SMEs* (Brussels: EU).

Sonnenblick, R. and Euchner, J. (2013) 'Addressing the Challenges of Portfolio Management', *Research-Technology Management*, **56**(5), 12–16.

Spekman, R. E. and Isabella, L. A. (2000) *Alliance Competence: Maximising the Value of your Partnership* (New York: John Wiley & Sons).

Spivey, W. A., Munson, J. M., Flannery, W. T. and Tsai, F. S. (2009) 'Improve Tech Transfer with this Alliance Scorecard', *Research-Technology Management*, **52**(1), 10–18.

Steele, L. W. (1989) *Managing Technology* (New York: McGraw-Hill).

Straker, D. (1997) *Toolbook for Quality Improvement and Problem Solving* (New York: Prentice Hall).

Tao, J., Daniele, J., Hummel, E., Goldheim, D. and Slowinski, G. (2005) 'Developing an Effective Strategy for Managing Intellectual Assets', *Research-Technology Management*, **48**(1), 50–58.

Tao, J. and Magnotta, V. (2006) 'How Air Products and Chemicals "Identifies and Accelerates"', *Research-Technology Management*, **49**(5), 12–18.

Taylor, M. and Taylor, A. (2012) 'The Technology Life Cycle', *International Journal of Production Economics*, **140**(1), 541–553.

Teece, D. J. (1986) 'Profiting from Technological Innovation', *Research Policy*, **15**(6), 285–305.

Teece, D. J. (2006) 'Reflections on "Profiting from Technological Innovation"', *Research Policy*, **35**(8), 1131–1146.

Teece, D. J. (2007) 'Explicating Dynamic Capabilities: The Nature and Microfoundations of (sustainable) Enterprise Performance', *Strategic Management Journal*, **28**(13), 1319–1350.

Teece, D. J. (2014) 'The Foundations of Enterprise Performance: Dynamic and Ordinary Capabilities in an (Economic) Theory of Firms', *Academy of Management Perspectives*, **28**(4), 328–352.

Teece, D. J., Pisano, G. and Shuen, A. (1997) 'Dynamic Capabilities and Strategic Management', *Strategic Management Journal*, **18**(7), 509–533.

Teece, D. J., Pisano, G. and Shuen, A. (2000) 'Dynamic Capabilities and Strategic Management', *Nature & Dynamics of Organisational Capabilities*, **1**(9), 334–363.

Terwiesch, C. and Ulrich, K. (2008) 'Managing the Opportunity Portfolio', *Research-Technology Management*, **51**(5), 27–38.

Tidd, J. and Bessant, J. (2013) *Managing Innovation: Integrating Technological, Market and Organizational Change*, 5th edn (Chichester: John Wiley).

Thompson, J. and Martin, F. (2010) *Strategic Management: Awareness and Change*, 6th edn (Singapore: Cengage Learning).

Thongpapanl, N. (2012) 'The Changing Landscape of Technology and Innovation Management', *Technovation*, **32**(5), 257–271.

Thomke, S. and Manzi, J. (2014) 'The Discipline of Business Experimentation', *Harvard Business Review*, **92**(12), 70–79.

Thursby, M. C., Fuller, A. W. and Thursby, J. (2009) 'An Integrated Approach to Educating Professionals for Careers in Innovation', *Academy of Management Learning & Education*, **8**(3), 389–405.

Tobias, Z. (2000) 'Chief Technology Officer', *Computerworld*, **34**, 76–77.

Tödtling, F., Lengauer, L. and Trippl, M. (2008) 'Start-ups and Innovation in the Vienna ICT Sector: How Important is the Local Cluster?', *International Journal of Services Technology & Management*, **10**(2/3/4), 299–317.

Tschirky, H., Jung, H.-H. and Savioz, P. (2003) *Technology and Innovation Management on the Move* (Zurich, Switzerland: Orell Fuessli Verlag).

Tushman, M. L. and Andersen, P. (2004) *Managing Strategic Innovation and Change*, 2nd edn (Oxford: Oxford University Press).

Uijl, S. D., Bekkers, R. and Vries, H. J. D. (2013) 'Managing Intellectual Property Using Patent Pools', *California Management Review*, **55**(4), 31–50.

Utterback, J. (1994) *Mastering the Dynamics of Innovation* (Boston, MA: Harvard Business School Press).

Utunen, P. (2003) 'Identify, Measure, Visualize your Technology Assets', *Research-Technology Management*, **46**(3), 31–39.

Van der Boor, P., Oliveira, P. and Veloso, F. (2014) 'Users as Innovators in Developing Countries: The Global Sources of Innovation and Diffusion in Mobile Banking Services', *Research Policy*, **43**(9), 1594–1607.

Van der Hoven, C., Probert, D., Phaal, R. and Goffin, K. (2012) 'Dynamic Technology Leadership', *Research-Technology Management*, **55**(5), 24–33.

Van Wyk, R. J. and Gaynor, G. (2014) 'An Academic Template for Graduate Programs in Engineering and Technology Management', *IEEE Engineering Management Review*, **42**(4), 119–124.

Verganti, R. (2009) *Design Driven Innovation* (Cambridge, MA: Harvard Business School Press).

Von Hippel, E. (2005) *Democratizing Innovation* (Cambridge, MA: MIT Press).

Walsh, S. and Linton, J. (2011) 'The Strategy-Technology Firm Fit Audit: A guide to Opportunity Assessment and Selection,' *Technological Forecasting and Social Change*, **78**(2), 199–216.

Wang, C. L. and Ahmed, P. K. (2007) 'Dynamic Capabilities: A Review and Research Agenda', *International Journal of Management Reviews*, **9**(1), 31–51.

Weinzimer, P. (1998) *Getting it Right: Creating Customer Value for Market Leadership* (New York: John Wiley & Sons).

Wheelwright, S. C. and Clark, K. B. (1992) *Revolutionizing Product Development* (New York: Free Press).

Whitney, D. W. (2007) 'Assemble a Technology Development Toolkit', *Research-Technology Management*, **50**(5), 52–58.

Williams, F. and Gibson, D. V. (1990) *Technology Transfer: A Communication Perspective* (London: Sage).

Willyard, C. H. and McClees, C. W. (1987) 'Motorola's Technology Roadmapping Process', *Research Management*, **30**(5), 13–19.

Wingfield, N. and Guth, A. (2006) 'IPod, TheyPod: Rivals Imitate Apple's Success', *Wall Street Journal, Eastern edn*, **248**(66), B1–B5.

Winter, S. G. (2000) 'The Satisficing Principle in Capability Learning', *Strategic Management Journal*, **21**(10/11), 981–996.

Wright, M., Piva, E., Mosey, S. and Lockett, A. (2008) *Academic Entrepreneurship and Business Schools* (Oslo: The Changing Role of Universities in Innovation Systems Conference).

WWF. (2010) *Living Planet Report 2010. Biodiversity, Biocapacity and Development* (Gland, Switzerland: WWF International).

Zahra, S. A. (1996) 'Governance, Ownership, and Corporate Entrepreneurship: The Moderating Impact of Industry Technological Opportunities', *Academy of Management Journal*, **39**(6), 1713–1735.

Zeschky, M. B., Winterhalter, S. and Gassman, O. (2014) 'From Cost to Frugal and Reverse Innovation', *Research-Technology Management*, **57**(4), 20–27.

INDEX